PRAISE FOR MAKING HISTORY; CREATING A LANDSCAPE: THE PORTUGUESE AMERICAN COMMUNITY OF SOUTHEASTERN NEW ENGLAND

A masterful portrait of Portuguese Americans and the places they call home. By chronicling the presence and contributions of the Portuguese in America, this book makes a solid contribution to our understanding of the American ethnic tapestry. Never before has someone pulled together such a variety of information on the Portuguese and their place in American culture.

Donald Zeigler, Professor of Geography, Old Dominion University and author of numerous publications on American ethnic groups

James Fonseca has written a highly informative, lively account of the Portuguese in southern New England. In fact, he has produced the best volume on the history and cultural geography of the region's Portuguese communities that I have read.
He convincingly shows how a distinctive ethnic landscape emerged across southern New England. Fonseca accomplishes more. He compares the experience of the region's immigrants and their offspring to Portuguese communities in other parts of the United States, particularly California. This book should interest anyone engaged with the Portuguese experience. It offers a model for students of ethnic studies.

Joseph Conforti, Distinguished Professor of American and New England Studies, Emeritus, University of Southern Maine, author of Imagining New England, and Another City Upon a Hill, a memoir of growing up in Fall River

This book paints an up-to-date and accurate description of Portuguese communities, not only in New England, but throughout the United States. I say this as someone who immigrated from Portugal in 1956 at the age of 10 and lived in southeastern New England since then.

Tobias Paulo, former Regional Director of the Massachusetts Migrant Education Program

Jim Fonseca has written an exceptional book that fills a void in the literature with this captivating story of Portuguese immigrants who came to the United States, put down roots, and held on to their cultural identities despite the inherent pressure to assimilate into American society. This book details the evolution of these bicultural Portuguese Americans who have tenaciously remained in the New England towns they settled, despite high unemployment and poverty. It is a testament to the resiliency of these families.

Professor Fonseca describes these Portuguese American communities in such vivid detail that readers will become mesmerized and begin to imagine themselves strolling the streets of Fall River or New Bedford, looking for "three decker" houses. Readers will readily envision themselves in the backyard of a Portuguese American home enjoying the grape vines, gardens, and religious shrines, pondering what it must have been like for these families in their native Portugal.

Richard Greenlee, Professor of Social Work, Ohio University

James Fonseca skillfully presents important aspects related to the Portuguese presence in Southeastern New England where the Portuguese already left their "ethnic imprint" in the complex and rich cultural landscape/mosaic that characterizes these unique cities in the USA.

This book represents an excellent study of the Portuguese American community of Southeastern New England, a specific group of immigrants that until now has been largely ignored in migration studies. The choice of the study areas also provides excellent laboratories for the study of multiculturalism in the USA and for how immigrants/ethnic diversity affects urban structures and processes.

Fonseca's timely study makes a very strong contribution to scholarship by focusing in a very important concentration of Portuguese located in a "corner" of southeastern New England. This book is thus valuable in that it fills a major gap in the Portuguese migration literature in the United States. Fonseca offers an impressive depth of historical and empirical detail about the Portuguese settlement and presence in these cities, including their histories, demographic structures, Portuguese culture, urban, social and cultural geographies, economic geography/ethnic entrepreneurship, religion, patterns of community life, politics and citizenship, urban challenges and changing the urban landscapes.

Fonseca brings in-depth knowledge about these culturally diverse cities, the role and impact of the Portuguese Americans upon their urban institutions and structures, how they are evolving and how cultural differences are negotiated. His rich, well organized manuscript also looks at the numerous challenges facing the Portuguese communities in this region and how the local communities are evolving to accommodate the social, cultural and economic needs of the new generations of Portuguese Americans.

This book has a wealth of useful information, as well as policy implications. It is recommended as a resource for scholars and students of Portuguese migration studies. It would also be enjoyable and accessible to the general reader interested in this fascinating aspect of the Portuguese diaspora.

Carlos Teixeira, Professor of Geography, University of British Columbia and co-editor of *The Portuguese in Canada*

MAKING HISTORY; CREATING A LANDSCAPE
THE PORTUGUESE AMERICAN COMMUNITY OF SOUTHEASTERN NEW ENGLAND

BY

JAMES W. FONSECA

GeoImpressions Publishing

Making History; Creating a Landscape:
The Portuguese American Community of Southeastern New England

by
James W. Fonseca
© 2018 by James W. Fonseca
ISBN 978-1722258467
CreateSpace Independent Publishing Platform

ACKNOWLEDGMENTS

Going way back… I thank my grandfather, Jaime Alberto da Fonseca, and my father, James Albert Fonseca, Jr., for instilling in me a love of all things Portuguese.

Going back… I thank three professors who were instrumental in my education: Agrippina Macewicz who answered my question "What is graduate school?" and Manny Maier, both at Bridgewater State University, and my Ph.D. thesis advisor, Saul Cohen at Clark University.

Recently… I thank many colleagues and friends who read the manuscript and gave me critical comments and advice. I owe a particular debt of gratitude to Joe Conforti, Professor of New England and American Studies at the University of Southern Maine who gave it a very close reading and gave me continued encouragement through the writing process. I also thank Rich Greenlee, Social Work, and Jim Newton, Geography, both professors at Ohio University; Tobias Paulo, who has worked with Portuguese migrants in Massachusetts; Bill Pylypciw, a retired history teacher in upstate New York, and geography professors Carlos Teixeira at the University of British Columbia and Don Zeigler at Old Dominion University.

I thank my wife Elaine and son James E. who also read the manuscript and gave me many useful comments and edits. I also thank Cassandra Rice for her valuable help in formatting the book for print and electronic versions.

ABOUT THE AUTHOR

James W. Fonseca is Dean Emeritus at Ohio University – Zanesville where he served as Dean and Professor of Geography from 1998 to 2011. He was Executive Dean of Regional Higher Education at Ohio University until 2013.

Prior to coming to Ohio University Jim Fonseca spent 25 years as an administrator and faculty member at George Mason University in Virginia where he taught and held administrative positions including Director of Individualized Studies, Associate and Acting Dean of the Graduate School, and Founding Director of the University's Prince William Campus in Manassas.

Jim grew up in New Bedford's North End Portuguese community and graduated from New Bedford High School in 1965. He commuted to Bridgewater State University for his bachelor's and earned his Ph.D. in Geography from Clark University in Worcester, Massachusetts in 1974. Along the way he worked in warehouses, grocery stores, the Titleist golf ball factory, a bakery, a soda-canning plant, a plastics factory and as a cab driver. He also taught geography as an adjunct at Clark University, American International College in Springfield and Rhode Island College in Providence.

Jim Fonseca's publications include (with Alice Andrews) the Atlas of Higher Education and the Atlas of American Society both published by New York University Press, and World Regional Map Skills: Student Supplement to de Blij's Geography: Regions and Concepts published by John Wiley, and a monograph, The Urban Rank-Size Hierarchy by the Institute of Mathematical Geography, Ann Arbor.

Jim lives in Ohio and Florida and spends time in Maine and Newport Rhode Island. He and his wife Elaine, have one son, Jim, who lives in Chicago. Jim Fonseca visits family in New England several times each year where he stocks up on linguiça, chourico and bacalhau.

CONTENTS

1. INTRODUCTION — 1
    The Organization of this Book — 5
    The Portuguese Diaspora — 7

2. HISTORICAL BACKGROUND — 7
    Initial Settlement and Waves of Immigration in the United States and New England — 9
    Origins, Destinations and the Island Connection — 15
    Island Population and Density — 21
    History and Poverty of the Islands — 23
    Immigration from Cape Verde — 28

3. GEOGRAPHICAL CONCENTRATION AND NEIGHBORHOODS — 30
    Geographical Concentration — 30
    The Development of Neighborhoods — 36
    The Location of Neighborhoods — 40
    Maintenance of Ethnic Neighborhoods — 48
    Landscape Concepts: Overt and Subtle Symbols — 51

4. THE HYBRID LANDSCAPE — 51
    The Residential Environment — 55
    A Hybrid Landscape — 64
    Gardens, Shrines and Flags — 66
    Cultural Entropy — 70
    Ethnocultural Space: The Portuguese Archipelago and an Emerging Ethnic Substrate — 72
    Religion in the Landscape — 77

5. HOW RELIGION HELPS SHAPE THE LANDSCAPE — 77
    Churches and Neighborhoods — 78
    Religious Feasts, Festivals and Processions — 85
    Cemeteries — 90

6. SEMIOTICS: SIGNS, SYMBOLS AND MONUMENTS ... 93
Signs ... 94
Cultural Symbols ... 97
Song and Dance ... 101
Monumentalization of the Landscape ... 103
Naming and Renaming ... 115

7. PORTUGUESE CULTURE AND ASSIMILATION ... 119
The Continuing Construction of "Portuguese American" Culture ... 119
The Complexities of Assimilation ... 122
Portuguese American Culture in the Context of Assimilation ... 126
Politics and Citizenship ... 129
The Role of the Portuguese National Government ... 136
Patriarchy ... 138
Prejudice ... 142
A Large Community with a Low Profile ... 148
Historical Conditions of the Economy
in the New England Community ... 151

8. THE ECONOMIC GEOGRAPHY OF THE PORTUGUESE AMERICAN COMMUNITY ... 151
The Portuguese Community within Its
Local Economic Geographical Setting ... 157
Employment and Unemployment ... 158
Income ... 159
Educational Attainment ... 164
Employment and Occupational Specialization ... 168
The Fishing Industry ... 177

9. FUTURES ... 181
Concentration, Dispersal and Ethnic Vitality ... 183
Growth, Decline, or Steady-State? ... 185
The Growth of Transnationalism, Return
Migration and Impact on Both Communities ... 191
Cultural Promotion ... 195
A Proposal for a Portuguese Heritage District ... 199
Summary ... 201

ENDNOTES ... 206

1
INTRODUCTION

The Portuguese Americans set out to create a community, not a landscape, but that landscape has become the most visible manifestation of their community

Since the mid-1800s Portuguese Americans have been quietly at work, adjusting to a new culture and adapting a pre-existing American landscape to suit their needs. In the process, they have created a hybrid Portuguese American landscape quite different from both standard American urban landscapes and the landscapes they left behind in Portugal.

The three states of southern New England -- Massachusetts, Connecticut, and Rhode Island -- are now home to more than 467,000 persons of Portuguese ancestry, 88,000 of whom were born in Portugal. The main concentration of Portuguese Americans, the largest cluster in the United States and the main focus of this book, is nestled in a corner of southeastern New England along the Massachusetts-Rhode Island border. The cities of Fall River and New Bedford in Massachusetts and nearby East Providence, Rhode Island are the main urban centers housing large numbers of Portuguese. These cities are connected by Interstate 195, the "Portuguese American Interstate Highway."

Much has been written about American ethnic groups and the landscapes they have created in their new land. Ethnic groups set out to create a community, not a landscape, but that landscape is the visible manifestation of their community interaction.[1] There have been a few geographic studies of Portuguese in the United States, especially Portuguese from the Azores Islands, who make up the bulk of Portuguese residents in southeastern New England, but most of these studies are now very much dated.[2] This book helps fill that void by exploring the geographic and historical aspects

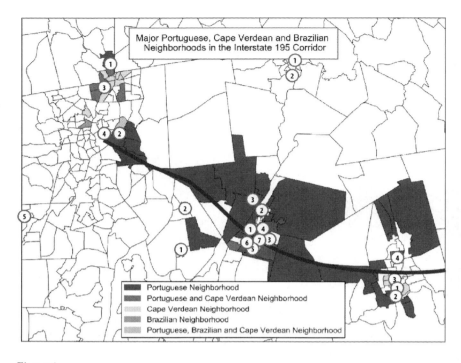

Figure 1
The "Portuguese American Interstate Highway," I-195, runs from Providence on the west through Fall River and New Bedford towards Cape Cod. The neighborhoods shown are defined primarily on the basis of foreign-born Portuguese, Cape Verdean and Brazilian residents as discussed on the city maps in Chapter 3. The dots illustrate church locations.

as well as the sociological and economic characteristics of the southeastern New England Portuguese community.

The Portuguese came to southern New England (and to Hawaii and California) because of whaling connections with New Bedford. They left lives as poor peasant farmers on tiny plots of land to come to urban areas in America. At the time of the greatest waves of immigration, Portugal was one of the poorest countries in Europe and the Portuguese islands of the Azores, Madeira and Cape Verdes were even poorer. Educational levels reflected their poverty; many had only a grade school education and many had never had any formal schooling. Their low level of educational attains has dogged the Portuguese to the present day and is still reflected in their occupations and their levels of income.

While whaling opportunities ended, jobs opened in New Bedford and Fall River with the great textile boom. Mainland Portuguese came as well as islanders. The Portuguese settled in the distinctive New England style of housing, wooden three-deckers within walking distance of the mills. Settlement spread with the expansion of mills to other southern New England cities, especially in Rhode Island. Amazingly, Portuguese neighborhoods today remain in these same neighborhoods more than a century later; an unusual occurrence in the history of American ethnic groups as normally, newly-arriving lower income groups displace earlier immigrants who assimilate and move to the suburbs.

The landscape these Portuguese immigrants created is an American landscape, but a hybridized landscape showing Portuguese cultural influences. The landscape is characterized by the distinctive three-deckers and by Portuguese iconography in the landscape especially in cultural symbols such as shrines, flags, architectural embellishments, and gardens. Some of these features were not just importations into the American landscape but reactions to it.

The Catholic religion of the Portuguese was instrumental in shaping the landscape of the immigrant communities. Churches were built around initial clusters of immigrants and large neighborhoods developed around those churches. So well-connected were the immigrants, due to chain migration from their villages, that the immigration process almost represented the transplantation of villages and parishes from the islands to America. Religious feasts, church festivals and processions marked the community.

Throughout the community, signs and cultural symbols such as the Portuguese flag, the black rooster the Cross of St. John's mark the ethnic group's territory. Over time, as Portuguese Americans accumulated some amount of wealth and political power, and with the help of the governments of Portugal and the Azores, the community has been building monuments and museums. Originally monuments to "great men" these commemorations have diversified over time to celebrate immigration and the Portuguese experience in the New World. One monument, in particular, Dighton Rock, can be seen as another reaction to American culture; in this case an "answer" to Plymouth Rock barely 40 miles away.

Portuguese Americans in New England still struggle to assimilate into American culture. Their lower levels of educational attainment and corresponding lower levels of income have kept the suburban American dream out of reach of some, but not all, of the immigrants. Lower levels of obtaining citizenship have kept the Portuguese a generation or more behind in assuming political power comparable to their numbers. Patriarchy, still strong in the culture, presents barriers to equal achievement by women. Prejudice against the community is still strong in some places. Even within the Portuguese community itself, there are complex prejudices between

Figure 2
Statues of Prince Henry the Navigator erected in 1940 in Fall River (left), and in 1996 in New Bedford (right). Both statues feature distinctive black and white tiling and a compass rose. New Bedford's statue looks direcly east over the harbor toward Portugal.

mainlanders and islanders, among immigrants from various islands, and between Portuguese and the linguistically affiliated Brazilian and Cape Verdean groups. Assimilation comes slowly and when it comes the Portuguese must struggle to avoid downward assimilation into a perpetual lower-class status.

The Portuguese in New England rode the economic waves of southern New England's booms and busts. Just as the whaling industry that had brought the early Portuguese died out, the textile mills began to move to the Southern states or go bankrupt. For a generation, the apparel industry blossomed by moving into the abandoned textile mills. (Textile workers make fabric; apparel workers make clothing from fabric.) When that industry declined, some plastics and electronics activity moved in but largely the heyday of manufacturing was over, jobs went not only to the South but overseas and to increased mechanization. Even the fishing industry that employed many Portuguese in New Bedford and in smaller towns such as Gloucester and Provincetown fell upon hard times.

With their low levels of educational attainment, many Portuguese, especially women moved into low-paying service jobs in retail and healthcare. But higher-paying professional and administrative jobs have been difficult to obtain especially for Portuguese men. An analysis of the occupational specializations of the Portuguese in Metropolitan Providence bears this out and shows the Portuguese to be behind the general population as well as comparative ethnic groups such as Greeks, Italians, Irish and French Canadians. The average income of the Portuguese Americans in southern New England remain behinds national averages, metropolitan averages, state averages and behind their California counterparts where the Portuguese have done quite well economically, exceeding both state and national averages.

What does the future hold for Portuguese Americans? With continued effort, they can increase their levels of educational attainment and take advantage of the metropolitan Providence-Boston job market. Portuguese immigration into the area has almost ceased while return migration has increased. Azoreans, in particular, are establishing a transnational culture that impacts both southeastern New England and the islands. Cape Verdean and Brazilian immigration is increasing but mostly in areas of Massachusetts outside the southeastern Massachusetts and Rhode Island core area. Economic development in the future can't be predicted but offshore wind or oil developments could possibly bring more jobs to the area. A Portuguese Village tourist development could take advantage of the cultural riches of the area and attract more tourists and produce jobs as well.

As we will see, whatever the future holds, the Portuguese Americans will continue on their path of making history and creating a landscape.

THE ORGANIZATION OF THIS BOOK

After this introductory chapter, Chapter 2 will examine how and why these Portuguese American communities developed in southeastern New England; why they have been so persistent; where migrants came from, and what drove individuals to emigrate. Some comparisons will also be made with the very few other areas of original Portuguese settlement in the United States, California, and Hawaii. Chapter 3 looks at the remarkable concentration (clustering) of Portuguese Americans, where large neighborhoods are located, and how they developed. In Chapter 4 we will discuss some concepts from scholarship in the field of geography about landscape and look at the hybrid landscape of the neighborhoods of the Portuguese Americans. Religion, churches, and religious festivals are so important to the community that Chapter 5 will focus on these factors. In Chapter 6 we will look at semiotics or the iconography of Portuguese

Figure 3
The Ponta Delgada Gates; Portas da Cidade. A reproduction of the Gates of the City in Ponta Delgada on the island of Sao Miguel in the Azores was constructed in Fall River in 2006. In the background is the Braga Bridge.

culture expressed in the landscape through signs, symbols, and monuments. Chapter 7 discusses the complexity of assimilation into American culture and how the Portuguese manage issues such as patriarchy, prejudice, American politics and acquiring citizenship. The economy and economic geography of the region is discussed in Chapter 8 where measures of educational attainment, income, and employment are analyzed. The last chapter, Chapter 9, speculates about the future of the community particularly in light of decreased Portuguese immigration and increased Brazilian and Cape Verdean immigration into southern New England.

2
HISTORICAL BACKGROUND

> *Portugal has been a nation so characterized by out migration that one may rightly speak of a Portuguese diaspora.*

Much has been written about many American ethnic groups and the landscapes they have created in their new land. As landscape scholar John Brinckerhoff Jackson noted, ethnic groups set out to create a community, not a landscape, but that landscape is the visible manifestation of their community interaction.[3] There have been a few geographic studies of Portuguese in the United States, especially Portuguese from the Azores Islands, who make up the bulk of Portuguese residents in southeastern New England, but most of those studies are now very much dated.[4] And there have been some geographic studies of the Portuguese of California.[5] Unlike the Portuguese in Canada,[6] Portuguese Americans and their landscape impact remain largely unstudied by academic researchers, especially the southern New England community, even though it is the largest. This book helps fill that void by exploring the geographic as well as the sociological and economic characteristics of the southeastern New England Portuguese community.

THE PORTUGUESE DIASPORA

Before focusing on Portuguese settlement in southeastern New England, it is helpful to put that stream of immigration into its longer-term international context. Portugal has been a nation so characterized by out-migration that one may rightly speak of a Portuguese diaspora.[7] Since the era of Portuguese worldwide discovery and colonization, and later, massive emigration to take advantage of overseas employment, the Portuguese have scattered around the world. Like the early Irish and Italian emigrants, the Portuguese left behind an impoverished, primarily rural, nation. Like the British and French, the Portuguese sent large numbers of people overseas as colonial officials and settlers. Like the Lebanese, Chinese and Jews, the Portuguese have settled around the world in numerous small communities as merchants and middlemen.

The result is that today there are large numbers of Portuguese and their descendants on every settled continent: in Asia in Macao, Timor, Sri Lanka and coastal India; in Africa in Angola, Mozambique, South Africa and Cape Verde; in Australia, and in South America, not only in Brazil (138,000 Portuguese-born in 2011), but in numerous other countries such as Venezuela which is home to about 37,000 individuals who were born in Portugal and another 400,000 people of Portuguese ancestry. In Guyana, the Portuguese form the largest European group of that nation's "Six Peoples." [8]

In Europe outside of Portugal, there are more than 200,000 Portuguese-born individuals in Switzerland and more than 100,000 in Spain, the United Kingdom, and Germany.[9] France is an especially favored destination for Portuguese emigrants. Almost 600,000 Portuguese-born individuals live in France. In 2012 the 18,300 new Portuguese immigrants were the largest immigrant group arriving in France from any nation that year.[10] Of 32 immigrant groups in Paris with more than 15,000 people in 2012, the 229,000 Portuguese were second in number only to the Algerians with 286,000.[11] Canada had 430,000 people of Portuguese ancestry in 2011, including 140,000 born in Portugal. The largest communities are in Toronto and Montreal. For comparison, the number of Portuguese-born residents in the United States is about 190,000.

One striking aspect of Portuguese settlement is the proportion of overseas settlement relative to the home nation. Among the 34 mainly European nations of the OECD, the Portuguese have sent proportionately more people overseas to the United States (14%) than any other countries except New Zealand and Ireland. About one of every seven people born in Portugal lives abroad.[12] We can also calculate the Portuguese foreign-born population in the United States relative to Portugal's national population. The number of Portuguese-born residents of the United States equals approximately 2% of the present-day population of Portugal (about 10,500,000 people).

The Diaspora is even more true of the Portuguese Atlantic islands since most American Portuguese came from the islands, not the mainland. Although accurate historical figures are not available for the regions of Portugal where emigrants originated, it is estimated that about 70% of American Portuguese immigrants were born in the Azores, a number that represents close to one-third of the population of the Azores.[13] As early as 1912 the Portuguese consul in Boston had reported that his district, comprised of the six New England states, housed 70,000 native-born Portuguese and 80,000 American-born descendants, of whom 75% were Azorean.[14] It has been estimated that the number of Azorean-born Americans and their descendants represent today more than four times the population of the Azores.[15] No wonder the southeastern New England Portuguese community has been called the "Tenth Island" of the Azores![16]

INITIAL SETTLEMENT AND WAVES OF IMMIGRATION IN THE UNITED STATES AND NEW ENGLAND

Portuguese settlers have been in the United States since the seventeenth century; indeed, probably the "first New Yorker," was a Portuguese man named Jan Rodrigues who settled in New York in 1613.[17] Another early cluster of Portuguese settlers within what is now the United States included Portuguese Jews who arrived in New York via Brazil in 1654. Other Portuguese Jews came to Newport, Rhode Island in the late 1600s where they were joined by Jews from Portugal and the Caribbean island of Curacao. In Newport, they established the Touro Synagogue in 1763, the first synagogue in the United States. A few of these Portuguese Jews were involved in whaling and may have been among some of the first whalers to begin the custom of stopping at the Azores for provisions and deckhands. Portuguese were recruited to cut lumber in New Jersey before 1830 and they gave their name to the settlement of New Lisbon, east of Philadelphia. Several hundred Madeirans who had converted to Protestantism were driven out of Catholic Madeira and arrived in Springfield and Jacksonville, Illinois in 1849 under Presbyterian church sponsorship.[18] A colony of several hundred Portuguese was recruited as contract laborers to cut sugar cane in Louisiana around 1840, despite the existence of slavery in Louisiana at the time. Around 17,000 Portuguese, mostly from Madeira, were recruited to migrate to Hawaii as contracted sugar cane cutters around 1880.

But it was the connection to the whaling industry that prompted a persistent stream of Portuguese migration to the United States. The Governor of the Azores reported as early as 1780 that Azorean men were on more than 200 American whaling ships.[19] All in all, however, Portuguese emigration to the United States was very limited before 1860 and, in addition to the few special groups cited above, consisted mainly of Portuguese men from the Atlantic Islands of the Azores, Madeira, and the Cape Verdes who signed on as deckhands and cabin boys aboard whaling ships, some of whom remained in the United States at the end of the voyage.[20] The first Portuguese name in New Bedford city directories appeared in 1817 and by the end of the Civil War, there were 800 Portuguese in the city.[21]

Undoubtedly some Portuguese and Cape Verdeans were living in the "New Guinea" section of the city shown on a British map of the town made during the Revolutionary War when the British invaded and burned much of Bedford Village. The terms "New Guineas" and "Guinea Towns" were generic terms used at that time to indicate settlements of Africans, American Indians, and southern Europeans; Guinea referring to West Africa.

The whalers sailed out of New England's southern ports, especially the "whaling capital" of New Bedford, Massachusetts, but secondary cores of early Portuguese settlement were also established at other New England ports where whalers operated, especially in Connecticut and Rhode Island. The whaling vessels went on two- and three-year voyages, stopping at ports around the world to make repairs and to take on provisions with a particular focus on the San Francisco Bay area and Hawaii. The "heyday" of American whaling, generally defined as 1840-1860, was short-lived, but indelibly imprinted small Portuguese communities upon the landscape in coastal southeastern New England, the San Francisco Bay area and Hawaii. These three areas formed the main settlement cores for later expansion of Portuguese immigration.

By 1870 there were about 9,000 Portuguese-born living in the United States, about equally divided between southern New England and northern California. The southern New England core was set for Portuguese immigration to grow substantially in the late 1800s with increased demand for low-wage textile workers. The numbers of Portuguese exploded in southeastern New England in response to this demand. The growth is illustrated by Fall River where the number of Portuguese-born residents grew from about 100 in 1880 to 500 in 1900, to 5,000 in 1905 and then to more than 12,000 in 1920.[22] In New Bedford, the numbers grew even faster and that city had 17,200 Portuguese-born immigrants by 1920. With the textile worker boom, now both men and women arrived and one sociologist noted that emigration became a viable option for Portuguese widows. In 1918-19, while only about 2% of single Portuguese men who immigrated were widowers, 13% of female immigrants were widows.[23]

Figure 4
Who were the Portuguese who immigrated to the United States? These photos show two relatives of the author's grandmother who emigrated from northern Portugal in the early 1900's.

After the three initial cores of the settlement were formed in southern New England, northern California, and Hawaii, two large waves of Portuguese immigration occurred. As shown in Table 1, the first wave started around 1870 and peaked during 1910-1920, a decade when almost 90,000 Portuguese immigrated.[24]

But this expansion of immigration by the Portuguese and other southern European groups led to federal legislation to restrict, slow or eliminate the flow of migrants. First, a literacy test for immigrants and new fees were imposed in 1917. After the implementation of the literacy requirement, non-US citizens even stopped returning to visit Portugal and the islands for fear they could not re-enter the United States if they left.[25] Then a eugenic quota system was put in place by 1924. The quota system limited immigration from each nation to 2% of its share of immigrants based on the Census of 1890.[26] Such a system obviously was intended to favor immigrants from regions with long-established patterns of immigration to the United States such as Great Britain, Germany, and Scandinavia at the expense of southern Europeans whose nations had miniscule quotas. There was a dramatic drop in Portuguese immigration after 1917 due to these restrictive measures.[27]

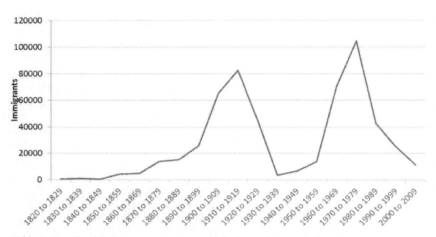

Table 1. Graph of Portuguese Immigration by Decade 1820 to 1910

Nationally, an average of more than 8,000 Portuguese immigrants had been arriving each year during the decade 1910-1920,[28] a number that fell to less than 400 annually, during the decade of the Depression, 1930-1939. Slow immigration persisted through most of the 1950s, which averaged about 1,400 immigrants each year after some revision of the quota system in 1952.[29]

The second great wave of Portuguese immigration began in 1958 with a lifting of the immigration quota specifically for Azoreans. This occurred after a series of volcanic eruptions off the island of Fayal displaced about 25,000 Portuguese. Collectively they were known as the "*Capelinhos,*" after the name of the volcano.[30] The sheer numbers of Portuguese already living in southeastern New England at that time led Massachusetts and Rhode Island politicians (including then-Senator John F. Kennedy of Massachusetts) to co-sponsor a bill, the Azorean Refugee Act of 1958, that allowed 1,500 additional visas for Fayal residents to be used by 1960. Various amendments added to the quota when the island of San Jorge was hit by an earthquake in 1964. This second bill was sponsored by Senator Edward M. Kennedy after the assassination of President Kennedy. Most of these Azorean immigrants came to southeastern New England; a smaller number went to California.

Coincidentally, shortly after these Azorean-specific legislative acts were passed, in 1965 the national origin quota immigration system was significantly revised allowing greatly increased immigration from Portugal. The numbers of Portuguese arriving in the United States shot up to from 2,000 in 1965 to about 9,000 in 1966 and grew to between 10,000 and 16,000 every year from 1967 until the mid-1970s.[31] The 1970s was a decade during which 105,000 Portuguese arrived in the United States. The large settlement cores in Fall River and New Bedford greatly expanded. This second wave reinforced the already strong connections between the Atlantic islands and southeastern New England. The two cites of New Bedford and Fall River were literally swamped with immigrants. To cite just one impact, the city school systems that had been seeing declining school populations suddenly were enrolling up to 1,000 new pupils per *month*, adding modular classrooms in school parking lots and playgrounds as fast as they could be installed.

Since that second wave ended, Portuguese immigration has fallen dramatically and continuously from about 4,000 per year in the 1980s to 2,500 per year in the 1990s. From 2010 to 2013 only about 850 Portuguese have immigrated annually, a figure so low that, considering return migration, it is fair to say that net immigration has effectively ceased. As of 2010, about 189,000 persons residing in the United States were born in Portugal and the vast majority of these, 84%, had immigrated before the year 2000.

During the second wave of immigration, the earlier established patterns of origin and destination of emigrants were largely maintained: immigrants to the United States came primarily from the Islands, especially the Azores, although emigration from "the Continent" was also increasing each year. The destinations of the Portuguese in the United States were primarily the same well-established historic cores. On average, for example, for a series of sample years from 1968 to 1974, most immigrants went to Massachusetts and Rhode Island (about 3,600 each year, combined), more than twice as many as those who went to California (about 1,400 each year). By 1974 however, a shift of destination was apparent -- a harbinger of more dramatic trends to come. Immigration to Massachusetts and Rhode Island had greatly slowed; immigration to California was declining, while immigration to New Jersey was increasing each year, almost equaling the numbers going to California.[32]

Portuguese immigration followed the usual pattern outlined by sociologists who have identified four stages in the transnational migration process.[33] First, there is what is intended to be (both by the migrants and by the host society) a temporary labor migration of young, mostly male, workers, with a strong orientation to their homeland, a concern to save money for return to the home country, and a wish to send remittances back to their families.

The second stage in the model emerges when those who are supposed to be temporary migrant laborers begin to prolong their stay and develop social and mutual help networks among those with the same ethnic origin. Once the immigrants prolong their stays, stage three begins to emerge, as the family reunion is attempted and there is a growing consciousness of long-term settlement and more concern for the norms of the receiving society. Ethnic communities begin to emerge, equipped with their own institutions. The final stage of the model is reached when the settlement has become permanent. Here, however, two contrasting outcomes can be seen – one in which the migrants attain a secure legal status and eventual citizenship; the other in which permanent settlement occurs in an environment of political exclusion and socio-economic marginalization, creating a situation in which ethnic minorities emerge.[34] These divergent outcomes will be discussed later in the book in a section on assimilation.

Figure 5
The author's grandparents (center with bouquet) pose with their wedding party in front of a three-decker in New Bedford's north end Portuguese community in 1919.

In retrospect, we can see the second wave of Portuguese immigration as part of the last great wave of European immigration to the United States. During the first wave, the Portuguese had joined an on-going influx of immigrants who were almost totally European in origin. During the decade of the 1890s, 97% of immigrants arriving in the United States had been born in Europe. Huge numbers were still arriving then from Great Britain, Germany, Scandinavia, Ireland, and Italy. Even as late as the decade of the

1950s, 56% of American immigrants were still arriving from Europe. After the national origin quota system was eliminated in 1965, Europe's share of American immigration fell to 13% in the decade beginning in 2000 and was as low as 9% in 2013. In that latter year, persons from Asian nations made up the largest proportion of immigrants (33%) followed by those from Mexico (14%), the Caribbean (12%), Central and South America (12%) and Africa (10%). Thus we can see discussion of the two great waves of Portuguese immigration within the context of the shifting geographical origins of American immigrants.

ORIGINS, DESTINATIONS AND THE ISLAND CONNECTION

Because of the key role that whaling played in Portuguese immigration, and because of whaling's connection to the Portuguese Atlantic Islands, the pattern of the predominance of Portuguese emigration to New England from the islands, rather than continental Portugal, was established very early.[35] The Portuguese arrived from different islands and from Continental Portugal with different customs and accents. Even within an island grouping, immigrants were disconnected or even factionalized by the long-standing island and village rivalries. Of course, every immigrant group experiences this to some extent. Among Italian immigrants to the United States, for example, northern groups such as the Tuscans looked down on the Neapolitans who in turn looked down upon Sicilians and, to some extent, didn't even consider the last group as Italians.[36] This factionalism was evident among the Azoreans where many immigrants identified themselves not as Portuguese or even Azoreans but as *Faialenses* or *Micaelenses*, depending upon their island of origin. Arriving in southeastern New England, Portuguese immigrants found themselves in a crucible of ethnic and cultural interaction, where people born on the island of Pico, for example, interacted for the first time on a regular basis with not only Maderians and Cape Verdeans but also with *Micaelenses* and *Faialenses* from their own island group.

In analyzing Portuguese emigration to the United States, it is helpful to keep in mind the context of New England immigration within the larger, macro picture of Portuguese emigration. First, Brazil, not the United States, was the primary long-term destination of most Portuguese emigrants. Second, very early, it was clear that the destinations of emigrants born in continental Portugal differed from the destinations of those born on the Atlantic Islands. Of the approximately one million Portuguese who left their native country between 1892 and 1921, 86% of emigrants from continental Portugal went to Brazil, while, due to the history of whaling connections, 82% of Azorean emigrants went to the United States (as did 34% of Madeirans). [37]

The varied distribution of origins meant that of Portuguese immigrants during the period 1892-1921, 63% were arriving from the Azores, 26% from the Continent and 11% from Madeira.[38] This trend was already evident during the period 1913 to 1917 when only about one of ten Portuguese emigrants from the mainland were coming to North America, but nine of ten Atlantic Islanders who emigrated headed to North America. Individual island and island cities were even more oriented to the United States, such as the city of Ponta Delgada on St. Michael's, where 96% of emigrants went to North America and the city of Horta on Fayal where 98% did so.[39] Specific islands were connected to specific destinations in the United States. By far, immigrants to Fall River had been born on the western Azorean islands such as St. Michael's and Saint Mary's.[40] The preponderance of Island emigration to the United States is also shown by the following statistics: in 1920, there were 106,400 Portuguese Americans who had been born in Portugal; 39% of these had been born in the Atlantic islands even though the combined population of all the islands at the time was only about 15% of Portugal's population.[41]

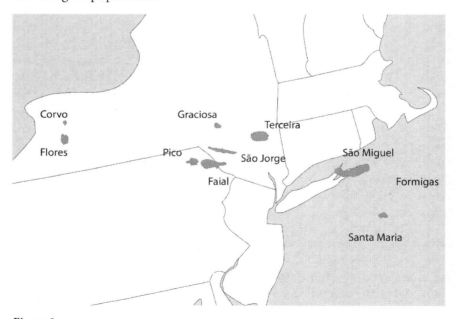

Figure 6
The Azores overlaid on a map of New England and New York State. Size of islands and distances between them are correct but latitude is not; the Azores are east of the area approximately from central New Jersey to southern Virginia.

The proportions of islanders and continentals also varied greatly by the region where the immigrants arrived in the United States. In 1920 when 26% of California Portuguese had been born in the islands, 50% of Massachusetts Portuguese immigrants had been born there. In 1920 when New Bedford had 17,200 Portuguese-born residents, 57% were from the islands as were more than half of Fall River's 12,000 Portuguese and more than half of Taunton's 3,200 Portuguese residents. On the other hand, in Bristol, Rhode Island, only 13 miles west of Fall River, only 3% of 2,300 Portuguese-born residents were from the islands; the vast majority were from continental Portugal.[42]

In addition to clustering at a macro level by state, Portuguese immigrants from different cities towns, islands, and villages clustered at a more micro level in different areas in New England. Provincetown attracted islanders born in the Azores and fishing towns of the Algarve region of southern Portugal. A jute mill, manufacturing burlap, in Ludlow outside of Springfield, Massachusetts, attracted about 1,500 immigrants from the *Tras-os-Montes* region of northern Portugal. In Valley Falls, north of Providence, Rhode Island, most of the settlers originated in Beira Alta province in northern Portugal. Just ten miles away in Central Falls, Rhode Island, immigrants were from the island of Madeira. Most Portuguese in Hartford, Connecticut were born in the Mira district north of Lisbon but those in Danbury, Connecticut came from the Gouveia district in north-central Portugal.[43] The large Portuguese immigrant community in New Bedford was geographically diverse. The city's North End attracted Madeirans, Continentals, and Azoreans from St. Michaels while the South End attracted almost entirely Azoreans but mainly those born on the islands of Pico and Fayal. Immigration could be so location-specific that sometimes not only villages but church parishes were recreated. An example is the Espírito Santo parish in Fall River which is a transplantation of Bretanha parish on the island of St. Michael's.[44]

Among the Portuguese Americans, island rivalries and divisions *within* island groups (for example, *Micaelenses* and *Terceirenses*, the names for people from the Azorean islands of St. Michael's and Terceira) are intensified by divisions *between* island groups (Azoreans and Madeirans). There is also a split between continentals from mainland Portugal and Atlantic islanders, a social division described in Frank Gaspar's novel, *Leaving Pico,* where the continental Portuguese were derisively referred to as "the Lisbons." Over time, of course, these divisions lessen as immigrants and the second generation come to think of themselves as Portuguese Americans even though some groups, such as social clubs and their associated soccer teams, oriented by island, remain evident in the landscape.

Regardless of whether they came from the Atlantic Islands or mainland Portugal, where the Portuguese arrivals settled in the United States mattered immensely in terms of whether their future employment would be oriented to "farm or factory." While this book is focused on the Portuguese in New England, it is informative to briefly contrast the outcome of

Figure 7
While much of this book will focus on Portuguese Americans in the Providence-Fall River - New Bedford corridor, impressive landscape features are found elsewhere in southern New England. Top, the Portuguese Cultural Center in Danbury Connecticut. Middle left, the Holy Ghost Society Club in Stonington, Connecticut. Middle right, the Grupo Amigos da Terceira Club in Pawtucket, Rhode Island. Bottom, the Portuguese American Civic League in Lowell, Massachusetts.

Portuguese settlement in this region with Portuguese settlement in the two other traditional cores, California and Hawaii. The contrast between West Coast and East Coast Portuguese immigrants was striking. Geographer Jerry Williams, who has written two books [45] about Azorean immigrants noted that in 1960 87% of Portuguese Americans who were classified as farm residents lived in California. Only 1% of Portuguese in southern New England were farmers.[46] The California Portuguese largely stayed on farms and became the most rural of California's numerous ethnic groups.

Although those Portuguese who immigrated were mainly farmers from rural areas and villages, those who came to southeastern New England largely settled in urban areas and primarily worked in the textile and apparel industries; the whaling industry had died out in the late 1800s. Those in Hawaii arrived as pineapple and sugar cane cutters to fill the need for low-wage agricultural workers after the legislative exclusion of Chinese immigrants. Many of those in northern California arrived as laborers engaged in dairying, horticulture, and viticulture (grape-growing). In each of these three core regions, the interaction of the Portuguese with the American economy and with American culture was different eventually resulting in a different experience of assimilation into American culture.

In Hawaii, the Portuguese, many of whom were Madeirans, arrived as low paid laborers on sugar cane and pineapple plantations and were treated more like the native non-white "Kanaka" population than as white Europeans. While some Portuguese achieved success in agriculture by eventually acquiring land and running sugar, pineapple, cattle or coffee operations, most eventually left these rural jobs and migrated to Honolulu. Here they adopted an urban lifestyle where they largely shed their Portuguese culture.[47] A few migrated to rural jobs in California. In fact, Leo Pap, a scholar who wrote the book, *The Portuguese-Americans*, noted that their experience of prejudice resulted in the "de-ethnicization" of those Portuguese who remained in Hawaii, although there were signs of an ethnic revival.[48]

Portuguese in northern California mainly worked initially as agricultural laborers, clustered around San Jose, Oakland, and the northern central valley. Eventually many bought land and became successful farmers of a variety of crops including fruits, nuts, and vegetables. In particular, the Portuguese controlled California's dairy industry for a long time. They surpassed their East Coast countrymen in prosperity as measured by US Census data showing above-average incomes for Portuguese Americans compared to both national populations and for residents of the state of California. High school completion rates for Portuguese in California approached the national average, although college graduation rates remained low.

The rural experience impacted Portuguese American culture differently than the urban experience in other ways. The relative isolation of the Portuguese on farms in rural California meant they were not exposed as much to competing ethnic groups as were the New England Portuguese who were surrounded by Italians, Irish, Poles, French Canadians and many other groups. Unlike the situation in New England where many Portuguese immigrant women worked in textile mills, there was less of a tendency for women to work year-round off of the farms, although many Portuguese women in California did work seasonally in factories canning fish and produce. Perhaps because of their relative isolation and the need to form friendships and alliances outside of the home, women's ethnic associations, especially the *Sociedade Portuguesa Rainha Santa Isabel* (Portuguese Society of Queen Saint Isabel), flourished in California in a way they did not in the urban East Coast cities where women could interact with each other on a daily basis.[49] In the east, Portuguese social associations were largely men's ethnic clubs.

In the urban environment of the small cities of the East Coast, the Portuguese found work in textile and apparel mills but accompanied by continuous economic struggle. The first blows to economic security were cycles of wage cuts and strikes, in which the Portuguese participated. Then the Great Depression hit. Some Portuguese workers relocated to Newark, New Jersey to get jobs, although most returned to southern New England. Then textile mills began moving to the Southern states but growth in the apparel industry temporarily replaced many textile jobs. In turn, when apparel jobs began to be lost to overseas competition, some plastics and electronic component firms moved into the giant vacant mills for a decade or so before those jobs moved overseas.

The second great wave of immigrants arrived primarily from the Azores and moved mainly into southeastern New England while the economic downturn continued, so unemployment remained very high in the area, usually double the national average. Trapped in low paying jobs with few possibilities for advancement, incomes for Portuguese Americans in New England remained well below state and national averages, unlike the situation in California. Also, unlike California, high school and college graduation rates remained well below national averages and exceptionally far below Massachusetts state averages. With low incomes and low levels of educational attainment, assimilation into the middle class and attainment of the "American dream" remained problematic. Unlike their California cousins, the Portuguese Americans of southeastern New England found themselves challenged to avoid "downward assimilation" into permanent lower economic class status. Yet, for the most part, the Portuguese Americans who came to southeastern New England greatly improved their economic situation compared to what it had been back in Portugal and on the islands, and, with few exceptions, choose to stay in their new homeland.

ISLAND POPULATION AND DENSITY

To better understand these varied geographical origins and the reasons the Portuguese had for emigrating, it helps to understand how individual islands varied greatly in size, population, and population density. The island of St. Michael's, for example, is home to more than half of the population of the Azores, 138,000 of 247,000 people in 2011 (the latest official statistics available). St. Michael's is the island from which most American island immigrants came, including most of the Azoreans who came to southeastern New England. St. Michael's has a population density of more than 500 people per square mile. Madeira has 268,000 people on 310 square miles giving it one of the highest population densities (867 people per square mile) of all political units in the European Union.

Since all of the Portuguese Atlantic Islands are steep volcanic islands, the effective density of population is really much greater than that indicated by simple figures of population per square mile. Geographers have developed the concept of physiological density, a measure of population per square mile of cropland. Because only about one-third of the area of the islands is arable, even when pastureland on steep hillsides is included, many islands have a physiological density about triple that of continental Portugal. Historically this physiologic density was immense; up to 700 people per square mile in the mid-1800s.[50] For a population largely dependent upon subsistence agriculture, this simple fact of density helps to explain much of the relative historical poverty of all of the islands and the propensity toward out-migration. Even in 1965, when the land tenure system had dramatically improved and 80% of the land was held by individual families, three-fourths of these landholdings were still inadequate to provide livable incomes for the families who worked them.[51] Were other economic options available related to urbanization and industry, sheer density would not have had such a significant impact.

We have seen how the loss of population to emigration was 50% greater on the islands than on the continent during the time of peak emigration.[52] Yet with birth rates historically and currently higher than continental Portugal, the island populations have remained relatively stable despite this massive out-migration. For example, the population of the Azores in 2011 as noted above (247,000) is just about what it was in 1864 (249,000); again in 1904 (248,000) and again in 1920 (232,000).[53] On the other hand, because of such substantial out-migration and consequent population stagnation, the population of the Azores has been only stable while Portugal's population grew. For example, in 1920 the Azores represented 3.9% of Portugal's overall population, but that proportion fell to 2.3% in 2011. These figures constantly change with Portugal's sharply declining birthrate, now the lowest of all nations in Europe, and with its continued high rate of emigration.[54]

Figure 8
Tiny plots of land on the island of Corvo, Azores. Although small plots have been consolidated on the larger islands such as Sao Miguel, tiny Corvo Island still illustrates how small the plots were originally; many are hardly larger than the houses. Image courtesy of Goggle Earth.

It is helpful too, to have an idea of the populations and areas of Portuguese regions relative to areas of the United States. The population of Portugal, including the Azores and Madeira, is approximately 10,500,000 people. Portugal's area of 35,600 square miles gives the nation a population density of about 300 people per square mile. These statistics make Portugal very comparable to the total population, area, and density of the state of Ohio. For a comparative area for the Atlantic islands alone, it is useful to switch the analogy to a much smaller state, Rhode Island. As shown in Figure 6 the combined areas of the Azores (906 square miles) and Madeira (309 square miles), a total of 1215 square miles is remarkably similar in size to Rhode Island's area of 1212 square miles. In 2011, as noted, the Azores had 247,000 people and Madeira had 268,000. The combined population of the two island groups is about 515,000 people, almost exactly half of Rhode Island's population of 1,050,000 people.

HISTORY AND POVERTY OF THE ISLANDS

The Azores, Madeira and Cape Verdes were all settled by the Portuguese in the early fifteenth century, around 1430-1440. While there may have been ancient inhabitants on some of the islands, they were unpopulated when discovered by the Portuguese. Population growth was slow at first. Pico and Fayal, for example, each had populations estimated at only 1,500 in 1490. When we consider that the islands had no population in 1400 and grew to a quarter million in the late 1800s when substantial emigration to North America started, the islands can be envisioned in a historical sense almost as "way stations" for the Portuguese on their way to America. Hans Leder, an anthropologist, and author of the book *Cultural Persistence in a Portuguese-American Community* notes that mainland Portuguese resettlement to the Azores had always been regarded as emigration, rather than internal migration, and thus the settlement of the Atlantic Islands can be seen as the first chapter in a historical Portuguese westward migration.[55] The Azores had become more densely populated than Portugal itself, and with incomes substantially less than even impoverished mainland Portugal, the islanders were ripe for an outlet for emigration.[56]

When large numbers of people leave one area for another, there are always numerous "push" and "pull" factors that lead people to make the decision to uproot their home and go to a foreign land. There were numerous "pull" factors – mainly the opportunity for work and a better economic life presented first by the whaling industry and the California gold rush, and then by the fishing industry and jobs in textile and apparel factories.

There were many "push" factors as well: the great physiological density of the island; an unfair land tenure system and accompanying poverty; crop plagues and crop failures; unpopular national policies on taxation and conscription for guerrilla wars in Africa, and finally, natural disasters due to volcanoes and earthquakes.

The Portuguese were among the last major groups of the European wave of immigration in the opening three decades of the twentieth century. The other late-arriving groups included Poles, Italians, Greeks, Slovenians, Croatians, Hungarians, Slovaks, Czechs, and Russian and Polish Jews.[57] While many European immigrants during the great waves of immigration in the late nineteenth century came from poor rural village environments, it is still hard to imagine the conditions that the typical emigrant was leaving behind on the Portuguese Atlantic Islands even as late as the time of World War I. In the mid-1800s, even on the better-off mainland Portugal, a traveler noted that one only had to travel a short distance from Lisbon to encounter peasants holding a goad over an ox cart with solid wooden wheels, just as one might have seen in the Middle Ages.[58] Nobel Prize-winning Portuguese author, Jose Saramago, wrote of the dire rural poverty, starvation, child labor and brutal mistreatment of peasants, on the rural latifundios in Portugal from the period of World War I until the 1974 Revolution in his novel, *Raised from the Ground*.[59]

On most of the Portuguese Atlantic islands, the economic situation of the people was worse than in mainland Portugal. Why were the islands so poor? In addition to the high physiological density that we have discussed, on the islands, most land was owned by large absentee landowners. Peasants worked the land with no remuneration other than the right to work it and to grow crops. In effect, they lived under conditions of feudal serfdom. While all land tenure systems are onerous to some degree, that of the Azores was particularly so. First, the land was inequitably distributed: three percent of the population owned all of the Azorean land in 1840. Secondly, the system of tenure, known as perpetual leasehold, required the peasant to pay a fixed amount of rent in cash or in crops, rather than a proportion of the crops, so while the peasant might benefit slightly in a good year, the fixed burden was onerous in bad years.[60] This system led to such exploitation that peasants at the time of the late nineteenth century, the first major wave of American emigration, were described as "abjectly and miserably poor." [61]

As with many islands worldwide, the economic history of the Azores and Madeira proved to be a search for export corps that would pay for needed imports. Throughout most of their history the situation was aggravated by a distant mother country that treated the Islands as true colonies; for example, taxing both imports and exports and requiring certain trade to go through Lisbon, adding to the excessive transport costs and consequent high costs of living faced by inhabitants of all small islands, worldwide.

Over the centuries, the agricultural export specialties of the islands, while never bringing true long-term booms in prosperity to the inhabitants, did bring devastating economic busts. In the Azores sugar cane was one of the first crops planted after the islands were settled, but it was quickly replaced by the woad plant, a source of the blue dye in the fourteenth and fifteenth centuries before indigo from the American colonies displaced Portuguese indigo in world markets.[62] Due to the historic trade connections developed between continental Portugal and Britain in wine, Britain was usually the main importer of Azorean and Madeiran products. Thus vines and lemons trees were planted for the British market until the lemon market collapsed in the early 1800s as Britain found other suppliers. The islanders experimented with everything from tea and tobacco to pineapples and oranges. Oranges gradually replaced the Azorean lemon market through the late 1800s. Madeira specialized more in growing pineapples, an agricultural skill that would later make Madeirans in demand for pineapple cultivation in Hawaii. The demand for wood for the manufacture of packing boxes for orange and lemon export denuded hillsides. Cattle grazing took over the upper slopes, a process that continues today with the expansion of beef exports to the mainland Portugal market.[63]

Various plant diseases had devastating impacts on the food and export crops of the Islanders. Three plant diseases hit in the mid-1800s spreading from island to island: an orange fungus, first noticed in 1835; potato rot (similar to that which hit Ireland) in the early 1850s, and grapevine rot in 1853.[64] The devastation of the two export products (oranges and wine) and the major food crop (potatoes) coincided with increased demand for male labor on the whaling vessels as well as with the California gold rush. The double attractions of whaling and the gold rush offered a combined opportunity: many Portuguese islanders signed on to whaling vessels and hopped ship in San Francisco, along with their American counterparts, to search for gold. The loss of both American and Portuguese whaling hands in San Francisco fueled the demand for more Portuguese labor on the whaling ships. Those Portuguese emigrants arriving in San Francisco helped form the core of modern-day Bay Area Portuguese settlement as the Azoreans shifted from whaling to panning for gold to agriculture.

Another way that whaling brought Atlantic islanders to California was through shore whaling, the practice of spotting whales from shore, rowing out to kill the whale, and rowing the carcass back to the island for processing. This technique was introduced to California by Portuguese from the Atlantic islands where shore whaling was carried out. By 1879 the Portuguese had set up 27 shore whaling stations along the Pacific coast including San Diego, San Luis Obispo, Monterrey, Crescent City and Portuguese Bend near San Pedro.[65]

Besides the abject poverty caused by the limited agricultural opportunity, another incentive for Portuguese to emigrate, especially for men, was military conscription. Compulsory military service for a distant mother country was an onerous burden for the Atlantic Islanders. All males at the age of sixteen faced three years of military service. That obligation was increased to four years in 1967 with a mandatory service period of two years in Africa. A substitute to serve could legally be bought but this was an option open only to the wealthy. In 1880 the Portuguese government tried to prevent illegal emigration by forcing families with male children to post a substantial bond when the male turned 14. The family would forfeit the bond if the youth emigrated surreptitiously.[66] While the term of service and penalties for not serving changed over time, in the 1960s and 1970s, the serious probability of actually fighting in a guerrilla war in Mozambique or Angola continued to encourage maximum legal emigration and much illegal emigration. As the practice of paying substitutes ended, more wealthy families used their affluence and influence to gain emigration permits for their sons. Thus there was an upswing in the numbers of wealthy and educated Portuguese male emigrants arriving in New England communities.

Of course, generalizing about all of the Portuguese Atlantic islands ignores substantial differences among them. St. Michael's and St. Mary's, two of the islands that sent the largest proportion of emigrants to New England, had the worst conditions of serfdom and poverty, whereas some other islands, such Fayal, had slightly better conditions with a few independent landowners. Yet travelers and observers in the late 1800s and early 1900s reported that, without exception, the island population appeared underfed. Typical household conditions were that families with many children lived in a single room and shared a single mattress in a whitewashed but windowless house. Rural households housed animals under the main floor. Cooking was done over a central hearth made of stones. The floor was dirt strewn with pine needles. The family was either entirely shoeless or owned a single pair of shoes shared by members of the

Figure 9
Portuguese immigrants in Fall River in 1921. The full caption written by the photographer tells us a lot about moral judgements made at the time: "Evening recreation of the "Young Holy Ghosters" - Ages 15 - 25, average is 18 - all mill workers - all Portuguese. Whole House on George Street. Great need of leadership." Photo by Lewis Hine, Courtesy of Library of Congress.

family. Women did heavy agricultural work as well as quarry work and rowing heavy barges, particularly in fishing villages where men were often at sea.[67]

The poverty appears in Portuguese American literature: the dismay of a second-generation woman visiting the islands for the first time as described in Sue Fagalde Lick's volume, *Stories Grandma Never Told*,[68] or the dream of having enough bread, sugar, and coffee, a mantra repeated a dozen times in Alfred Lewis' autobiographical work, *Home Is An Island*.[69] With poverty and relative rural isolation came illiteracy. In 1911 about 70 % of Portuguese islanders were illiterate. On many islands, such as Funchal, Madeira, only one-third could even sign their names on a marriage certificate, although the literacy rate was even higher (up to 70%) in Horta on the island of Fayal. Illiteracy rates among Portuguese immigrant women were as high as 83%, although there is evidence that on some islands, women, at least, may have been more literate than women in continental Portugal.[70]

IMMIGRATION FROM CAPE VERDE

Cape Verdeans, an ethnic group linguistically and culturally affiliated with the Portuguese, deserve special note. These individuals of Portuguese and African ancestry were sometimes called "Black Portuguese" or "Bravas" (from the name of one of the Cape Verde Islands). Like the Azores and Madeira, the Cape Verde islands suffered from poverty and high population density. Today almost 500,000 people live on this chain of volcanic islands totaling only 1550 square miles, giving the former Portuguese colony (now the nation of Cabo Verde, independent since 1975) a population density of about 310 people per square mile. Almost all Cape Verdeans immigrants before 1950 initially arrived in New Bedford because of the whaling industry and most remained in that city or within thirty miles of it. During 1911-1921 of 102,500 Cape Verdean emigrants, 70% were destined for Massachusetts or Rhode Island. The next largest destination, California, saw only 14% of the total of Cape Verdean emigrants.[71]

A number of New Bedford immigrants step-migrated to Providence and founded communities in that city. Currently, with almost 3,000 Cape Verdean immigrants arriving annually, almost all into in Massachusetts and Rhode Island, their numbers represent about seven times that of Portuguese immigration in recent years. As we will see shortly, Cape Verdeans, as well as the Portuguese, are two of the most concentrated of American ancestry groups and, if anything, Cape Verdeans are becoming more so as 95% of immigrants since 2000 are now arriving in these two states.

Even today, southeastern New England remains the only area of the United States that is home to historic Cape Verdean communities of any size. New Bedford, Providence, and East Providence are home to the older communities and through step-migration and direct migration, other Massachusetts cities including Brockton and Dorchester (in Boston) as well as to Pawtucket, Rhode Island have developed large communities. Eighty percent of the approximately 100,000 persons reporting Cape Verdean ancestry in the United States still live in Massachusetts and Rhode Island and more than half of these individuals live in three adjoining counties of Bristol and Plymouth in Massachusetts and Providence County in Rhode Island. In 2009 about one-third of the students in Brockton High School, the largest high school in the state of Massachusetts was Cape Verdean immigrants or of Cape Verdean ancestry.[72] There are some small rural Cape Verdean communities near the urban concentrations, such as in Wareham, between New Bedford and Cape Cod, where Cape Verdeans found jobs as cranberry workers.

In her study of the Cape Verdeans, Marilyn Halter, a historian, and American Studies scholar noted that the Cape Verdeans were the first black group to voluntarily migrate to the United States.[73] Cape Verdean entrepreneurs created a packet trade by purchasing derelict New Bedford whaling ships, refurbishing them as passenger vessels, and creating a business transporting immigrants between the islands of Cape Verde and New Bedford.[74] During this period, roughly, 1895 to 1920, the Cape Verdeans also become the only group of immigrants of African ancestry to control their own means of transport to the Western Hemisphere. Today, Cape Verdeans and their descendants overseas outnumber those living on the islands.[75]

3
GEOGRAPHICAL CONCENTRATION AND NEIGHBORHOODS

The persistence of neighborhood domination by the Portuguese for so long a period, more than 100 years now in most cases, is highly unusual among American ethnic groups.

Like many other American ethnic groups in many other cities, the Portuguese concentrated within specific neighborhoods. Portuguese settlement in the United States occurred primarily in northern California, Hawaii, and the northeastern United States, especially southeastern New England and New Jersey. In New England, they are located specifically in southeastern Massachusetts and adjacent parts of Rhode Island and Connecticut, the focus of this book

GEOGRAPHICAL CONCENTRATION

Today the Portuguese Americans are one of the most geographically concentrated of all American immigrants, especially among those with European ancestries. One study found that the Portuguese were the second-most geographically concentrated of 35 American ethnic and racial groups based on an index of spatial dispersion. Based on their analysis of the internal movement of 25 of these groups from 1975 to 1980, or in the case of the Portuguese, the relative lack of such movement, the authors showed that the Portuguese were likely to become the most concentrated group.[76] A 1988 study showed that the Portuguese clustered in so few locations that an index of geographic concentration listed the Portuguese the second least geographically dispersed of more than 50 ethnic groups studied.[77] (Interestingly, Cape Verdean was the group that had the highest index of concentration.) Another study in 1987 showed the Portuguese to be one of the most clustered populations in both the United States and Canada.[78] Because measures more recent than 1988 were not available, the author conducted his own study using 2010-2014 ancestry data by state. He found that with 65% of those with Portuguese American ancestry residing in just five states, they remain the most concentrated of 48 European ancestry groups identified by the Census Bureau. With the exception of a sub-group of very recently arrived refugees from Syria, Cape Verdeans had the highest index of concentration of all 102 ancestries listed.

Geographic concentration is normally a trait of small, newly arrived groups that have concentrated in one or two focal areas before dispersing geographically, such as the Syrian subgroup noted above. But the Portuguese and the Cape Verdeans, remain quite geographically concentrated despite the relatively large numbers of immigrants and the considerable amount of time the group has been in this county. Also, consider that waves of Portuguese immigration began in the late 1800s and early 1900s, so many of the Portuguese have been here as long as many of the Italians and some of the Irish who are extremely well-dispersed throughout the country, especially the eastern half of the nation. Interestingly, the Portuguese are similarly very concentrated in the Melbourne and Sydney urban areas of Australia compared to other ethnics,[79] and they are one of the most concentrated ethnic groups in Toronto.[80]

Why have the Portuguese remained so concentrated relative to other European ethnic groups? Income, education and strong family ties are undoubtedly the most important reasons. The Pew Research Center conducted a study in 2008 based on a survey and on US Census Bureau data[81] and they defined characteristics of two groups that they called "movers" and "stayers." Those with a college education tended to move more often than those with only a high school education. They tended to have higher incomes than stayers due to their higher levels of educational attainment. They also tended to move greater distances. Once someone moves to a distant area, they are also more likely to move again.

Movers gave economic opportunities – jobs --- as the main reason for moving. Given the educational levels among Portuguese Americans that have been mentioned and as we will shortly see in detail, there is not much incentive to move out of the area for hourly wage jobs. Stayers reported more family ties to an area; 40% of stayers reported ten or more relatives within an hour's drive of where they currently live and the majority had at least six relations nearby. The majority of movers had five or fewer relatives in the local area and 25% reported none. Stayers tended to report family ties as the reasons for staying put, in comparison to movers who sought better jobs. The strong family ties of Portuguese Americans, their lesser incomes, and educational levels combine to create strong incentives for them to remain in southeastern New England.

Census Bureau ancestry data in Table 2 (Portuguese Americans by State) show how Americans who identify themselves as having some Portuguese heritage are distributed in the United States. According to the 2010 American Community Survey Census, 1,443,000 American residents report some Portuguese ancestry with California home to the largest number, about 375,000. The phrase "some ancestry" means that those surveyed listed an ancestry among three allowed. That is, someone who responded to the ethnic heritage question as listing Irish, Portuguese and Italian ancestry would be counted among those with Portuguese ancestry in this book. Massachusetts follows California with 312,000 persons of Portuguese background, followed by Rhode Island with 101,000. With Connecticut's 54,000 persons of Portuguese ancestry, the tri-state region of southeastern New England has a combined total of 467,000 Portuguese Americans, a much larger figure than that for California and almost one-third (32%) of all those with Portuguese ancestry in the United States. As a proportion of the total population in these three states, Rhode Island has the largest percentage of persons with Portuguese ancestry, almost 10%, followed by Massachusetts with 5% and Connecticut with 1%.

Southern New England is home to an even larger proportion of persons born in Portugal than that shown by ancestry figures. Of the 189,000 American residents in 2010 who were born in Portugal, almost half (47%) live in southern New England: about 58,000 in Massachusetts, 17,000 in Rhode Island and 13,000 in Connecticut. As we will see in more detail later in this book, other than the three states of southern New England and California, Portuguese Americans reside in only a few other states in any significant numbers, mainly New Jersey, New York, Hawaii and Florida.

In addition to a concentration in a few states, the Portuguese have also settled in large numbers in only a few cities, making them the predominant ethnic group in those cities and differentiating them from a very large number of other European urban ethnic communities in the United States.

		Residents with Portugese ancestry		Residents with Portugese Ancestry Born in Portugal		Percent of total Portugese-Americans Living in each State
		Number	%	Number	%	%
1	California	374,602	1.0%	27,693	7.4%	26.0%
2	Massachusetts	311,767	4.8%	58,001	18.6%	21.6%
3	Rhode Island	101,095	9.6%	16,944	16.8%	7.0%
4	New Jersey	79,499	0.9%	35,345	44.5%	5.5%
5	Florida	69,472	0.4%	7,878	11.3%	4.8%
6	Hawaii	58,791	4.3%	159	0.3%	4.1%
7	Connecticut	54,477	1.5%	13,438	24.7%	3.8%
8	New York	52,947	0.3%	13,303	25.1%	3.7%
9	Texas	26,974	0.1%	1,278	4.7%	1.9%
10	Washington	22,051	0.3%	500	2.3%	1.5%
	MA, RI, CT (combined)	467,339	4.2%	88,383	46.9%	32.4%
	USA Total	1,442,896	0.5%	188,590	13.1%	100.0%

Source: Census Bureau: American Community Survey, Ancestry Data, 2010

Table 2. Portuguese Americans by State

Metropolitan Providence, Rhode Island, which, as of the 2010 Census includes Bristol County Massachusetts, including the cities of Fall River and New Bedford, and is thus the most convenient geographic unit to discuss population figures. Metropolitan Providence, with a population of 1,601,210 is the 37th largest metro area in the United States. Table 3 shows that the 259,000 people in the metropolitan area reporting Portuguese ancestry make up 12.7% of the population. This percentage is greater than that for any other ethnic group except the Irish with 14.7%, and it is higher than Italian ancestry at 12.1%. However, if we look only at first or primary ancestry listed, the Portuguese are the largest ethnic or racial group in metropolitan Providence: 13.2% compared to 12.1% for Italians and 12.0% for Irish.

		First Ancestry		All Ancestries	
		Number	%	Number	%
1	English/British	98,764	6.2%	166,925	8.3%
2	French/Fr. Canada	172,806	10.7%	254,816	12.7%
3	German	43,917	2.7%	81,545	4.1%
4	Irish	190,116	11.9%	292,284	14.6%
5	Italian	196,447	12.2%	245,378	12.2%
6	Polish	41,374	2.6%	65,870	3.3%
7	Portuguese	198,194	12.4%	248,126	12.4%
8	Brazilian	5,505	0.3%	6,394	0.3%
9	Cape Verdean	31,037	1.9%	35,429	1.8%
10	Hispanic or Latino	180,037	11.2%	*	*
11	Black or Afr. Amer.	109,421	6.8%	*	*
12	Port, Braz and C.V. (combined)	234,736	14.6%	289,949	14.5%

* not reported for Hispanics and African Americans

Source: Census Bureau, Census Reporter, American Community Survey 1-Year Ancestry Data, 2013

Table 3. Metropolitan Providence Ancestries (2013)

In terms of the preponderance of the dominant ethnic group, the Portuguese Americans in the two largest urban clusters -- the cities of New Bedford and Fall River, Massachusetts -- make up the greatest concentrations of such an urban ethnic group in large- or medium-sized cities anywhere in the United States, with only one exception. That exception is the concentrations of Hispanic persons in various cities of the American Southwest, and of Hispanics (Cubans) in some cities in the Miami area.[82] In Fall River, 40,000 of that city's 89,000 people report Portuguese ancestry (46%) and in New Bedford 36,000 of that city's 95,000 people report Portuguese ancestry (38%). These data are shown in Table 4 (Portuguese Ancestries in New Bedford and Fall River). For comparison with some other popularly-known ethnic concentrations, the percentage of people with Irish heritage in metropolitan Boston is 19%, whereas New York has 12% of its population with Italian ancestry and Milwaukee has 29% German ethnicity. And, if we add to the Portuguese totals the culturally and linguistically affiliated groups of Brazilians and Cape Verdeans, the Portuguese ancestry figures in Fall River and New Bedford rise to 49% and 48%, respectively as also shown in Table 4. Persons of Portuguese ancestry and culture dominate in these two communities.

GEOGRAPHICAL CONCENTRATION AND NEIGHBORHOODS

New Bedford		Population:	94,855
Ancestry		Number	%
Portuguese		35,577	37.5%
Brazilian		538	0.6%
Cape Verdean		9,470	10.0%
	Combined	45,585	48.1%
Fall River		Population:	88,705
Ancestry		Number	%
Portuguese		40,322	45.5%
Brazilian		1,563	1.8%
Cape Verdean		1,944	2.2%
	Combined	43,829	49.4%

Source: Census Bureau, Census Reporter, American Community Survey 3-Year Ancestry Data, 2010-2013

Table 4. Portuguese Ancestries in New Bedford and Fall River

Connections to Portugal are not only by ancestry: According to 2010-2014 data shown in Table 5 (Countries With More than 4,000 Foreign-Born Residents Living in the Providence Metropolitan Area). About 51,000 residents of Metropolitan Providence were born in Portugal. The 51,000 residents born in Portugal dwarf the numbers of every other group; the next closest number is the 23,000 residents born in the Dominican Republic. No other European country even has more than 4,000 foreign-born residents. And, as Table 5 shows, both Cape Verdeans (11,000) and Brazilians (4,600) are also major groups in Providence. Although not shown in the table, the majority of those born in Portugal in Metropolitan Providence reside in Bristol County, Massachusetts (36,000) with the largest clusters in Fall River (11,500) and New Bedford (10,000).

	Birth Country	Number		Birth Country	Number
1	Portugal	51,183	7	Brazil	4,558
2	Dominican Republic	23,341	8	Canada	4,551
3	Guatemala	17,924	9	Cambodia	4,217
4	Cape Verde	11,067	10	India	4,202
5	China	5,565	11	Mexico	4,026
6	Colombia	5,279			

Source: US Bureau of Census, Place of Birth for the Foreign-Born Population in the US, 2010-2014 American Community Survey 5-Year Estimates

Table 5. Countries with More than 4,000 Foreign-Born Residents Living in the Providence Metropolitan Area

THE DEVELOPMENT OF NEIGHBORHOODS

Portuguese neighborhoods in Fall River and New Bedford have housed the greatest number of immigrants and have been most frequently studied so those can serve as good examples of settlement patterns. The first detailed study of a Portuguese neighborhood was done by Donald Taft in the 1920s. He studied a 15-block Portuguese neighborhood in Fall River bounded by Hunter, Broadway, Columbia, and Division streets. This district was an area of heavy immigration from the Azores and, even then, specifically from the island of St. Michael's. Eighty of the 88 fathers of the 120 families he studied had been born on St. Michaels's.[83] Today, almost 100 years later, this neighborhood is still an area of Fall River that is a prominent Portuguese community, particularly for immigrants from St. Michael's.

In a 1960s study, Ira Sharkansky used Fall River City Directories to look for 16 specific Portuguese surnames.[84] He identified four districts based on common Portuguese surnames that were clustered around Portuguese churches in Fall River. He traced the percentages of these surnames in the four districts over ten-year intervals from 1890 to 1959 and showed that Down North and North Flint, as well as Fall River as a whole, had an even denser concentration of Portuguese with these surnames in 1959 than in 1890, and that only the Below the Hill neighborhood (also known as the Columbia Street neighborhood) showed a decline in Portuguese names.

Then in the 1970s sociologist, Dorothy Ann Gilbert took the same four Fall River neighborhoods clustered around the four churches and administered a city-wide survey asking if the head of household was Portuguese or Azorean.[85] She identified four vernacular neighborhoods with extensive concentrations of Portuguese: Below the Hill, focused on Santo Cristo Church, where 80% responded that they were Portuguese or Azorean. In Down North, centered around St. Michael's Church, 50% to 72% in two census tracts responded that they were Portuguese. In West Flint, focused on Espírito Santo Church, 42% were Portuguese and in North Flint, focused around St. Anthony of Padua Church, the figure was 58%. In addition, the area between the Down North and North Flint neighborhoods was 48% Portuguese.

She also showed that within these neighborhoods, immigrants clustered as extended families recreating their island communities and parishes block by block and neighborhood by neighborhood. Residents of island neighborhoods or parishes (*freguesias*) clustered by neighborhood in Fall River, usually on a few adjacent streets or city blocks. She found, for example, that 137 of 149 residents (92%) from one island neighborhood lived within a short distance of each other, and in the case of another *freguesia*, 150 of 180 of islanders (82%) did so. In another way of measuring the same phenomenon, she found that of 902 immigrants from St. Michael's only 16% were *not* located on the same street or between two intersections of other households from the same *freguesia*. Of a further subgroup of immigrants, 31% lived not only on the same street but within the same tenement house.[86] This immigration phenomenon also called "chain migration" [87] was really a process of transplanting Azorean island *freguesias* to Fall River neighborhoods.

Since new immigrants tend to cluster by region of origin, they maintain the identities and village rivalries that they brought with them into the new land. Gilbert cites many examples to show how Italians clustered by home village and district in Italian neighborhoods in New York. She noted a similar pattern of strong family and geographic village co-existence among Portuguese immigrants not only in Fall River but also in New Bedford.[88] Island and even village origin forms the core of identity that is carried to the new nation. Pap cites this extreme regionalism or factionalism of the Portuguese islanders, calling it *barrismo* from the term *barrio* or village neighborhood. Residential immobility in rural Portugal promoted such village allegiances and parochialism. For example, Portuguese census data from 1900, at the time of the first great wave of immigration to the United States, showed 94% of residents still living in the village of their birth.[89]

In New Bedford, Fonseca, the author of this book, showed neighborhood persistence over time in his study of that city's three major Portuguese communities. One neighborhood in the South End of the city was focused around Mt. Carmel Church; one in the North End of the city was focused around Immaculate Conception Church, and one, a Cape Verdean community between downtown and the South End Azorean community, was focused on Our Lady of the Assumption Church. In New Bedford's case, the South End community was comprised of many Azoreans, particularly from Fayal and Pico, but the North End community had many more Madeirans and Continental Portuguese as well as Azoreans from St. Michael's. Like Sharkansky, Fonseca used Portuguese surnames from a City Directory to identify Portuguese neighborhoods in New Bedford in the 1960s and showed how they corresponded with historic sites of Portuguese settlement in the city dating back to the mid-nineteenth century. With the exception of retreat from some neighborhoods around the downtown historic port area, the three major Portuguese communities were substantially the same ones found in the city in the 1860s.[90]

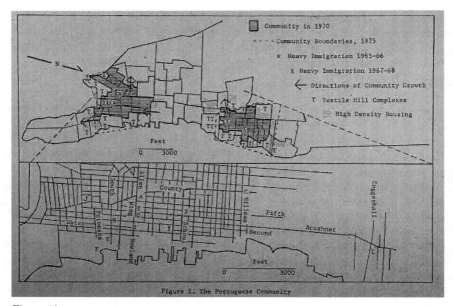

Figure 10
This map shows New Bedford's two main Portuguese communities in 1970 and how they had expanded by 1975. The communities are still centered on these two neighborhoods but have shifted somewhat. The inset map shows important historical sites of the community in the earliest days when a single community was focused near the waterfront between downtown and the docks.

This persistence of neighborhood domination by the Portuguese for so long a period, more than 100 years now in most cases, is highly unusual. Waves of neighborhood succession, one ethnic group displacing another, are common in most American cities and among most ethnic groups.[91] This phenomenon is also called sequent occupance, an academic phrase for the displacement of one ethnic group in a neighborhood by another, a staple of study by sociologists and geographers. There are hundreds, perhaps thousands, of ethnic neighborhoods in American cities but few persist with the same occupants for 100 years. The sequence of Irish, Germans, Italians, East Europeans, Jews, African-Americans, Hispanics, and East Asians saw in several American metropolitan areas is one example. Boston has neighborhoods that have housed in turn, over time, Irish, Italians, African Americans, and Hispanics. As cultural geographer Wilbur Zelinsky noted, neighborhoods, including even churches, can be recycled through a varied succession of immigrant groups.[92]

For an ethnic neighborhood to persist, geographer Allen Noble noted that even a relatively small ethnic group may compensate for small size by density. However, population numbers must be large enough to repel competition from other ethnic groups – that is, they have to effectively dominate the settlement area. He asked why some rural ethnic islands have persisted and others have disappeared and believed that the strength of religious conviction helps groups persist, citing the Welsh, Germans, German-Russian Mennonites, as well as persistence and extent of poverty, citing the Irish and Spanish-Americans. Also important is the timing of settlement; that is, the first effective settlement, meaning that the groups first on the scene (if they arrived prior to the English) have the greatest and longest-lasting impact in determining the cultural landscape of an area. Examples illustrating the last point are Germans in the central Texas hill country and the Scots-Irish in Appalachia.[93]

The Portuguese certainly had large numbers in the areas they settled. And the more-or-less continuous arrival of new immigrants, and especially the influx from 1960 to 1980, strengthened the traditional Portuguese ethnic elements in their neighborhoods and also may have delayed assimilation.[94] Perhaps also the more or less continuous economic recession/depression in old New England "mill towns" such as New Bedford and Fall River, due to the decline of the textile and apparel mills, has discouraged in-migration of other groups and protected the Portuguese neighborhoods from ethnic succession. And there is the unusual tendency, or at least the statistical tendency, of the Portuguese to "stay in place," more than most other ethnic groups. These factors contribute to this relatively rare phenomenon of ethnic neighborhoods persisting in place for more than a century.

So far, we have focused primarily on Massachusetts where most Portuguese immigrants settled. Neighboring Rhode Island's main attraction for the early Portuguese was simple proximity to southeastern Massachusetts and a similar initial economic focus on textiles and later, apparel. Some Portuguese spilled over the border to work in farming in nearby Portsmouth where they were the only immigrant group, unlike in the urban areas where they were one of many ethnic groups. As early as 1920 they constituted half of that small community's population. In Providence, which was a larger urban area than either New Bedford or Fall River, the earliest Portuguese were mainly day laborers employed as deckhands, longshoremen and meat packers or workers in coal and brickyards. By 1930 there were about 30,000 Portuguese in Rhode Island, mainly in the eastern part of Providence and working in textile mills in nearby Pawtucket, East Providence, and Bristol, stretching south to the farming cluster in Portsmouth and nearby Newport.[95]

THE LOCATION OF NEIGHBORHOODS

Where are these Portuguese neighborhoods located today? In Figure 1 we saw a map showing the clustering of neighborhoods in the three major urban areas along Interstate 195. Figures 11 through 14 offer a more detailed look at these neighborhoods in the four major urban areas of Portuguese concentration in southeastern New England: Fall River, New Bedford, Providence, and Taunton. The maps show major Portuguese, Cape Verdean and Brazilian neighborhoods based on census tract data from the 2010-2014 American Community Survey. Census tracts are areas defined by the Bureau of Census with populations of about 5,000 people although in these southeastern New England cities these vary from about 2,000 to 7,000 total population. Tracts are often bounded by features visible in the landscape such as major streets, highways, and parks. In urban areas, census tracts are primarily made up of clusters of city blocks.

Since the intent of these maps is to show "core" ethnic neighborhoods, the number of residents in each tract born in Portugal, Cape Verde or Brazil, and the percentage of each tract's population they represent were used to define neighborhoods. This measure of foreign birth was used, rather than using those who list Portuguese ancestry because so many people in all these cities have Portuguese ancestry that it is difficult making distinctions using that measure. Ancestry data are also less reliable data than the country of birth because people may report ancestry differently over time. In addition, the neighborhoods housing the most people of foreign birth are arguably the most vibrant neighborhoods because they house the most recent arrivals from Portugal, Cape Verde, and Brazil.

In each city "Portuguese Neighborhoods" were defined in both absolute and relative terms: census tracts with at least 400 persons born in Portugal and where those residents make up at least 8% of the tract population. Because the numbers of people born in Cape Verde or Brazil are less than residents born in Portugal, "Cape Verdean Neighborhoods" and "Brazilian Neighborhoods" were defined by tracts housing at least 100 residents born in those countries and where they made up at least 3% of tract population. In tracts where residents born in Portugal did not total 400 residents but still outnumbered those born in Cape Verde or Brazil, the tract was labeled as a "Portuguese and Cape Verdean Neighborhood" or as a "Portuguese and Brazilian Neighborhood." This method recognizes that many neighborhoods have mixed Portuguese, Cape Verdean, and Brazilian populations.

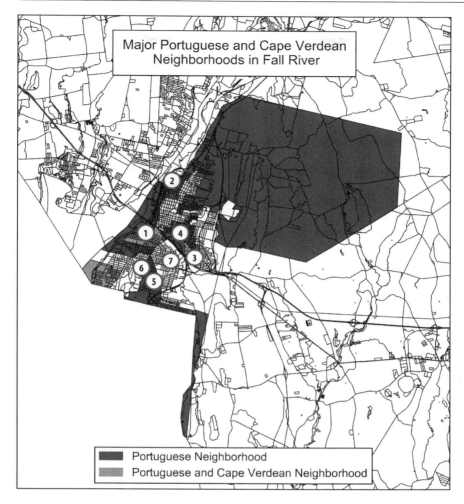

Figure 11
Major Portuguese, Brazilian and Cape Verdean neighborhoods in Fall River.

In Fall River with about 11,400 residents born in Portugal, the majority of the census tracts met the criteria for inclusion as a Portuguese neighborhood; 18 tracts of a total of 25. Almost the whole city is in one or another Portuguese neighborhood, although the size of these neighborhoods is exaggerated on the map by a large single census tract in the northeast part of the city that is largely rural and thus non-urbanized. Every census tract in Fall River has at least 100 people born in Portugal and every census tract has at least 5% of its population born in Portugal. In Fall River Portuguese have permeated every census tract in the city and the city is truly deserving of its designation in a National Geographic Magazine article in 1975 as "New England's Little Portugal." [96]

Portuguese-affiliated parishes labeled on the map are as follows: Santo Cristo (#1); St. Michael (#2); Espirito Santo (#3); St. Anthony of Padua (#4); St. Elizabeth (#5); Our Lady of the Angels (#6) and Our Lady of Health, which closed in 2006, (#7). Even though all these churches were founded between 1876 and 1924, all the areas around them remain Portuguese neighborhoods today.

Most notable is the neighborhood around Santo Cristo Church (label # 1) which is the tract with the highest percentage of persons born in Portugal (23%). This is the main Portuguese district in Fall River, the Columbia St. neighborhood, which is also designated by the City as a cultural heritage district. Santo Cristo was the first Portuguese parish in the city and historically it was the first district to be home to large numbers of Portuguese immigrants in the late 1800s. It is the same district that was intensively studied by Taft in the 1920s and then by Gilbert in the 1970s.

Keeping in mind that each of the 25 census tracts in Fall River is home to at least 100 people born in Portugal, it is perhaps easier to discuss what neighborhoods are *not* designated as Portuguese neighborhoods. These census tracts and neighborhoods are of three types. First is the traditionally highest-income area of the city called the Highlands, north of downtown and east of St. Michaels Church (label # 2 on the map.) Today this area remains a collection of large, ornate single-family homes, often historical mansions formerly owned by the elite of Fall River, many of them textile mill owners.

The second type of neighborhood is where Portuguese may have originally lived in large numbers but have been displaced by more recently arriving groups such as the area along the Taunton River north of St. Michael's (#2). Here small communities of Filipinos, Turks, Jamaicans and other West Indians now live. Another such neighborhood is in downtown Fall River east and northeast of Santo Cristo Church (#1), the main Portuguese Columbia Street district. Here are communities of Haitians and Vietnamese.

The third type of neighborhood is where other European ethnic groups have traditionally lived. Most of these groups are now fairly-well assimilated, such as French Canadians. One such area is at the far eastern end of the city, just east of Espirito Santo Church (#3). Before the influx of the Portuguese, Fall River was largely a city of French Canadian immigrants. In 1900 it was estimated that 40,000 of the city's then-100,000 residents were French Canadian immigrants and their descendants.[97] This neighborhood still has many residents of French Canadian ancestry. Another example is the area west of Our Lady of the Angels (#6) which at one time had large numbers of Polish residents.

Because of the domination in numbers by Portuguese, the city has a relatively small number of Cape Verdean (about 1,260) and Brazilian residents (about 540). These immigrants are clustered as shown on the map but are well-mixed in with Portuguese neighborhoods throughout the city.

Although New Bedford has almost as many residents born in Portugal as does Fall River (10,100 compared to 11,400) these residents are not as equally distributed across New Bedford as they are in Fall River; thus they are more concentrated in certain neighborhoods. In a cycle of cause and effect, New Bedford has many fewer Portuguese parishes. As in Fall River, these neighborhoods remain closely connected to churches but more clustered neighborhoods meant fewer churches are needed to serve the residents. New Bedford has only two active Portuguese Catholic parishes and one Cape Verdean parish compared to six in Fall River.

Nor are the Portuguese neighborhoods concentrated in the center of New Bedford; in fact, they appear to have pulled away from the center, although this is not a recent development. If we compare this map with that of Portuguese neighborhoods in the city in 1975 (Figure 10), we see that there were two distinct neighborhoods and neither was located in the center of the city. One was in the north end of the city around the Church of the Immaculate Conception (label #4) and one in the south end around Mt. Carmel Church (#2). Portuguese had already moved away from their initial settlements established during whaling days that were located near the harbor and close to the center of the city where St. John the Baptist Church (#2) had been built. With the loss of parishioners St. John's closed in 2015. But Cape Verdean residents remained near the center of the city and near their parish, Our Lady of the Assumption (# 1). New Bedford has nearly twice as many residents born in Cape Verde as does Fall River; about 2,300 compared to 1,260.

Another factor that has reduced the Portuguese presence in some areas is displacement by more recently arrived groups. New Bedford has an amazing number of small communities of immigrants from all over the world, perhaps reflecting its maritime economy and those international connections. The city is home to more than 1,000 resident born in Asia, mainly Indians and Cambodians; almost 2,500 from Central America, especially Guatemalans and Mexicans, and almost 1,000 from Caribbean countries, especially immigrants from the Dominican Republic. So there has been some displacement of Portuguese. For example a generation ago the Portuguese neighborhood in the north end would have been equally large south of Immaculate Conception church as north of it, extending south to Coggeshall Street, about twelve city blocks south of Immaculate Conception Church.

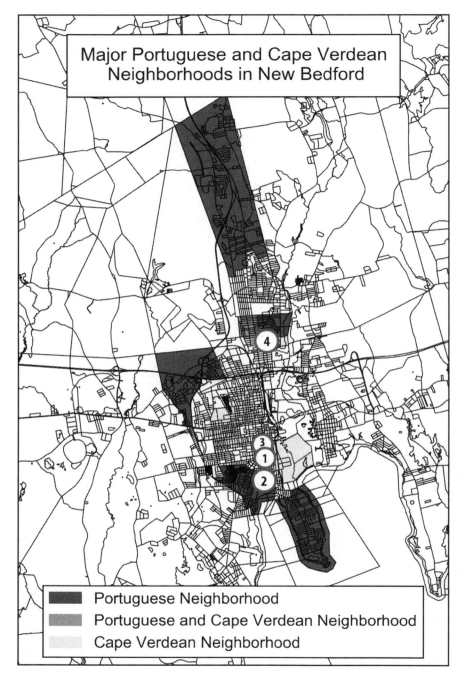

Figure 12
Major Portuguese and Cape Verdean neighborhoods in New Bedford

It is instructive to look at that area of New Bedford in detail because it shows how a Portuguese neighborhood can change over time as the oldest Portuguese residents die or move away and as newer immigrants move in. Specifically, this area in New Bedford is Census Tract 6512, an area of approximately 30 city blocks bounded by Coggeshall Street on the north, the Acushnet River to the east, State Route 18 to the west and Wamsutta Street to the south. It is bisected by Interstate 195 and it's various entrance and exit ramps which take up a considerable amount of space. Noise from the highways reduces its attraction as a residential area. It is primarily an area of three-deckers interspersed with retail and some wholesale and industrial buildings. While this tract is still home to more than 100 persons born in Portugal and about 30 born in Cape Verde, there is a wider variety of newer immigrants: about 300 born in Guatemala; 80 from El Salvador; 50 from Mexico and 30 from Honduras. In total, 25% of the tract's 2,400 residents are foreign-born.

A similar process of increasing diversity in Portuguese neighborhoods is going on, for example, in two census tracts in the northeastern corner of the city's south end community. While these two tracts are still part of the heart of the community, with (combined) more than 1,100 residents born in Portugal and more than 100 born in Cape Verde, several other immigrant groups have located there as well. Like the north end community discussed above, there are more than 200 residents born in Guatemala and about 100 born in each of three other Latin American countries: Mexico, Honduras, and El Salvador. But there are also 30 or 40 immigrants from countries such as Nigeria, Chile, and Vietnam.

Twenty-three of the 141 census tracts in Providence County met the criteria to be mapped on Figure 13. Of the county's 10,800 residents born in Portugal, a little more than half live in the neighborhoods defined by census tracts on the map. The largest cluster of residents lives in several census tracts in the East Providence area around the St. Francis Xavier Church (label # 2). This is the part of the metropolitan area closest to Massachusetts and to Fall River. These two cities are separated by only 15 miles along Interstate I-195 and many residents in East Providence live literally two or three minutes from the Massachusetts state line. The second largest community is in the northern part of Providence County in Cumberland/Valley Falls around Our Lady of Fatima Church (#1). As many Portuguese have moved out of the center of the city itself, there is no longer a large number of Portuguese-born living around the first Providence church established to serve them, Our Lady of the Rosary (# 4). Large numbers of Portuguese-born also no longer reside around St. Anthony's in West Warwick (# 5) although that church still holds an

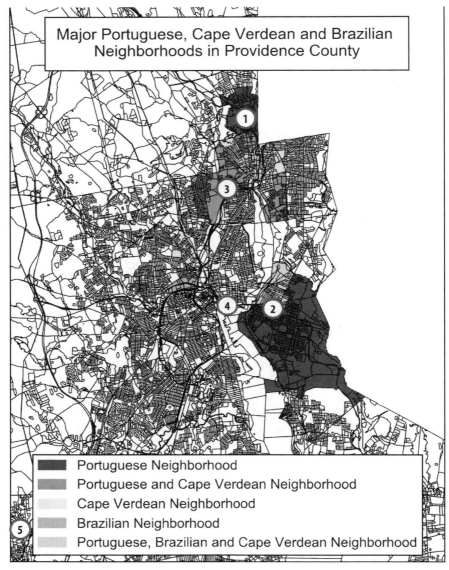

Figure 13
Major Portuguese, Cape Verdean and Brazilian neighborhoods in Providence County.

annual *festa* and procession.

An even larger number of census tracts, seven, are neighborhoods housing communities of both Portuguese and Cape Verdeans residents. This is particularly true of the area around St. Anthony's in Pawtucket (# 3). In all there about 7,400 residents of Providence County who were born in Cape Verde and about 70% of them live in mixed Portuguese/Cape

Verdean neighborhoods or in the nine tracts that define the Cape Verdean neighborhoods shown on the map. There is also one census tract in East Providence that is a Portuguese/Cape Verdean/Brazilian neighborhood. Large clusters of Cape Verdean residents are also located in the northern part of East Providence and some reside near the center of the city of Providence.

Relatively few residents of the County were born in Brazil; only about 1,100; but about 30% of these live in two census tract shown in neighborhoods on the map. One of these is a Brazilian neighborhood near the center of Providence and one is the neighborhood of mixed Brazilians, Portuguese and Cape Verdeans in East Providence mentioned above.

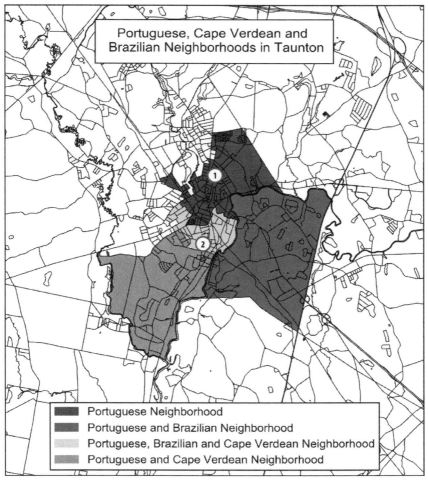

Figure 14
Major Portuguese, Cape Verdean and Brazilian neighborhoods in Taunton.

Taunton, with a population of 56,000, is substantially smaller than either New Bedford or Fall River. It is 17 miles north of Fall River and 23 miles from New Bedford. The city is also different from the other three urban areas looked at so far, in that those residents of Taunton born in Portugal are much more evenly distributed among its 11 census tracts than in the other cities. Five of Taunton's eleven census tracts are shown as a Portuguese neighborhood in Figure 14. The two largest tracts are clustered around St. Anthony Church (label #1) and those two tracts are home to 25% of Taunton's 3,600 residents born in Portugal.

Our Lady of Lourdes Church (label #2) is located in a mixed Portuguese, Cape Verdean, and Brazilian neighborhood. Two of Taunton's census tracts have substantial numbers of Cape Verdeans and those two tracts house almost 75% of the city's 375 residents born in Cape Verde. Similarly, two census tracts have large numbers of Brazilians and the two tracts shown as Brazilian neighborhoods are home to two-thirds of the more-than 500 Taunton residents born in Brazil.

MAINTENANCE OF ETHNIC NEIGHBORHOODS

As we will see in detail in our discussion of the economic geography of the community in Chapter 8, one often-overlooked consequence of the more-or-less continuously depressed economic environment in southeastern New England is that the Portuguese ethnic neighborhoods were relatively protected from succession by other ethnic groups. Ethnic succession, also called sequent occupance, means that one ethnic group moves out of a neighborhood and another moves in. Usually, the incoming group is of lower socioeconomic status than the one it is displacing. In Boston, for example, some neighborhoods have transitioned or changed the dominant occupying group many times, such as from Irish to Jewish to African American to Haitian. But persistently high unemployment in the southeastern New England cities for decades, from the Great Depression through the present, may be the predominant phenomenon that has discouraged other ethnic groups from migrating into these cities in large numbers. Few low-level jobs are available for newcomers because the Portuguese still occupy those jobs.

In New Bedford and Fall River, many of the earliest Portuguese neighborhoods that were established in the late 1800s and early 1900s remain as Portuguese neighborhoods today, more than 165 years after the initial settlement was established. For example, neighborhoods in New Bedford that had high concentrations of Portuguese-born in 1850 are the same ones that have high concentrations of foreign-born Portuguese today. And the 15-block Fall River Portuguese neighborhood studied by Taft, bounded by Hunter, Broadway, Columbia and Division streets, was an area of heavy immigration from the Azores and specifically from the island of St. Michael's (São Miguel) in 1920.[98] Today, almost 100 years later, this area is still a prominent Portuguese cultural community, particularly for immigrants from St. Michael's. Columbia Street remains a commercial focus for Portuguese restaurants and other businesses.

This continued neighborhood vibrancy of the Portuguese in southern New England cities is in sharp contrast to Little Italy in New York City, for example, where, other than a commercial strip of restaurants, only a few hundred persons of Italian heritage actually live today. According to the 2010 Census, only about 5% of the neighborhood's population reports Italian ancestry and not a single resident was born in Italy. This is in sharp contrast to the 40,000 Italian residents at the height of the neighborhood's size in the late 1800s and 10,000 Italian residents in 1910.[99] New York's Little Italy today is largely occupied by immigrant and first-generation Chinese and Koreans.

There has been some displacement of Portuguese by African Americans and Puerto Ricans in the urban core of central New Bedford in the neighborhood closest to the docks. This area just west of the waterfront was described as the original "Portuguese Quarter."[100] In some parts of the South End community of the city Portuguese have been displaced by Puerto Ricans, and on the southern fringe of the North End Portuguese district, by Hispanics. Fall River has many fewer African Americans, Puerto Ricans, and Hispanics than New Bedford, but there has been some displacement of Portuguese by Cambodians in that city. African Americans and Hispanics number 12,000, about 13% of New Bedford's population, whereas, in Fall River, those two groups comprise only about 7% of that city's population and the original Portuguese neighborhoods have been even less displaced. However, both cities have seen the demolition of three-decker neighborhoods for construction of Interstate 195 and connecting highways. But all in all, the preservation of the three-decker residences that comprise the cores of the Portuguese American neighborhoods have helped keep neighborhoods alive.

This "stickiness of place," if you will, is clearly related to the numbers, density or concentration and the amount of recent immigration of Portuguese within the neighborhoods.[101] As we have seen, the Portuguese very much tended to settle in neighborhoods near the old brick textile mills, living in three-story wooden tenement buildings, known locally as "three-deckers" or "triple-deckers," one family per floor. Their communities are marked by distinctive landscape features including grapevines, shrines, and gardens.[102] Starting out as renters, the Portuguese who dreamed of home ownership eventually acquired these buildings and rented other floors to family and acquaintances from their villages, a model that has worked for over a century.

4
THE HYBRID LANDSCAPE

The Portuguese American landscape is enriched by large and small reminders contributed by successive generations of immigrants: ethnic landscape signatures.

LANDSCAPE CONCEPTS: OVERT AND SUBTLE SYMBOLS

Frank Gaspar, mentioned earlier as the author of *Leaving Pico* is also a poet. In his poetry, the ear can pick up the sadness, the cultural longing, the hardships of the Portuguese community, even though the word *Portuguese* is never written. Nowhere, as Alice Clemente, former Chair of the Department of Spanish and Portuguese at Smith College notes, does Gaspar ever specifically mention Portugal, the Portuguese language, or the Portuguese community that is the object of his artistic focus.[103] But many clues tell us that this is no generic Old World, despite the similarity to other European Old Worlds, but a specific Old World within the New World: a Portuguese American world in Provincetown, Massachusetts, in the era just after World War II.

In a similar fashion to looking for cultural clues in poetry, the eye of the trained observer can find Portuguese influences in the landscape, large and small, blatant and subtle, even when no billboard announces, "Entering the Portuguese American community." As Michael Conzen, a geography professor at the University of Chicago notes, the American landscape is enriched by large and small reminders contributed by successive generations of immigrants. He calls these features "ethnic landscape signatures."[104] Cultural geographer Pierce Lewis suggests that ethnic cultural landscapes present us with a series of sedimentary layers of social accretion.[105] The landscape reflects the major cultural signifiers of the Portuguese community just as poetry reflects those cultural signifiers in coded sign and symbol: this is the semiology of culture. Semiology (or semiotics), the use of cultural signs and symbols in the landscape, builds on the work of French philosopher and linguist Roland Barthes.[106] Not all symbols are self-evident; some knowledge of Portuguese culture is necessary to recognize many of these symbols. And with a few clues, a guidebook so to speak, signs are present everywhere in the panorama we see around us in southeastern New England.

So, how would a casual visitor to New England know he or she was in a predominantly Portuguese American area? Geographers have listed five major contemporary public expressions of ethnic culture: ethnic heritage celebrations, landscape, museums, ethnic voluntary associations and homeland visits.[107] These scholars divide cultural markers in the landscape into two subcategories, overt and subtle. In the case of the Portuguese American landscape, overt signs include such things as monuments, religious shrines, distinctive Portuguese gardens and signage in the Portuguese language. Subtle signs might include such things as the sidewalk display of retail goods and the large satellite antennas used to receive Portuguese television broadcasts (especially soccer games) found on the grounds or roofs of Portuguese social clubs. Landscape elements have also been divided into fixed and semi-fixed features. Fixed features, such as building style and street patterns, are hard to change and may not reflect any obvious Portuguese influence. But semi-fixed features, such as symbols and names on storefronts, lawn ornaments and yard shrines, house colors, national flags, signs with ethnic names (such as political posters), fences and gardens are easier to install and to change and thus tend to reflect Portuguese culture more often and more overtly.[108]

Other common indicators of Portuguese influence that can be seen in the landscape but are more subtle than such obvious structures as churches are benevolent associations and social clubs. Benevolent associations, as among other immigrants groups, were formed to assist the newly arrived immigrants with housing and employment information, banking services, life insurance (originally burial insurance), and English language classes. While some benevolent associations still exist, such as the *Associação Academica* of Fall River, Portuguese credit unions, often affiliated with churches, are a modern-day offshoot of the benevolent societies. An example is the Espírito Santo Credit Union in Fall River, associated with the church of that name. Another iteration of the benevolent associations has resulted in youth organizations, some sponsored by social clubs.

Subtle signs of Portuguese American culture also include the busy mixed pedestrian and auto landscape that mark many Portuguese American neighborhoods and which keep downtowns more vibrant than is the case in cities without Portuguese neighborhoods. These "streetscapes," and "yardscapes" give a distinct character to the Portuguese American landscape. In addition to dense pedestrian and vehicular traffic, a healthy mix of residential and commercial land use, and the sidewalk display of goods impart a European feel to many of these streetscapes. Compared to other distressed and sometimes deteriorated neighborhoods in many other old New England mill towns, most Portuguese neighborhoods have held up well. Given the reputation of the Portuguese for the upkeep of their properties, and, until recently, the continuous infusion of new arrivals, the Portuguese communities remain occupied and vibrant, not blighted and abandoned. This vibrancy supports the preservation of nearby downtowns and traditional neighborhood shopping districts. The ethnic neighborhood shopping districts in the Portuguese districts and the downtowns of New Bedford and Fall River do not have as many vacant buildings and are not as economically distressed as many other New England cities of equivalent size that were similarly dependent upon textile, apparel or other factory employment in the past.

One scholar uses the term streetscape to summarize these characteristics and notes that every urban neighborhood has a principal commercial street which, in an area of immigration, is often converted into an "ethnic main street." Within these neighborhoods, ethnics make their presence known to co-ethnics through business signs and names of businesses that reflect place names from the home country or significant cultural artifacts. National flags, national crests, and religious symbols are displayed, and colors of the national flag may be found in places such as store awnings.[109]

Geographers use a variety of tools to explore the cultural landscape, a concept that has been defined as the artificial landscape created by people in their re-shaping of nature.[110] While the work of many traditional geographers initially focused on the physical terrain and the environmental impact of the cultural landscape,[111] the bulk of modern work studies culture itself in the landscape, in both urban and rural settings. Following the pioneering work of J. B. Jackson,[112] who, to put it broadly and simply, saw landscape as a reflection of society, geographers have realized the tremendous source of information and clues about the culture that is inherent in the vernacular or "every day" scenery that we take for granted. He asked how should we think of landscapes? This means not merely how they look, but how they satisfy the elementary or basic needs: the need for sharing some of those sensory experiences in a familiar place including popular

Figure 15
A dual flag logo on the sign of a social club in New Bedford. The club's name translates as "memories" or "remembrances" of Portugal. The members of this club are mainly from mainland Portugal.

songs, common food dishes, and sports and games. Jackson believed that these things remind us that we belong to a specific place: a country, a city or a neighborhood. He also believed that a landscape should establish bonds between people through language and customs or manners. He further wrote that a landscape should foster the type of spatial organization that encourages experiences and relationships, that is, it should offer special spaces for gathering to celebrate; but also spaces to be alone, and spaces that remain the same so that when we come back to them at some time in the future, they are as we remember them and hopefully, we will again feel an emotional attachment to the landscape.[113]

Cultural geographers have written that many Americans are oblivious to their everyday environments: like fish, they can't see the water all around them.[114] Landscapes, whether created or modified, are made by human beings and are human-made artifacts that are cultivated and reflect human values. For example, the scenery we think of as characteristic of the English countryside is almost wholly human-made; it is tamed nature used for human needs and pleasures.[115] Geographer Peirce Lewis created a list of "axioms for reading the landscape" that characterize the concept as a clue to culture.¹¹⁶ His major premise was that the man-made vernacular landscape – the collection of ordinary run-of-the-mill material things that humans have created and put upon the earth – provides strong evidence of the kind of people we are, and were, and are in the process of becoming. In short, landscape reflects present, past and future.

The culture of any nation is unintentionally reflected in its ordinary or vernacular landscape. Nearly all items visible as you take in the panorama around you reflect the culture in some way. Most items in the landscape are of equal importance meaning that most are *not* more important than others. Different observers bring preconceptions to what they observe, as geographer Donald Meinig notes. These different individuals may interpret what they find in a landscape as nature, human habitat, artifact, environmental or cultural system. Or they may interpret what they see as "a problem," a place, a historical remnant, or an aspect of wealth, ideology or aesthetics.¹¹⁷ He encourages observers to abandon the stance of a spectator and to try to experience the panorama in terms of its inhabitants, which means asking ourselves how a person who has to live in it fares. What chances, for instance, does the landscape offer for making a living? What chances does it offer for freedom of choice of action? What chances exist for meaningful relationships with other people and with the landscape itself? What are the opportunities for individual fulfillment and for social change?¹¹⁸

With such a wealth of multi-layered cultural meanings, the geographical setting of the Portuguese American community of southeastern New England is a vernacular landscape that provides the scholar with an excellent opportunity to study the manifestation of Portuguese culture within its larger American context. This is especially true in aspects of the landscape related to semiology (signs and cultural symbols), land use and architecture. Geographers call such a landscape the spatial expression of societal organization.

THE RESIDENTIAL ENVIRONMENT

The new living arrangements that the Portuguese encountered in New England brought challenges to their culture in many aspects of their day-to-day living arrangements. First and foremost for many was the transition from rural village island culture to all of the good and bad aspects of modern American urban life in a medium-sized New England city. The largest city in the Azores, Ponta Delgada with about 70,000 people, is smaller than the legal cities of either New Bedford or Fall River. Without attempting to catalog all these dramatic changes, just a brief listing of some of the more important ones shows us challenges that are daunting, if not overwhelming, to the new rural immigrant, and even to those Portuguese who came from small cities. Consider urban density, automobile ownership, traffic congestion, street violence, drugs, neighborhood gangs, HIV/AIDS, Fordism (especially production lines and night shift factory work), women working outside the home, and changes in dress and courtship rituals for young people. Any one of these cultural shifts, such as rural women working outside the home for the first time, undoubtedly introduced stress and change into the home and challenged traditional patriarchic arrangements perhaps in the same way that was experienced by Cubans who immigrated to the United States after Castro.[119]

But it is at home that we can learn a lot about the Portuguese. Landscape scholars tell us that the dwelling should be the primary focus of study by human geographers because a house is a microcosm of human efforts to organize the environment to suit their biological, social and spiritual needs. The collective structure we call landscape is the result.[120] Look for difference: it is the individual house that stands out from the majority of American buildings in design or construction that best shows ethnic influence in the landscape.[121] But the urban Portuguese, unlike, say rural Finns or Norwegians in northern Minnesota, occupied an already-built environment.[122] The Portuguese were not shaping a rural landscape from scratch by recreating their housing style, settlement pattern and rural central place system. Urban-dwelling immigrant groups such as the Poles did not initially homestead or own their own land; they accepted whatever housing already existed when they arrived. Consequently, Polish neighborhoods in large American cities are usually difficult to distinguish from those of other communities.[123] Urban living quickly integrates immigrants into architectural norms, so vernacular housing in cities tends not to have the strong ethnic peculiarities of rural housing. Urban ethnics move among houses and neighborhoods and participate in the existing city-wide housing market, unlike rural ethnics, who may live a lifetime in a home they constructed themselves. At best ethnic decorations on traditional housing stock may mark ethnic territory and this is mainly the case with the Portuguese in southeastern New England, even though an occasional single or multi-family home can be found that shows distinctive Portuguese architecture.[124]

It is fascinating to note that the style of the basic housing stock in the cities primarily settled by the Portuguese in New England is uncommon by national standards. The predominant style of housing in the Portuguese neighborhoods, as it is for many other middle- and lower-income residents of the area is the wooden three-story tenement house colloquially known as the "three-decker." [125] These structures were built as worker housing within walking distance of the textile mills complexes and they remain the predominant type of housing in all the Portuguese neighborhoods of New Bedford and Fall River. Joseph Conforti, a professor of American Studies whose mother was Portuguese and who grew up in Fall River, has written about the distinctive New England landscape created by the combination of three-deckers neighborhoods and the dense ethnic-immigrant-Catholic culture of the Portuguese and others living in them.[126] Portuguese building preferences even game a name to a particular architectural style, the "Portuguese dormer." [127] The construction of three-deckers closely coincided with mill construction, especially during the second wave of the textile mill boom, 1901 to 1925. In 1910, the peak year of mill construction in New Bedford, building permits for three-deckers reached their peak, 290 permits.[128]

Figure 16
Portuguese dormers. The attic of what otherwise would have been a two-decker is expanded outward, effectively making the house a three-decker. Located in New Bedford near Mt. Carmel Church in the south end Portuguese community.

Each family occupies a single floor of a three-decker. The interior of a typical three-decker usually includes only six or seven rooms: a dining room or parlor; a living room or family room; three bedrooms, a kitchen (often too small for a dining table) and one bathroom. While many Portuguese are tenants in these houses, some own the houses, living on one floor and renting out the other two floors, often to relatives. In the local idiom, people will say "I live over my mother on Nash Road" or "She lives under her sister on Tinkham Street." The three-deckers are densely packed. About one-half acre of land will sprout four three-deckers housing twelve families. With three families per house, increasing auto ownership, and limited parking on the street, many front yards, and some backyards have been turned into driveways and parking lots.

The vertical residential structure of these three-story buildings, rather than the traditional horizontal structure of homes in rural areas and villages in Portugal, provided another challenge. Yet, in some ways, the structure was not all that different from what the immigrants had left behind on the Atlantic islands. In the typical village, houses were clustered closely or attached to each other. Walls of houses may extend to the street. Extended families lived next door or nearby and moved freely in and out of the neighboring houses of relatives. Neighborhoods (*freguesias*), which were often synonymous with parishes, had a high kinship density and almost all inhabitants of a village were relatives or distant relatives to some degree.[129] The three-decker environment of New Bedford and Fall River allowed villagers to replicate these relationships, one might say, with "more verticality and less horizontality." The parcel of land for a garden, never large anyway, was reduced to at most perhaps 1,000 square-feet in the backyard of a three-decker. This change in style of living, however, created additional problems and opportunities for the immigrant such as learning to share the yard and more exposure to landlord-tenant relations. The Portuguese have also adapted to more widespread auto ownership than in the islands and the attendant social disruptions produced by the auto.

The three-deckers are close enough to each other for casual conversation over the fence, from a front window or door to the street, from porch to porch, and from house to house when women hang clothes from upstairs windows. One family's laundry may hang over a neighbor's yard because of shared clothesline poles (of three-story height). Since yards are small, to begin with, and are occupied by gardens and outdoor furniture, children seldom have large spaces to play unless they happen to live near a city park or schoolyard. Children often play in the street. While the majority of these homes in the working class neighborhoods are three stories, some are four- and some are two-stories; some are "doubles," in effect, contiguous three- and occasionally four-deckers housing six or eight families, respectively. The three-decker neighborhoods grade into two-decker neighborhoods and then single-family homes. Two-deckers and even an occasional single-family home are interspersed among the three-decker neighborhoods. And, of course, many Portuguese Americans live in single-family homes and in more traditional low-rise apartments, condominiums, and townhouses. Both Fall River and New Bedford have medium-rise apartment buildings of eight to ten stories, usually comprised of units offering federally-assisted rents, especially for the elderly. Often these more varied styles of housing are usually outside of the districts defined as Portuguese American neighborhoods, although there are exceptions such as the ten-story apartment building in Fall River's Columbia Street Portuguese district.

Figure 17
A view showing the density of three-decker housing in Fall River. All three-deckers were built within walking distance of the textile mills.

Daily living arrangements in this triple-decker housing in the new country produced new stresses and opportunities such as learning to share the yard. If all three tenants are related, as is often the case, the yard is used as a communal property of the extended family. Otherwise, sharing the yard of a three-tenement home takes some doing. If the owner is not a family member and lives in the tenement, regardless of what floor he or she lives on, the yard will be used almost exclusively by the owner, except for necessary functions of other residents such as putting out the trash or connecting a garden hose to wash a car. When the owner does not live on the property, one family often functions as caretaker of the property for the owner. They shovel snow, cut the grass and put out the trash, often earning the exclusive right to use of the backyard and to parking, if any, on the property.

The front yards of the three-deckers may sport grass, flowers or a shrine, or space may be used for parking. It is the backyard that provides more privacy and is used for family activities such as child play, gardening, barbecuing, drying clothes or carpets. The typical yardscape also includes grapevines, kitchen gardens, religious shrines, food preparation areas and often an "outdoor room" as an appendage to the house. Backyards are filled with lawn chairs, plastic wading pools, and barbecue grills. Clotheslines are omnipresent, as four three-tenement homes will spout twelve clotheslines. Even in this era of clothes dryers, the Portuguese often economize by hanging laundry outdoors if the weather is pleasant. Pigeon coops are still sometimes seen in Portuguese American backyards, but they are increasingly uncommon and never were as common in the Portuguese community as in Italian immigrant neighborhoods.

Backyards of three-deckers are crowded, yet neat, and multi-functional. This multifunctional yard calls to mind J. B. Jackson's musing that what we need is not an aerial perspective of the globe but an aerial perspective of our own backyard. We can't understand that the world is our home and that we should love it until we learn to love our own corner of it.[130] Like some Latino landscapes, such as those of East Los Angeles, signs or landmarks may not identify a Portuguese neighborhood, but what distinguishes it is the use of space enabling people to congregate around the home. Occasionally tables and chairs in the front yard incorporate that space into the home and effectively move the threshold of the home from the front door to the front gate.[131]

Portuguese Americans aspire to home ownership as much as do Americans. Nationally, according to the most recent data available by ancestry, the 2006-2010 American Community Survey, almost as many persons of Portuguese ancestry own homes (66%) as do all Americans (69%). Homeownership

Figure 18
The backyard of this three-decker in New Bedford is crowded yet neat and multifunctional including an old garage now serving as a storage shed, a shrine, dog house, picnic table, grapevine, hanging laundry, trash can storage, toys, lawn ornaments and garden (behind the fence).

figures for Portuguese Americans are fairly consistent across southern New England with 65% owning homes in Massachusetts, 66% in Rhode Island and, a slightly higher number, 73% in Connecticut. (And they are consistent with statistics for Portuguese in Canada.[132]) Even in Bristol County, Massachusetts, 63% of Portuguese Americans are homeowners and only 37% are renters. In the three-decker environment of Fall River and New Bedford, home ownership figures are lower, as would be expected because only one household of the three occupied floors can be an owner, although some individual floors of three-deckers are now being sold as condominiums. But even in these two core cities of Portuguese Americans, home ownership prevails in New Bedford (55% owners, 45% renters), although that situation is reversed in Fall River (52% renters, 48% owners).

Portuguese American homes are well cared for, and, in owner-occupied units, sometimes the exteriors are decorated with architectural touches as if they were single-family homes. White or cream stucco may replace siding; brick or stone steps may be added along with mosaic work, wrought iron, and red clay roof tiles. Outdoor rooms may be built in the backyard. These Mediterranean (technically, Southern European) influences are increasingly added to both three-deckers and single-family homes to make them more reminiscent of homes in the old country, a recently occurring phenomenon akin to the concept of "cultural rebound" where, over time, a cultural or ethnic group has greater financial means to reestablish or to revert to ethnic ways.[133] The interiors of Portuguese American single-family homes may show hybridized culture by having an "American style" upstairs where visitors are greeted, and a "Portuguese style" downstairs leading out to the outdoor room of the backyard where the family spends most of its time.[134] It is also interesting to note that such diffusion in housing styles has developed into a two-way, trans-Atlantic exchange. Portuguese American emigrants returning to their homeland are known for building American-style single-family houses in Portugal, called *casa do emigrante,* an emigrant's home.

The gated or fully-fenced yard is common in Portuguese American neighborhoods, just as it is a recognized feature of Spanish and Mexican American landscapes. Daniel Arreola, a geographer writing about Mexican American neighborhoods in the Southwest, traces these enclosures to Iberia and suggests the feature goes back to Islamic influences upon Spain,[135] but the same could be said of Islamic influences upon

Figure 19
Portuguese homes are well-cared for. Owner-occupied three-deckers are sometimes decorated as if they were single family homes. Here the owner has added southern European touches including an arch, red clay tiles, curved masonry walls, decorative spheres and wrought iron fencing.

Portugal. He notes that the origin of this architecture, where dwellings and walls form enclosures, served to give privacy to women and families, a strong tradition in Islamic culture. *Azulejos,* the blue and white tiles with yellow and white borders that are indigenous to Portugal, are an additional detail found in Portuguese homes and often in their exterior decoration.[136] These polychrome tiles also trace their origins back to Muslim influence. Other aspects of Islamic landscapes exported to the Iberian Peninsula include plazas, tiles, water, fountains, geometry and the veneration of trees. These features are encapsulated in the "paradise garden" that celebrates the effect of irrigation on an arid world, another cultural influence brought by the Muslims of North Africa to the Portuguese and Spanish and then to America.[137]

The physical structure of Portuguese neighborhoods has remained relatively intact with the exception of some urban renewal of the very oldest buildings and swaths in each city that were cleared for the construction of Interstate 195 and connecting arteries in the late 1950s through the 1960s. Indeed, I-195, bisecting the three cities that house the largest concentrations of Portuguese Americans – East Providence, Fall River, and New Bedford – has become the "Portuguese American Interstate Highway." Otherwise, there has still not been the massive replacement of these structures that have occurred in other urban areas with greater population growth as noted by geographer Arthur Krim.[138] In brief, the relative lack of economic growth that we will discuss in a later chapter is a factor in the preservation of the area's landscape including its three-deckers.

Nor have areas become blighted, as one might expect of neighborhoods composed of the old industrial housing adjacent to mills and factories that have shed most of their employees.[139] Also contributing to neighborhood preservation are social characteristics of many Portuguese Americans. The Portuguese are known for their ethic of hard work, improvement of their homes and neighborhood, and their unwillingness to accept social services and welfare. While this may sound like a benign ethnic stereotype, both Leder and Muller found these traits to be statistically true in the Portuguese communities they studied on opposite coasts, San Jose, California and Newark, New Jersey, respectively. Muller credits the Portuguese with helping revitalize Newark by fixing up their neighborhoods, helping that city improve its image, creating a net surplus in social services by paying taxes but not accepting welfare, sending their children to parochial schools rather than to public ones, and underutilizing police services due to their low crime rate.[140] Again, perhaps this lack of economic dynamism in these old textile towns has helped to preserve the landscape and thus created a sense of historical continuity. Geographer

David Lowenthal tells us that knowing that our neighborhood structures are durable gives us a better sense of being rooted in a place.[141]

A HYBRID LANDSCAPE

At first appearance, the Portuguese American landscape of southeastern New England is a distinctive landscape, neither typically American, nor Portuguese, but a hybrid creation combining elements of the two cultures. But ultimately it is an American landscape providing American solutions to American problems. There are many sections of American cities where immigrant groups and their descendants make up all or most of the population, with distinctive ethnic markers such as shop signs, religious objects, festival decorations, cemetery features, and historical monuments, but Zelinsky wrote that he has never found a "non-American" ethnic landscape in any American city. He even specifically noted the use of color in Portuguese communities, calling them a "chromatically adventurous group." But the buildings turn out to be compromised structures, a blending of styles and construction techniques from two contrasting ethnic worlds. He wrote that "...we are dabbling with cosmetics instead of basics." [142]

Geographer Joseph Wood also noted that there is no such thing as a truly non-American ethnic landscape. Instead, there are ethnic markers and compromises and manipulations of pre-existing forms, such as shopping plazas.[143] Thus we can safely say that the Portuguese Americans have created a hybrid landscape that is neither a typical American one nor a typical Portuguese landscape. Rather, it is a unique American landscape that blends and reflects both American and Portuguese cultural values. The continuous work of shaping the material things of the landscape into more familiar forms reduces the stress or the discordance induced by the immigration process. Ethnic groups, like everyone else, try to shape their corner of the world into something "distinct and memorable." [144] This effort may be made deliberately or even unconsciously.

A helpful metaphor in understanding how the Portuguese American landscape is an *American* landscape comes to us from literature where there is a similarity between discussions of American ethnic literature and discussions of ethnic landscapes. Reinaldo Francisco Silva, the author of the book *Portuguese American Literature*, has pointed out how American ethnic literature is *American* writing.[145] It is the ethnic or cultural outsider who can best tell us what it means to exist within American culture; literature about those who are on the edge of American culture, written by those on that edge, can tell us volumes about what happens within that culture.[146] Francis Rogers wrote that the ethnic literature of Americans of Portuguese descent and birth forms part of American literature, not of Portuguese literature. It treats American problems, not Portuguese problems.[147] And Almeida reminds us that there are also some works about the Portuguese American immigrant experience published only in the Portuguese language.[148] The dozen or so autobiographies of Portuguese immigrants all tell one *American* story: that of the struggle to achieve the American dream and the success or partial success of the author in achieving it.[149] Using these concepts of ethnic literature as a metaphor we can apply them to the Portuguese American area of southeastern New England and explicitly state that the landscape is an American one, not a Portuguese one. Thus what we see in this Portuguese American region can tell us a lot about American landscape; indeed it is an American landscape.

A significant factor affecting this landscape is that the Portuguese arrived in an area that had already been settled for centuries. Zelinsky tackled this issue by developing a theme that he called "the Doctrine of First Effective Settlement." Simply stated, the concept is that the first cultural group to effectively settle and control an area sets the rules of the game for future settlement to which all other groups must adapt.[150] These rules include the dominant language, type of political system and land use policies. As if to illustrate this concept, in Frank Gaspar's poem *Beachcombing*, a Portuguese boy and his grandfather find in the Provincetown sand rusted Yankee artifacts from long before they came. And a considerable time it was, given that the British had a 250-year head start in New England, arriving in Plymouth, symbolically touching first in Provincetown in 1620, long before the great number of Portuguese began arriving in the late 1800s. Metaphorically and literally, the puritanically stern Pilgrim Monument, the tallest structure in Provincetown, overlooks the community like a watchful eye; an ever-present reminder to the Portuguese of who was here first and of their place in New England society.

Thus, the Portuguese arrived in a setting in which the dominant culture was already in place. English speakers had pre-established the cultural framework ranging from the political system and language to building codes, architectural style and system of land tenure. Houses were already built, streets were already named, and capitalist systems such as factory employment and methods of dividing the profits from whaling voyages were all in place. Groups that came in later, or much later like the Portuguese, faced the proverbial uphill battle in their exertions to adapt to that dominant culture and social system and in their attempts to adapt the accumulated cultural artifacts, including housing stock, to their needs.

The Portuguese, like many other American immigrant ethnic groups, were adapting their culture to the framework established by the preceding culture; not only the English but also the Irish, French Canadians, and Poles who had settled many of these neighborhoods before the Portuguese.

GARDENS, SHRINES AND FLAGS

The Portuguese American landscape is a complex hybridized landscape that defies simplistic explanations. It is easy, but, as we shall see, simplistic, to assume that Portuguese cultural artifacts in the landscape were "transplanted" to America. Three examples showing the complexity of these unique blends of culture are demonstrated by Portuguese American gardens, religious shrines and the display of the Portuguese flag. To the tourist and the casual visitor, gardens, shrines, and flags are quaint re-creations of cultural items brought from the home country to the United States to make strange surroundings more familiar to the immigrants. In reality, these cultural artifacts are often used in ways *unlike* they were used in Portugal and, to some extent, represent a *reaction* to American culture.

Take the Portuguese American garden. J. B. Jackson noted the importance of gardens to American ethnic groups. He wrote that the garden may be the only visible link a group can retain with its past and that beyond the practical purpose of supplying foodstuffs essential to the traditional diet, gardens re-establish family cooperation in work and leisure, and serve as a place for the older generation to pass on food and horticultural traditions to the younger American-born generation.[151] One scholar cited Portuguese Americans as one of a number of ethnic groups having gardens distinctive enough that a trained observer can identify them as being "Portuguese gardens." [152]

Since most Portuguese immigrants, particularly the Islanders, came from rural traditions, the initial lack of access to a household garden was a significant loss for both men and women. The household garden is an important and defining expression of culture tied to national identity (especially grape-growing and wine-making) and a necessity in the rural culture, not at all equivalent to the usual American hobby garden. In the three-decker environment, if the whole building is occupied by an extended family, all residents share in the work and bounty of the gardens. Non-family residents may have a garden or assist in gardening at the home of a relative who has access to land. This recreates the island situation where most village residents have a plot of land outside of town where vegetables such as potatoes, corn, and kale are grown. Many Portuguese islanders fortunate enough to

Figure 20
In New Bedford a whole backyard has been devoted to a garden including kale, center left. Note also the grapevines and hanging laundry.

have access to land attempt to re-create the vegetation of their home island landscape. In so doing, they do more than replant the household gardens they left back home. Instead, as Huse and Sears have shown, many island immigrants create a miniature whole-island landscape -- a unique re-creation of whole-island vegetation, to the extent that climate and special techniques of over-wintering allow.[153] Portuguese American writer Darrel Kastin wrote a short story, *The Exile*, in which an Azorean man living in California literally has soil shipped to him from the island of Pico.[154] Portuguese American gardens often include husbandry of small animals such as rabbits, ducks, and chickens, even in urban areas, where municipal laws permit.

The Portuguese American garden thus combines the functions and characteristics of the island *horta* (kitchen garden) and *jardim* (formal flower garden) into a *quintal* or "backyard garden." The resulting garden is yet another example of a unique hybrid cultural expression that is neither solely American nor Portuguese. As Huse and Sears show, the Portuguese American gardens reflect more than a copy of the *quintais, hortas* or *jardims* found in mainland Portugal or on the islands. They see the gardens as an expression of *saudade*, a yearning for the homeland left behind. The gardens generate a memory of the whole landscape and a way of life left behind in Portugal or the Azores. The variety of plants are intended not just to re-create what was planted in the home garden back in the village but to celebrate the whole landscape.[155]

The Portuguese garden is also a way for the Portuguese Americans to reaffirm their identity and national origin in response to the pressure they feel to assimilate into American culture.[156] Silva writes that in Portuguese American fiction the garden is not just a place to grow flowers and vegetables; rather it helps preserve the ethnic identity and honor the rural way of life of one's ancestors. It is a way to retreat from the daily grind and the alienating conditions imposed by the factory or commercial fishing.[157] The garden and the ethnic meal are intimately connected: the eating experience with home-grown food is an opportunity to recollect and to reconstruct memories of the Old Country with family and friends.[158]

Portuguese American gardens, like their Old World counterparts, are intensive in both their cultivation practices and the use of space which often includes utilization of vertical space and "outdoor rooms." Alleyways among the trees are covered with vine crops. The grape arbor provides a type of "ceiling" that helps to divide the garden into a variety of well-defined spaces. Trellises and potted plants on the ground and on shelves on walls accentuate the design along with plantings of herbs and vines to create foliage walls. Apparently, the Portuguese were pioneers in this type of "green wall" written about by Huse and Sears in 1998 that has become popular among American gardeners and architects almost two decades later. Pole beans also utilize vertical space. Intercropping often occurs, such as kale planted under fruit trees. Some spaces may be double-cropped with kale, for example, planted later in the same space after other crops are harvested.[159]

In the Portuguese American garden, kale is the most common plant as it is a staple in Portuguese soups, especially kale soup, *sopa da caldo verde*. Peaches and pears are planted by themselves, or with under-plantings of kale. Multiple grafting of fruit trees, such as grafting a pear limb onto an apple tree, makes even more efficient use of space. Fava beans are planted as well as potatoes, sweet potatoes or yams, tomatoes, corn and many other vegetables. Frequently, herbs are grown for folk medicine use. In adapting to the shorter growing season and colder winter of New England, the Portuguese gardener is sometimes forced to use alternate plant varieties and to bury or cover plants to survive the winter.

The vineyard may be the most striking feature of the Portuguese American garden. If the available space is large enough, five hundred feet of row aligned north-south, providing maximum exposure to the sun, may produce a thousand pounds of grapes, more than enough to make a year's supply of wine for a family. A plot of land of this size is rare in the backyard of a three-decker, but even in the tiny backyards of these buildings, a 10 foot by 10-foot arbor is common. These plots in the backyards of the three-deckers have dimensions of at most forty or fifty feet, but they provide enough room to plant the kale and corn of Ernestina's garden in Gaspar's poem *The Shoemaker's Wife*.[160]

Like the Portuguese garden, display of the Portuguese flag is an important indicator of a Portuguese neighborhood. But again, a case can be made that this trait is not so much an importation or a simple transplantation of a cultural symbol as it is an example of a landscape symbol that can be interpreted as an acquired trait or even a *reaction* to American culture. While on one level, the Portuguese national banner is a cultural symbol to Portuguese like the American flag is to Americans, the semiotic meaning of the Portuguese flag in the Portuguese American context is different. Zelinsky has written about the display of flags in nations around the world. He notes that the United States is one of the nations where the appearance of the national flag is most common. Portugal, on the other hand (and Brazil, heavily influenced by Portuguese culture), is a nation where such private exhibition is much less common.[161] The Portuguese national banner is seldom seen on private residences and privately owned businesses in Portugal and the islands. However, private display of the Portuguese flag is common in the Portuguese community of New England, apparently in reaction to the common display of the Stars and Stripes. This is very likely a trait acquired or borrowed from American culture. Thus the private display of the Portuguese flag is probably more common in the landscape of the Portuguese American community of southeastern New England than it is in Portugal.

There is even an additional variant on the appearance of the Brazilian flag; the idea that it serves to demarcate shared or perhaps contested space among Portuguese-speaking subgroups: "We are Brazilians, not Portuguese." [162] This use of the flag as cultural symbol is thus similar to the way that various Hispanic communities mark their urban neighborhood turf vis a vis other Hispanics.[163] The Portuguese and American flags are also blended together in a dual flag logo frequently seen on signs of social clubs, war monuments, lapel pins and bumper stickers.

In a similar manner to flags, religious shrines, so typical of the yardscape of Portuguese American community in New England, are relatively uncommon in private yards on the Portuguese Atlantic islands. Instead,

Figure 21
The Portuguese and the American flags on display on a three-decker in Fall River.

religious shrines in Portugal and the Atlantic Islands are a common feature of the *public* landscape, especially in village squares and at road intersections. In New England, where such publicly sponsored religious display is prohibited, the Portuguese have adapted with a private display of shrines to preserve this important feature of their cultural landscape.[164] We will discuss shrines in more detail in the next chapter on How Religion Helps Shape the Landscape.

CULTURAL ENTROPY

While the non-Portuguese community often views the Portuguese community as both homogeneous and expressive of numerous (and

Figure 22
A shrine on a private home in Fall River.

often erroneous) traditional stereotypes, in reality, the community is extremely diverse in many of its socio-economic aspects and cultural traits. Before their transplantation from their traditional rural island environments, Portuguese islanders did not usually encounter persons from other Portuguese subgroups (Azoreans, Madeirans, Continentals, Cape Verdeans, Brazilians) as often as they now did in southeastern New England. Recall that in 1900 almost all Portuguese who immigrated had lived in the village of their birth.[165] Thus the regional subgroups that share Portuguese culture experience a great meeting, mixing and merging in their new setting in the United States, a kind of cultural entropy, or cultural hybridization, that is perhaps only found elsewhere in the large cities of Portugal itself. The Portuguese Americans acculturate to each other perhaps as much as they acculturate to American culture. As noted earlier, Gaspar makes many references to this intracultural friction between the Azoreans and "the Lisbons" in his novel, *Leaving Pico*.[166]

The diversity of the ethnic group and the ensuing trends toward cultural entropy constantly call into question "what it means to be Portuguese" simultaneously with the question of "what it means to be Portuguese American." This questioning is true for both the Portuguese American community and for those outside the community. Added to this is the constant re-shaping of the concept of Portugal as a nation which has been in flux in recent decades due to Portugal's loss of its colonies, the "Carnation Revolution" of 1974, Portugal's entry into the European Community, the switch of currency from the *escudo* to the Euro, and many other factors. There is some evidence to show the complex interplay of this re-shaping of nationalistic feeling among the immigrants. For example, Pap, writing in 1981, stated that Azoreans had less of a sense of the Portuguese nationality than did the Continentals. He cites linguistic evidence to show this by stating that allegiance to the concept of Portugal was so undeveloped on St. Michael's that the term that evolved to refer to Americans was "people from a nation," as opposed to the Portuguese, who apparently were "not from a nation." [167] At about the same time a study of eighty Portuguese women in New Bedford, many from the Azores, found that those who had immigrated earlier identified *more* closely with the Portuguese culture than did recent arrivals.[168] The long-term presence of Cape Verdeans and the on-going Brazilian immigration into Portuguese areas will very likely further promote cultural entropy or mixing among Portuguese-related cultures in the United States.

ETHNOCULTURAL SPACE: THE PORTUGUESE ARCHIPELAGO AND AN EMERGING ETHNIC SUBSTRATE

What can the geographical literature on ethnic groups and their cultural landscapes tell us about this hybrid landscape occupied by and adapted to their needs by the Portuguese Americans? While we cannot definitively answer this question, since there is disagreement over terminology even among geographers, the discussion can shed some light on the geographical nature of the landscape. The areas occupied by the Portuguese under study are much more than urban ethnic neighborhoods. What is the appropriate geographical terminology to use to refer to the Portuguese settlement in southeastern New England? Are these areas a Portuguese "heartland" or "homeland"? Or are they ethnic enclaves, or ethnic districts or ethnic provinces? Perhaps an ethnic substrate or cultural region? In short, what type of ethnocultural spaces do the Portuguese Americans occupy? [169]

Conzen[170] notes that the concept of American ethnic cultural regions first gained currency with Meinig's study of the Mormon cultural region[171] and later with the concept of a Hispano "stronghold" in reference to Hispanics in the Southwest.[172] Then another geographer, Nostrand, applied the term "homeland" to the Hispanic Southwest.[173] Both scholars recognized varying spheres of influence or distance decay from a cultural core. Meinig defined three zones of decreasing intensity of settlement for Mormons: "core, domain, and sphere," whereas Nostrand used the terms "stronghold, inland, and outland."

The categorization of types of ethnic areas in the United States has a long tradition of study within the field of geography. Some scholars defined an ethnic enclave as a transitional space where immigrants can find protection from an alien society until they are capable of affiliating with that society.[174] Earlier scholars wrote of ethnic islands[175] and ethnic provinces,[176] although both of these usages were in the context of American rural areas. The Portuguese in New England did create a few small rural islands where clusters of Portuguese farmers once dominated. An example is Portsmouth, Rhode Island, where the topiary gardens "Green Animals" created by Portuguese gardeners remains a tourist attraction. But a rural categorization of use of space is more appropriate for the Portuguese in California than for the primarily urban Portuguese communities of New England. And yet even the terms "Portuguese community" or "Portuguese neighborhood" seem strained to describe denser concentrations of Portuguese within these cities surrounded by the larger Portuguese substrate that now covers several urban areas. Perhaps the phrase "Portuguese neighborhood" might best be reserved for the area of newest and densest concentrations of recent immigrants.

The area of Portuguese influence is not large enough to constitute an ethnic "homeland," nor is it appropriate to call it an ethnic "hearth" or "heartland" because its spatial extent and numbers of people are not at all equivalent to the large territories of the United States occupied by groups such as the Hispanics or the Mormons. No American ethnic group has succeeded in establishing a "homeland" with exclusive control over their territory and therefore use of the term "homeland" for American ethnic groups is inappropriate.[177] This is true even though one of the hallmarks of such a homeland is "the production and veneration of nationalistic landmarks." But this is not what the Portuguese are doing with the construction of monuments; these are generally monuments to Portugal and its history and a celebration of immigration, rather than monuments to a "Portuguese territory" being created in the New World. Although we should note that, as strange as it sounds to American ears, the phrase "Portuguese colony" was commonly used in the Portuguese American press in the past to refer to the Portuguese in New England, and while not as commonly used today, can still be heard on occasion.

Figure 23
Green Animals is a topiary garden in Portsmouth, Rhode Island on an estate formerly owned by an executive of a Fall River textile company. The topiary figures were created by two Portuguese gardeners, Joseph Carreiro from 1905 to 1945, and his son-in-law, George Mendonca, until 1985. Photo: Green Animals Topiary Garden by Dhananjay Odhekar, Flickr Creative Commons, License 2, some rights reserved.

Even more terms and phrases have been proposed. Is this Portuguese American region then an "ethnic culture region" or, a "regional ethnic enclave" like dense areas of Mexican American settlement? [178] Or an "ethnic province?" The concept of an ethnic substrate is another geographical concept that may be the appropriate one to describe the areas of Portuguese settlement. An ethnic substrate is a large area where persistent migration of large numbers of immigrants, literally millions, over decades, has resulted in a particular ethnic group and their descendants scattered across the urban, rural and suburban landscape of a large multi-state region. Such is the case with Mexican Americans, German Americans, Scandinavian Americans and Italian Americans over regions of the United States.[179] Although they are not immigrants, the concept can also apply to regions of African Americans in the American South and in urban areas across the county.

At first glance, the Portuguese do not meet all the criteria for an ethnic substrate. There are certainly not "millions" of them. As we have seen, the extreme concentration of the Portuguese, more than most other ethnic groups, has discouraged their spread over large areas but over another generation or two, an ethnic substrate could be developing. At present, the

Portuguese are not numerous enough, nor widely dispersed enough, to form a national ethnic substrate, although clearly there is a regional ethnic substrate extending across a number of adjoining counties in southern and especially southeastern New England, and it is a multi-state region. Recall how spatially concentrated the Portuguese Americans are, more so than any other European group of immigrants. Perhaps an appropriate analogy is with the French Canadians spread across many counties of New England, especially the rural northern parts of the three states of Maine, New Hampshire and Vermont with a cluster in urban areas throughout New England.

And, while not millions, the sheer number of Portuguese in southeastern New England is impressive. If we compare the numbers of Italians in 1900, one of the nation's largest ethnic groups at the time, while the number of Portuguese did not approach the number of Italians in New York City (145,000 at their peak), numbers of Portuguese even now are roughly equivalent to the numbers of Italians in secondary cities that were foci of Italian immigration in 1900: 17,800 in Philadelphia; 16,000 in Chicago, and 14,000 in Boston.[180] And, of course, the Portuguese are focused in much smaller cities and therefore have an even greater relative cultural impact on those areas. Indeed, Noble cites the Fall River Portuguese as one example where a particular ethnic group comes to characterize the entire city, at least in the popular mind. This usually occurs with ethnic groups in small cities such as Greeks in Tarpon Springs, Armenians in Riverside California, Spaniards in Tampa and Italians in dozens of cities including Rome, New York.[181] Even at their peak, the populations of both New Bedford and Fall River only reached about 120,000 each, less than a tenth of the populations of the large American cities cited in reference to the Italians above. All in all the Portuguese American cluster in southeastern New England is clearly much larger than an ethnic neighborhood or an ethnic "quarter."

Since the Portuguese occupy a series of adjacent cities, a better case might be made for describing the Portuguese areas of southeastern New England as ethnic clusters, or as a series of "ethnocultural islands" or even a "cultural archipelago."[182] The best example of an ethnic archipelago is probably the pattern of Amish settlements in "islands" spread across the Midwest from Pennsylvania and upstate New York to Wisconsin and Missouri.[183] The Portuguese are spread among multiple cities and the population is both urban and suburban. The Portuguese Americans seem to fit the description of geographers Terry Jordan and Lester Rowntree that an ethnic island occupies an area smaller than a county and housing anywhere from several hundred to several thousand people.[184] The term archipelago seems appropriately fitting since most of the Portuguese in the region came from islands and to an extent, they have inadvertently recreated that spatial pattern in southeastern New England minus the intervening ocean. In fact, the phrase *Decima Ilha* (Tenth Island) is used on occasion among Azoreans, a reference to the fact that the Azores has nine major islands and a mythical tenth one -- the Azorean community in southeastern New England.[185] (Coincidentally the phrase has also been used to mean the "Tenth Island" of Cape Verde because that nation also has nine major inhabited islands.) And these ethnocultural islands lie within a sea made up of an emerging Portuguese American "ethnic substrate" in southeastern New England.

5
HOW RELIGION HELPS SHAPE THE LANDSCAPE

More than 95% of Portuguese Americans identify as Catholics. For almost all of the immigrants the Catholic parish and its church acted as a magnet for the development of neighborhoods.

RELIGION IN THE LANDSCAPE

In addition to the private display of religious shrines in the yardscape, there are a number of ways that more organized Catholic religious activity plays an important role in shaping the landscape of the Portuguese American community in southeastern New England. In this chapter we will look at three of these major factors in more detail: first, churches, particularly their impact in shaping the location of neighborhoods; second, feasts, festivals, and processions; and third, cemeteries. Most Portuguese are Catholic and Pap believes that the idea of Catholicism is so deeply ingrained in Portuguese culture that Protestantism itself is evidence of denationalization, although he wrote that in 1981.[186] A comprehensive survey of 400 Portuguese Americans in Taunton, Massachusetts conducted in 2000 found that more than 95% of those surveyed identified as Catholics.[187] The Portuguese Atlantic islanders have always demonstrated more traditional religious behaviors than the continentals and they adopted much less of the anti-clerical attitude that followed the 1910 Portuguese Revolution that overthrew the monarchy.[188]

For almost all of the immigrants, regardless of origin, the Catholic parish acted as a magnet for Portuguese settlement. Indeed, the circular causation effect of parish and neighborhood resulted in a close connection between dense Portuguese American settlement and Portuguese parishes, especially among the foreign-born Portuguese population. There are a few Protestants of traditional denominations among the Portuguese and some fundamentalist denominations and sects as well, particularly among the new Brazilian immigrants. In fact, given the low rates of church attendance of the Portuguese (lower than that of Americans, despite the stereotypes of Portuguese as devout Catholics) one scholar, Maria Gloria Mulcahy, a sociologist, wrote that Protestant churches, almost all run by Brazilian ministers, were to some extent, "re-Christianizing" the Portuguese community.[189]

CHURCHES AND NEIGHBORHOODS

Each of the major Portuguese neighborhoods in this study, two in New Bedford and three in Fall River, is focused around Catholic churches offering masses in Portuguese. In most cases, the establishment of the parish followed dense Portuguese settlement. One source stated in 2005 that there were 300 churches offering some masses in Portuguese or Brazilian Portuguese in Massachusetts and southern New Hampshire, although that number has undoubtedly declined since then.[190] Churches and parishes serve the Portuguese in varying degrees. Parishes may be Portuguese National Parishes specifically founded to serve the Portuguese population, in which case usually all parish priests are of Portuguese background and most masses are said in Portuguese. Or they may be regular Catholic parishes with a Portuguese-speaking priest or visiting priest that offer some regularly scheduled masses in Portuguese. Among the Portuguese National Parishes, while the exterior of the churches may give little evidence of their Portuguese nature other than written signs in the Portuguese language, the interiors of the churches often illustrate a variety of Portuguese religious iconography.

Once established because of the presence of some Portuguese immigrants in an area, in a cause and effect cycle, these churches became critical structures around which Portuguese American neighborhoods coalesced in southeastern New England. A study of the role of churches within the Swedish immigrant community in Minnesota showed that true immigrant social communities jelled around the old social networks maintained by the church. The immigrant church was the center of community life, charged with the responsibility of upholding values and preserving continuity with the cultural past. The church was the first and often the strongest bulwark against rapid change.[191]

For immigrants from countries that were dominated by a single religion, as was Portugal, religious affiliation became an even more emotionally charged issue after emigration to the United States. This is because of two major ways that religion differed between the two countries. First, the separation between church and state in the United States meant not only that private shrines had to replace public ones, as discussed earlier, but it also meant that private funding of churches had to replace public funding to construct, operate and maintain buildings and to fund priests and nuns. The second difference was the strong representation of Protestant denominations and churches in the United States that was lacking in Portugal. Although most other large immigrant groups in southeastern New England were also Catholic, such as Irish, Polish and French Canadians, there were an abundance of Yankee and northern European protestants groups and some other denominations (Greek and Lebanese Orthodox churches, for example), that emphasized the cultural differences the Portuguese already felt in their new land. This new religious environment probably resulted in a strengthening of the immigrants' religious feelings.

One challenge facing the new immigrant family from the Azores, perhaps unanticipated prior to emigration, was that daughter Maria might run off to marry a Madeiran, or worse, a German Lutheran! Such a thing would have been rare back in the Islands. The church was the symbolic and functional heart of the community. As such, the role of the church as a general conservative force acting to preserve traditional Portuguese culture cannot be underestimated. In addition to religion, the churches struggled with the all-important issues of preserving the language, values, and social traditions.[192] In many cases, parochial schools were established with all instruction in Portuguese.

All that being said, it should also be noted that many characteristics of the Portuguese and Portuguese Americans defy the traditional stereotypes that are often imposed upon them by the outside community. In Portugal, while surveys show 86% of the population to be nominally Roman Catholic, only 29%, predominantly women, regularly attend church compared to 39% who report regularly attending church in the United States.[193] The Portuguese are also relatively tolerant of marriage outside the ethnic group. Church records at St. Mary's Catholic Church in New Bedford recorded several marriages between Portuguese men and Irish women in the 1840s, which was very early in the history of Portuguese immigration into New England and at a time when few Portuguese women had emigrated. Taft cited a study that showed the Portuguese were the most likely of 55 ethnic groups in New York City to marry outside their group.[194]

The role of the priest in Portuguese culture also defies traditional stereotypes. Portugal had an era of anti-clericalism following the republican revolution of 1910. While priests are regarded as necessary and respected for their other-worldly knowledge, they are seen, particularly by men, as lacking in knowledge of "this" world. In Leder's view, Portuguese men see priests as "meddlers" and somewhat "womanly meddlers," at that. They are sometimes jokingly referred to as *sogra*, (literally, "mother-in-law").[195] Taft noted a difference between islanders and continentals in terms of religiosity. Mainland Portuguese often did not support the Church because of the anti-clerical movement that accompanied the Revolution. However, islanders remained much more supportive of the Church. This was true even though the Islanders were also more prone to the influence of folkloric beliefs and practices such as the "evil eye," folk healers, and image worship.[196] Anthropologist Caroline Brettell also noted this anti-clericalism and how it varied regionally in Portugal where it was much stronger in the south than in the north.[197] Those regional differences in religious attitudes in Portugal were carried over to the respective areas of immigrant settlement in the United States.

The need for church fund-raising was another American religious peculiarity to which the Portuguese had to adapt. Until the end of the Salazar dictatorship in 1970, Catholic churches were supported by the national government, so adapting to the American practice of private fund-raising to build local churches was difficult. The possibility that a local Portuguese church owned by the parish might be closed or turned over to another ethnic group was anathema that on occasion led to legal disputes with the diocese.[198] To cope with this new American custom, it was not unusual for Portuguese businessmen to buy and donate a structure to serve as a church. The former Baptist church in Fall River that housed the Santo Cristo parish was purchased by a Portuguese man who donated it to the diocese in 1889. The identical scenario occurred in Taunton, twenty miles north of Fall River when a Portuguese man purchased and donated the site of what became the Portuguese parish of St. Anthony in 1903 (replaced by the present structure in 1951). These scenarios show that as early as the closing of the nineteenth century there were at least some Portuguese Americans with the financial means to make such donations. Common church names for parishes serving Portuguese communities include Our Lady of Fatima and two saints born in Portugal, St. John of God and St.

Anthony of Padua. Table 6 provides a list of Portuguese churches in southern New England and their dates of founding.

MASSACHUSETTS

Boston:		Lowell:	
1873	St. John the Baptist (North End)	1901	St. Anthony
1921	St. John the Baptist (East End)	Ludlow:	
Cambridge:			Our Lady of Fatima
1902	St. Anthony	New Bedford:	
East Falmouth:		1871	St. John the Baptist
1921	St. Anthony	1903	Our Lady of Mt. Carmel
Fall River:		1905	Our Lady of the Assumption (Cape Verdean)
1876	Santo Cristo	1909	Our Lady of the Immaculate Conception
1902	St. Michael	Peabody:	
1904	Espirito Santo	1976	Our Lady of Fatima
1911	St. Anthony of Padua	Somerset:	
1915	St. Elizabeth	1928	St. John of God
1915	Our Lady of the Angels	Taunton:	
1924	Our Lady of Health	1903	St. Anthony
Gloucester:		1905	Our Lady of Lourdes
1889	Our Lady of Good Voyage	Provincetown:	
Lawrence:		1890	St. Peter the Apostle
1907	Saints Peter and Paul		

RHODE ISLAND

Bristol		Pawtucket	
1913	St. Elizabeth	1923	St. Anthony
Cumberland		Providence	
1953	Our Lady of Fatima	1885	Our Lady of the Rosary
East Providence		Warren	
1916	St. Francis Xavier	1952	St. Thomas the Apostle
Newport		West Warwick	
1926	Jesus Savior	1925	St. Anthony

CONNECTICUT

Bridgeport		Waterbury	
1926	Our Lady of Fatima	1969	Our Lady of Fatima
Hartford			
1958	Our Lady of Fatima		

A note on sources: Two sources were used to compile this list: The Harvard Encyclopedia of American Ethnic Groups, Stephan Thornstrom, ed., 1980, and Bearing Fruit by Streams of Water: A History of the Diocese of Fall River, Barry W. Wall, 2003. Many dates differ by one, two or three years between the two volumes based on what date is used: the authorization of the parish; the start or completion of construction of the church building, or the date of the first celebration of a mass. In the list above, and in the text, Wall's dates are used unless those are contradicted by church histories on web sites. Not all churches listed above were Portuguese territorial parishes (some were only for a period of time) and not all churches listed above are still in existence; some have been consolidated with other parishes. Nor do all churches listed still offer masses in Portuguese. The Harvard Encyclopedia lists only four Portuguese churches elsewhere in the United States: three in California (Oakland, Sacramento and San Jose), and one in Newark, New Jersey.

Table 6. Portuguese Churches Founded in Southern New England

Church histories provide information about the evolution of Portuguese American settlement especially before ancestry data were collected by the Census Bureau and in the days when almost all Portuguese immigrants were Catholics. The church's internal spatial organization by parish provides one definition of Portuguese neighborhoods. Records from the Diocese of Fall River, which includes Fall River, New Bedford, Taunton and Cape Cod, cover the bulk of the Portuguese community in southeastern Massachusetts. For example, records at St. Mary's Church in New Bedford show that in one month in 1861, nine children of Portuguese ancestry were baptized. One church source estimates that there were 800 Portuguese parishioners in the city by 1865. By 1866, Portuguese priests were regularly sought after and a formal congregation was established in 1869. In 1871, this congregation evolved into the first Portuguese parish in the United States, St. John the Baptist, on County Street, located just a few blocks from the main wharves in present-day downtown New Bedford.[199] The original church was built in 1875 but destroyed by fire and replaced by the present Romanesque style church in 1913.[200] The first American-born Portuguese priest of this parish was Father Manuel Candido Terra, who was born in New Bedford in 1862, sent to school in the Azores and to seminary in Montreal, before returning as a parish priest.[201] In 1875, an English-speaking priest was sent to Portugal to learn Portuguese. Unfortunately, as of 2015, the parish has been closed and the structure is in danger of being abandoned because of the cost of repairs and the declining number of parishioners.[202]

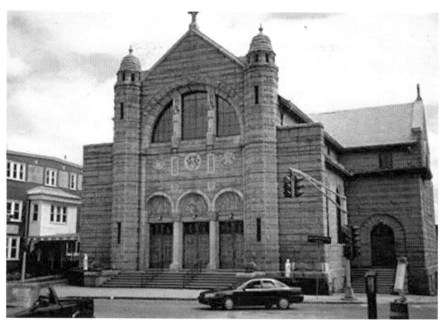

Figure 24
St. John the Baptist Church on County Street in New Bedford. This is the first Portuguese parish in North America, established in 1871. This building, constructed in 1913, replaced one destroyed by fire in 1875. Now the church is closed.

By the turn of the century, when St. John the Baptist had 7,000 parishioners, waves of Portuguese immigrants were arriving and expanding both north and south of downtown New Bedford. They moved from the dock-oriented downtown neighborhood into the three-decker neighborhoods adjacent to the textile mills that were being built along the north-south flowing Acushnet River. This movement resulted in New Bedford's two major Portuguese neighborhoods that still exist today. With this expansion of Portuguese settlement out from downtown and the continued new arrival of immigrants, a need evolved for a parish in both the South End and the North End of the city. A priest from St. John's had started holding masses for 600 families in a rented hall in the South End. In 1903 the cornerstone was laid for Our Lady of Mt. Carmel and the upper church was completed in 1913.[203] In the North End, Immaculate Conception parish was founded as a Portuguese National Parish in 1909 and the present church was dedicated in 1913. Immaculate Conception also operated a parish school until 1970. In 1905 Our Lady of the Assumption was also established in New Bedford specifically for Cape Verdean immigrants located between downtown and the South End's primarily Azorean community.

The Portuguese communities in Fall River started later than those in New Bedford and parish development evolved later as well. As the textile industry employment grew in Fall River many Portuguese moved there from New Bedford and in short order immigrants started arriving directly from Portugal and the Azores. By 1876 there were enough Portuguese that priests from New Bedford traveled weekly to celebrate a Portuguese mass. By 1890 there were an estimated 1,500 Portuguese Catholics in Fall River and a former Baptist church, as noted above, was purchased on the corner of Canal and Columbia Streets. A priest was assigned to the evolving parish in 1892. The parish was called *Senhor Santo Cristo dos Milagres* (Lord Holy Christ of Miracles), named after an Azorean convent.[204] Today the church is commonly known as Santo Cristo and remains the focus of Fall River's Columbia Street Portuguese community. Santo Cristo spun off its own satellite church, St. Anthony of Padua, which began as a mission of Santo Cristo in 1908 with masses celebrated in the basement of St. Rock, a non-Portuguese Catholic church. St. Anthony's became a Portuguese parish in 1911. A new church was built in 1913 and replaced with the present structure in 1969.[205]

By 1895 there were enough additional Portuguese in the North End of Fall River that St. Michael's parish was established by 1902 and a permanent structure dedicated in 1922. In keeping with distinctions among island cultures, just as the diocese established a parish in New Bedford specifically for Cape Verdeans, St. Michael's was served specifically by priests from the Azores. By 1903 there were also enough Portuguese in the neighborhood called Flint Village (today, more commonly called "The Flint") that a local priest from another Portuguese parish began saying masses at St. Joseph's Hall on Bassett St. The first *Espírito Santo* (Holy Spirit) church was thus founded in 1904 and replaced by the present structure in 1963. Three other Portuguese parishes were founded: Our Lady of the Angels in 1915 (with a church built in 1917); St. Elizabeth, also in 1915, and Our Lady of Health in 1924. Our Lady of the Angles was merged with two other parishes in 2002 into the Church of the Good Shepherd.[206] Thus by 1924 Fall River had seven Portuguese churches served by fourteen Portuguese priests.[207] In addition to churches, a Portuguese convent was established. Members of the Franciscan Sisters of Mary came to New Bedford in 1906 to do catechetical work among Portuguese children and they permanently moved to Fall River in 1910 to the Mercy Convent on Second Street. There they established the *Espírito Santo* School, the first Portuguese-speaking school in the United States.

As the Portuguese population grew outside of the urban cores of settlement in New Bedford and Fall River, churches were added in areas outside of the core neighborhoods. One of the first suburban churches was St. John of God in Somerset, a suburb of Fall River across the Taunton River, founded for the local Portuguese population in 1928 although priests had served locally a decade earlier, sometimes living in private homes. The contemporary structure was built in 1978.[208]

By 1890, the number of Portuguese in the fishing community of Provincetown who attended St. Peter the Apostle Church became large enough to demand a Portuguese-speaking priest. Father Terra from St. John's in New Bedford was reassigned to that new parish. St. Anthony's in East Falmouth on Cape Cod was established in 1921 for parishioners from Cape Verde and the Azores, many of whom were employed as cranberry pickers.[209] To accommodate Brazilian immigration, masses in Brazilian Portuguese began to be offered at St. Francis Xavier in Hyannis in 1991 after it was determined there were 200 Brazilian parishioners. As of 2010 masses in Brazilian Portuguese were being offered in Massachusetts on the islands of Martha's Vineyard and Nantucket and in the cities and town of Falmouth, Fall River, Framingham, Milford and Marlboro.

Portuguese parishes were established in Rhode Island communities as well including Saint Elizabeth's in Bristol (1913), St. Francis Xavier in East Providence (1916), and the Holy Rosary Church in the Fox Point neighborhood of Providence (1885). Over time, with the decline of new immigrants and the passing of the very oldest generation that only spoke Portuguese, masses in Portuguese churches have transitioned from Portuguese-only to where most masses are in English and only some masses at designated times are conducted in Portuguese. Of course, many other Catholic churches serve the Portuguese community as well. For example, St. Anthony of Padua, established as a French Canadian parish in New Bedford's north end, now offers Portuguese masses on holidays and prints church materials in English, Portuguese and Spanish to serve its diverse community.

RELIGIOUS FEASTS, FESTIVALS AND PROCESSIONS

In addition to relatively permanent religious structures in the landscape such as churches, and shrines in private yards, ephemeral landscape semiotics are present in temporary displays including religious processions. These processions are reminiscent of those in Portugal and the islands. They range from a simple street procession to more elaborate multi-day events such as those of the Feast of the Blessed Sacrament in New Bedford and the Festival of the Holy Ghost in Fall River where planning begins a year in advance of the events.

The Feast of the Blessed Sacrament, commonly known as the *Festa da Madeira* (Madeiran Feast), is held annually during August in New Bedford's North End Portuguese community. The event was started by four immigrants from Madeira who arrived in the early 1900s. Although there are other explanations of the origin of this feast, the most common legend has it that their ship encountered such rough weather that passengers feared for their lives. The four men, all with the given name of Manuel, made a vow to honor the Blessed Sacrament with a festival if they survived. The event is a recreation of the festival in Madeira, where on the day of the religious procession the street is decorated with boughs of trees and banners of the Order of Christ. The door of the neighborhood church, Immaculate Conception, is decorated with branches and the road is lined with elaborate colorful decorations made of chalk and flower petals. Residents hang bedspreads, flags, and rugs over porch balconies of the three-deckers in imitation of island customs.

Figure 25
A float in Provincetown's annual Portuguese Festival. Photo courtesy of Massachusetts Office of Travel and Tourism on Flickr Creative Commons, License 2.

Stephen Cabral, an anthropologist, explains how over the years the feast evolved from a religious procession to a parade, in large part because religious leaders felt that having the statue process through the streets without all on-lookers getting on both knees was sacrilegious.²¹⁰ So, since 1932, the sacred icon is only processed within the church. Attendance at the annual four-day festival grew from 2,000 in 1915 to 15,000 in the 1930s to more than 100,000 at present. Portuguese travel from as far away as Canada, California and Madeira by plane and chartered bus. The parade expanded with drum and bugle corps, veterans groups, color guards, motorcades, politicians, beauty queens and a car raffle.

The Madeira feast in New Bedford, under the leadership of 50 *festeiros* (male descendants of the original founders) became, in effect, a business, buying half a city block and establishing a covered pavilion, barbeque pits, restrooms, clubhouse and stage, and offering carnival rides, fireworks and continuous musical and dance performances. Scholars note that these festivals and parades, although temporary, define cultural identity in spatial terms by marking routes and attaching importance to the sites where events begin and end in the urban cultural landscape.²¹¹ To understand the importance of the connections between parades and ethnicity we need only think of the importance of St. Patrick's Day parades to the Irish, African American jazz funerals in New Orleans or Chinese New Year's Day parades.²¹²

These expanded activities reflect the Americanization of the procession as has been described by João Leal, an anthropologist at the New University of Lisbon, in his study of the *Império Mariense*, the Holy Ghost festival organized annually in East Providence. This event is run by Azorean immigrants from the island of Saint Mary's (*Santa Maria*) which has a population of less than 6,000.²¹³ These immigrants, known as *Mariense*, keep their Holy Ghost festivals alive by traveling to celebrate neighboring events and supporting them financially. The first celebration was held in Saugus, Massachusetts in 1927 and others are now held at Hudson and East Bridgewater, Massachusetts, Hartford, Connecticut and East Providence. In the last city the largest community of *Mariense* now live, numbering about 1,000 people.²¹⁴ There has also been a deliberate effort to consolidate some of the smaller festivals into the larger ones but with limited success.

The Holy Ghost festival (*Festa do Espírito Santo*) in Fall River is a large multi-day event comparable to the Madeira feast in New Bedford. In comparison to New Bedford's festival, colloquially known as the Madeira feast, the Fall River counterpart is sometimes called the Azorean feast. Holy Ghost Festivals are celebrated in all Portuguese American *Micaelenses* (St. Michael's) communities on both East and West coasts, but the one organized by Fall River's Santo Cristo church is particularly large, attracting thousands of celebrants. It serves as a focal point for *Micaelenses* from the United States and Canada just as the four-day Madeira feast in New

Bedford serves as the primary annual American gathering of Madeirans. There are many varying oral traditions about the origin of this event as it has been elaborated with numerous meanings and different symbolism in different communities. Like the Madeira Feast in New Bedford, the Fall River festival has developed the tradition that travelers in peril at sea pledged to start a religious celebration if they returned safely to land. The spirit of the Holy Ghost is particularly associated with protection against plagues and natural disasters. Perhaps, because so many Azorean islanders emigrated in response to the destruction wreaked by earthquakes and volcanic activity, this festival has assumed even more meaning among Portuguese Americans.

Other associations and symbolism associated with the Fall River festival include the feeding of the poor with soup, meat and sweet bread, a celebration of Saint (Queen) Isabel of Portugal, the coronation of a common person as a kind of King for a Day, a religious procession through the street, music, dancing, miraculous cures, roses, doves and a hexagonal crown. Although it had been celebrated in several localities in California as early as 1874, the first Holy Ghost festival on the East Coast took place in Gloucester, Massachusetts in 1902. By the 1920s this event was celebrated in all Portuguese American communities, although it has all but died out in Hawaii.[215]

It is interesting to note that historically such festivals grew in popularity on the islands when the tradition was dying out in mainland Portugal, and more recently, have been growing in popularity in New England while declining in some areas such as Madeira and on Santa Maria Island in the Azores.[216] This reminds us that immigrant groups in America can sometimes preserve Old World customs better than the Old World. It was said of Polish immigrants in Hamtramck, Michigan, that pre-Communist Polish culture was better preserved in that small city than back in Poland.

The recent revival of a particular religious procession shows how, far from dying out, the Portuguese cultural tradition of religious processions and festivals is still reinvigorating and re-inventing itself. Two Fall River men from the Azores missed the tradition of a Lenten religious procession they had engaged in during their youth on St. Michael's. They approached their parish priest about recreating this procession in 1984 and thus began the custom of *Romeiros* where men dressed in traditional capes and kerchiefs, and carrying stout walking sticks, march across the city stopping and worshipping at various Portuguese churches. This "new old idea" spread quickly through the New England communities. Now hundreds of men (and, again reflecting American influence, now including women) carry on the custom annually, not only Fall River but also at churches in New Bedford, Taunton, Pawtucket, and Bristol.[217]

Figure 26
The annual procession of Romeiros, held on Good Friday. The costumes in this photo from Sao Miguel, Azores, are identical to those worn in the New England processions. Photo from Rae Brune, courtesy of Antje, on Flickr Creative Commons, License 2, some rights reserved.

Various island-specific holy celebrations are staged, usually in association with holy images possessed by churches back in the islands. As noted above, the sacred image is not processed in the city streets in New Bedford's festival, and in Fall River, the Holy Ghost Feast similarly features the veneration of a replica of an image preserved in a convent in Ponta Delgada on St. Michael's, the namesake for the Santo Cristo church. Even smaller towns have their processions. St. Elizabeth's Church in Bristol, Rhode Island holds an annual procession for its image of *Senhor Santo Cristo dos Milagres* as does St. John of God in Somerset. Intra-island rivalry based on a competing St. Michael image at another parish led to the start of the *Festa do Senhor da Pedra* (Lord of the Rock) procession and feast in New Bedford, helped along by the felt need for the folks from St. Michael's to have a festival akin to that of the Madeirans in the same neighborhood. Gloucester's annual celebration at the church of Our Lady of Good Voyage also celebrates the Holy Spirit and features the crowning of a religious statue. This festival has become more popularly known among non-Portuguese for its annual Blessing of the Fleet of fishing vessels.[218]

Village and parish connections back to the home island frequently led to island-based social and cultural societies and "island day" celebrations. In this sense, the Madeiran Feast in New Bedford is not only a religious event but a celebration of Madeira. The Feast of the Holy Ghost in Fall River is clearly a celebration of St. Michael's. Yet Portuguese of all origins attend the festivities as well as many non-Portuguese who come for the food and festivities. The communities thus developed Madeira Day, St. Michael's Day (*Dia Micaelenses*), Terceira (Island) Day, and others – so many that the Portuguese government is encouraging consolidation into a single annual *Dia de Portugal* celebration. Celebrations of these island days are often synchronized in Portuguese communities on both coasts and in Canada. As communities become more affluent, associated fundraising efforts are held in conjunction with churches to send proceeds back to the home island parish often for a specific purpose such as to repair a church roof, to replace a church altar or to buy equipment for the village hospital.

CEMETERIES

Lastly, cemeteries, particularly those associated with Portuguese Catholic churches, are distinctive elements of the Portuguese American landscape showing the impact of religion. Folklore scholars remind us that cemeteries are much more than space set aside for the burial of the dead; they are cultural texts that can be read by anyone who takes the time to learn their semiotic language.[219] They are more important as fields of remembrance for the living than they are as areas of repositories for the dead.[220] The roles of Portuguese cemeteries are akin to those of Italian cemeteries, which seem to be not just to keep alive the memory of those who have died, but to prolong grief, as opposed to the Anglo tradition of softening grief and trying to forget the trials of death through contemplation of the beauty of the earth.[221] For Portuguese Americans, as for many Catholics, weekend visits to the plots of family members are frequent. Family care of the plot and frequent visitations by the family for decades after the death are characteristics seen in Portuguese American cemeteries. In one scholar's words, cemeteries and the religious culture associated with them are part of a religious culture creating a self-conscious awareness of the American ethnic groups' special identity and an opportunity for expression of their values and worldview.[222]

Figure 27
Family grave markers reflect changing linguistics and acculturation over time. This marker in New Bedford lists "sua esposa" for a wife who died in 1938 but "his wife" for a death in 1966. Very likely the first generation was born in Portugal (1885 and 1893).

In terms of aspects of cemeteries visible in the landscape, Portuguese headstones are recognizable not only by their ethnic names and frequent use of the Portuguese language but also by their color and by material objects placed on the stones and around the graves. Grave markers may also contain images of the deceased etched in granite.[223] On male headstones, it is common to include an etching indicating the occupation of the deceased, especially etchings of fishing and naval vessels. Gravestone photographs can be seen as images that serve as intermediaries between the material and spiritual worlds.[224]

Plants and flowers and other ornaments are maintained for decades after a burial. The Portuguese, like all ethnic groups influenced by southern Mediterranean culture, including Mexican Americans and Italian Americans, place fresh flowers and photographs of the deceased on the grave. Greeting cards, photographs and other personal memorabilia such as wedding announcements, religious articles, holiday decorations, miniature fences, pictures of local or patron saints, pictures of weddings, first communions, confirmations and graduations of relatives of the deceased are also displayed. Similar objects in honor of the deceased may also be displayed at shrines inside and outside of the family home.

Figure 28
A number of religious items and flowers mark a grave in New Bedford. The Portuguese inscription loosely translated reads "Don't cry if you did not have sons in this life because it is far worse to have had one and lost him."

6

SEMIOTICS: SIGNS, SYMBOLS AND MONUMENTS

The Portuguese American landscape is rich in overt and subtle cultural symbols. Some knowledge of Portuguese culture gives the observer a "dictionary" to help understand these cultural signifiers.

As noted in the discussion of the "hybrid landscape," signs and cultural symbols abound in the Portuguese American landscape. The concept of semiology, or semiotics, helps guide the observer to read this cultural evidence and to understand what these symbols mean to Portuguese Americans. The concept, including the use of language on signs as described below, builds on the work of the French philosopher Roland Barthes.²²⁵ And, as we know from the earlier discussion of the overt and subtle landscape, the semiotic glossary of the Portuguese Americans ranges from obvious and unmistakable symbols such as grand monuments to almost invisible cultural signifiers, such as the St. John's cross, that might easily be overlooked by a casual observer. Some knowledge of Portuguese culture is necessary to recognize many of these symbols just as some knowledge of the Portuguese language is necessary to read some signs. Some cultural symbols may be ephemeral, such as the religious processions of the *Romeiros* or the song and dance of *rancho*, described below. But with a few clues, an observer can read and understand many of the signs present everywhere in the landscape of southeastern New England.

SIGNS

Signage is one of the most obvious ways that a different culture presents itself in the American landscape. There are numerous varieties of Portuguese signs. Some are in the Portuguese language only; some are dual language with the message in both English and Portuguese; some are English language signs using Portuguese grammatical constructions or literal translations of Portuguese idioms, and some are mixed language or hybrids, primarily in one language or another, but using an English or a Portuguese word. Such signs are a reliable indicator of all American ethnic neighborhoods and the fact that the signs usually are in both languages is evidence that cultural assimilation is well underway.[226]

On mixed language signs, distinctive words stand out, such as *linguiç*a, and *chouriço*, types of Portuguese sausage. A sign at a tavern in Fall River reads "Billy's Fish and Chips – The Best Chourico in Town." Ethnic names are a subcategory of such signs provided that the observer recognizes Portuguese given names and surnames. Some signs in English with the unfamiliar grammatical structure or word usage reveal their origin in literal translation from the Portuguese. A shop sign in Fall River, "Gilda's Place of Bridals," is an example of such a literal translation from the Portuguese name for the wedding-related store, "*Casa das Noivas*," literally "house for brides."

Spelling used in signage provides additional cultural clues. Words may look odd to both the Portuguese and non-Portuguese observer. Words on signs may be spelled in accordance with English usage or Portuguese usage. Few signs have the accent marks common to the Portuguese language. But even Portuguese language signs may use Anglicized spelling. An example is the word "Portuguese" itself, which, correctly spelled in Portuguese, is "Português" lacking the final "e" used in English. A sign containing the word "restaurant" spelled correctly in Portuguese would be "*restaurante.*" One Fall River restaurant has a subtitle on its sign that says "*Restaurante Portuguese.*" Perhaps the owner thought that customers would recognize the Portuguese spelling of restaurant but also thought that it would look odd to American customers to exclude the final 'e' on Portuguese. The *Acores* Market uses the Portuguese spelling of Azores, yet lacks the cedilla on the "c," while a social club sports a sign that uses the adjective " *Açoreana*" correctly spelled with the cedilla. An English equivalent of that word would be "Azorean."

Figure 29
The Acores Market in Fall River features a map of the Azores on two sides of the building.

Interesting semantic structures abound. The warning sign, "Don't park in this (parking) lot," is translated into Portuguese as *"Não parque neste parque."* This is an example of a homonym, the appropriation of an English word into Portuguese because it sounds similar to the Portuguese. *Parque* is pronounced similarly to 'park,' but in formal Portuguese, it is a noun that has traditionally meant "park" in the sense of a recreational patch of greenery and not "parking lot." The word has worked its way into the language of American Portuguese as a verb meaning "to park a car."

Sometimes the observer needs a sharp eye to see the hints of cultural hybridization. Many stores post a sign that states *"Nos Falamos Português"* – "We Speak Portuguese." One scholar discusses such signage and symbols in the Hispanic context, noting that this is a way some firms try to expand clientele by adding *"Se Hable Espanol"* and *"Bienvenidos"* as an unobtrusive means of indicating a Latino-friendly environment.[227] Interestingly, the phrase *"Nos Falamos Português,"* while formally correct in the Portuguese language, still reflects an Anglicization. The grammatically "proper" usage would be *"Fala-sê Português,"* meaning "Portuguese is spoken here." The phrase *"Nos Falamos Português,"* while formally correct in structure (as an answer to the question "do you speak Portuguese?" directed to a group), is improperly used in this context. This particular phrase, "We speak Portuguese," is a word for word translation using English syntax.[228] Such adoptions of English ways of combining words have been called "loan translations." Another example is the phrase *escola alta*, used by many Portuguese Americans to mean high school; literally, "a school at a high elevation."[229] Often signs in the Portuguese American communities written in Portuguese, even in a formal context, contain some errors in spelling, grammar or diacritics."[230] Perhaps this is a reflection of the lesser years of formal education attained by many immigrants from Portugal. Many

Figure 30
Four signs illustrating various aspects of semiotics in the landscape. Top left, a "Customer only" parking sign in New Bedford. Top right, "Nos Falamos" is an example of grammatical structure borrowed from English. Bottom left, Portuguese sausages on sale at a Fall River market. Bottom right, an example of a literal translation from Portuguese to English of "house for brides" at Gilda's in Fall River.

Portuguese born in Portugal have only a grammar school understanding of their own written language.[231]

A landscape can be a hybrid creation using many of the same rules of hybrid language. Jackson writes that a landscape, like a language, has obscure and undecipherable origins and like a language, it is the result of a slow accretion of many elements in society. Landscape grows according to its own laws, rejecting or accepting new constructions as it sees fit, clinging to obsolete structures in some cases while inventing new ones in others. A landscape, like a language, reflects continuing conflict and compromise between what is formally endorsed by authority and what the vernacular prefers.[232]

Signage can also give clues as to how ethnic neighborhoods are perpetuated. A sign in Portuguese advertising a vacant retail store for lease on a main street shopping district, shown in Figure 31, obviously helps perpetuate the Portuguese nature of the shopping district. The building owner simply assumes the next tenant will be Portuguese-speaking. Non-Portuguese speaking observers of the sign would not understand it and thus would be unlikely to rent the vacant shop.

Figure 31
This polite sign on a vacant store on a main shopping street in a Portuguese neighborhood in Fall River illustrates how the neighborhood perpetuates itself. The owner assumes the next renter will be Portuguese. The sign reads "Please call. Thank you."

Portuguese destinations on travel agency storefronts are another interesting example that provides additional landscape evidence of the Portuguese connections of the community. Signs also give clues to changing linguistics and acculturation over time. On a single gravestone in the Portuguese section of New Bedford's Pine Grove Cemetery, information about the parents, the last of whom died in 1943, is given in Portuguese. Information on their children, however, the first of whom died in 1969, is given on the same stone in English. Borrowing a classification scheme developed by scholars studying Spanish language usage among Latinos, it may be useful to think of Portuguese speakers along with a language continuum of Portuguese Dominant, Portuguese Preferred, True Bilinguals, English Preferred and English Dominant.[233]

CULTURAL SYMBOLS

Another semiotic category showing the presence of the Portuguese American community is that of cultural symbols. Portuguese cultural symbols are common on signs, particularly those symbols showing Portugal's maritime heritage, symbols of modern Portuguese popular culture, and nationalistic and royal symbols. While often present in signage, these cultural symbols are not limited to signage, as they are also found on household items and on architectural features. Some of the more important symbols are the Portuguese flag; royal and national symbols within the flag, including the five shields of the national coat of arms; ethnic names with broader cultural meanings, such as Sagres and Fatima; and special ethnic symbols such as the black rooster, a symbol of good luck. These symbols, used separately or together, are often indicators of Portuguese cultural influence in the landscape just as much as distinctive terms such as *linguiça*, and *chouriço*. An awareness of this semiotic glossary can give important clues about the cultural landscape to the informed observer.

For example, St. John's Catholic Church located in a suburban setting in Somerset, Massachusetts, across the Taunton River from Fall River, gives no obvious clues to its ethnic connections. Even the name of the church does not give an apparent hint. Yet this church was founded as a Portuguese National Parish with masses offered in Portuguese. The semiotic clue to the cultural connection is found in the architectural design of the steeple that incorporates stylized sails marked with the Cross of St. John. This style of the cross has many other names: the Cross of Portugal; the Portuguese Cross of the Order of Christ and the cross formée. It is readily recognized as the only cross with arms that terminate in 45-degree angles. The cross is a common symbol of Portuguese culture found on monuments and especially on the sails of ancient and modern Portuguese sailing ships.

The name Sagres is another national cultural symbol. Sagres is the point of land at the southwestern tip of Portugal (also the southwestern tip of Europe) from which Prince Henry the Navigator dispatched explorers to discover the sea route around Africa to India. Sagres is also the name of the Portuguese navy's "tall ship" that travels to maritime celebrations around the world. Sagres is also the name of the best-selling national beer (the Portuguese equivalent of Budweiser). Names of famous Portuguese explorers are also used frequently enough to be seen as cultural symbols.

Figure 32
An awareness of the semiotic glossary of Portuguese culture can give clues to the casual observer. St. John's Catholic Church in Somerset gives no outward signs of its Portuguese connections other than this architectural design incorporating simulated sails decorated with the St. John's cross.

An example is Vasco da Gama, the first Portuguese explorer to round the Cape of Good Hope and reach India, whose name is used on restaurants and businesses.

Another cultural symbol connected to exploration is the compass rose, used frequently in architecture in Portugal such as the plaza surrounding Lisbon's Monument to the Discoveries in *Belém*. The compass rose is frequently used in similar symbolic settings in New England. For example, both statues of Prince Henry the Navigator in Fall River and in New Bedford are placed within settings of the compass rose tile work as are the re-created gates of Ponta Delgada in Fall River. At the Monument to the Portuguese Explorers in Newport, Rhode Island, stones representing the points of the compass are incorporated in the megalith-like structure.

Fatima is another name laden with Portuguese cultural symbolism and connotations because of the miracle and shrine at Fatima, Portugal. Catholics believe that in 1913 a vision appeared here of the Virgin Mary, known as Our Lady of Fatima. The name Fatima is also a common given name for Portuguese women. Six Portuguese churches in southern New England are named Our Lady of Fatima (Table 6). Portuguese churches and churchyards often display statues honoring Our Lady of Fatima as do many private homes. Statues of the Virgin Mary are common in the yardscape of the Portuguese community but the two girls and boy to whom the visions appeared, as well as lambs, identify the statue of Mary as Our Lady of Fatima.

Such statues are often displayed in plaster or concrete arches (and yes, bathtubs) with a protective glass or plastic sheeting and other items including photos of deceased family members and candles, constituting a shrine. Although Our Lady of Fatima is also associated with some Latino American communities,[234] it is generally as distinctive a marker of Portuguese American culture as is the Virgin of Guadalupe is for Mexican Americans and the Virgin of the Milagrosa for Puerto Ricans.[235] Interestingly, the name Fatima is itself reflective of cultural syncretism. The name Fatima came into Portuguese culture during the time of Moorish domination from the name of the Prophet Mohammed's favorite daughter.

Several important Portuguese cultural symbols derive from semiology incorporated into the Portuguese flag (Figure 34). The "five shields" symbol, one element in the iconography of the Portuguese flag, is part of the national coat of arms and a type of national shield for Portugal, in the way that the bald eagle on the Presidential Seal is for Americans. On the Portuguese flag, a large shield with a border of seven castles encompasses these five smaller shields in its center. The symbolism evolved from the coat of arms of Don

Figure 33
A shrine to Our Lady of Fatima in a three-decker neighborhood in Fall River.

Afonso Henriques, (King Afonso I) known as the father of the Portuguese nation. Legend has it that in 1140, he defeated five Moorish leaders in a series of battles, establishing the territorial core of what eventually became the modern Portuguese state. The five shields represent the kings he defeated. Each of the five shields contains five marks, (originally silver nails) said to represent the five wounds of Christ. The seven castles in a red border surrounding the shield represent military victories against the Moors in the Algarve by King Afonso III in 1249.

The ribboned armillary sphere is a later addition to the flag. It represents the exploration of the world by Portuguese navigators. The five arcs of the armillary sphere represent the Equator, the two Tropics, a meridian and the plane of the ecliptic. The background colors of the Portuguese flag, red and green, date from 1910 and celebrate the Republican overthrow of the monarchy in that year. The various shield symbols, the armillary sphere, and the colors of the flag, red, green and gold, used separately or together, are important indicators of Portuguese cultural influence in the landscape.

Figure 34
The Portuguese flag is rich in symbols: the colors red, green and gold; a shield; five smaller shields with five nails representing the wounds of Christ; seven castles and a ribboned armillary sphere.

SONG AND DANCE

The semiotics of the Portuguese community include music and dance. Portuguese music and dance are among the signs and symbols in the culture that have been imported into the landscape of southeastern New England. Like religious processions, song and dance are temporary but vibrant aspects of the ethnic landscape. There is a distinctive style of Portuguese popular music called *fado*. Interestingly, it is only within the past few decades that this Portuguese national style of song has become popular within the communities of southeastern New England. *Fado* evolved in nightclubs and cafes in Lisbon and Coimbra (Portugal's national university town) in the early nineteenth century. It had still not made its way to the islands by the first major waves of emigration. It is only very recently, since the 1980s, that American Portuguese communities, where Atlantic Islanders dominate, might feature this style of singing.[236] Meanwhile, *fado* is experiencing a renaissance across all of Portugal, the islands, and the immigrant communities after finally freeing itself from its reactionary political association with the long-time dictator Antonio Salazar.[237]

In addition to *fado,* folk dancing and village folk song is a part of the Portuguese culture that helps knit together Portuguese on both sides of the Atlantic. While just about all European immigrants in the United States express their culture through folk dancing, Kimberley DaCosta Holton, a scholar of Portuguese culture and literature, has studied how this "performancescape" has a particular meaning, and perhaps a unique meaning among America's Portuguese immigrants due to that nation's particular history.[238]

With the zest of genealogist on a quest, folkloric dance troupes in Portugal called *ranchos,* not only perform but also research these traditional dances. They interview the elderly, hunt for authentic musical instruments and scrutinize costumes in old photographs to reconstruct the traditional dances in each rural microregion of the nation. The typical *rancho* group has twenty or more performers including singers, narrators, instrumentalists, and dancers. In Portugal, the 3,000 or so Portuguese *rancho* troupes directly involve perhaps 100,000 people at any given time. Including the extended families, neighbors, and all the kids in tow, *rancho* rivals soccer as a national preoccupation. In the Portuguese American communities, the rancho dance troupes are often associated with social clubs. For example, the PYCO Club of Fall River sponsors the Lusitano Folk Dancers. (The acronym P.Y.C.O., Portuguese Youth Cultural Organization, is a play on words because Pico, an Azorean island, is one of the main origins of New England immigrants.)

Today, performing *rancho* in Portugal serves many roles in helping to preserve national identity and traditional Portuguese culture. *Rancho* performance stands against the onslaught of modernization spurred by the European Union within Portugal. In the immigrant communities, performing *rancho* helps preserve Portuguese culture including in DaCosta's home community of Newark, which she focuses on in her book. Almost every Portuguese festival in southeastern New England features the dancers. *Rancho* is performed each day of the four-day Madeira feast in New Bedford.

The "performancescape" also forges bonds between the overseas emigrant communities and the home country. Many Portuguese emigrants return home to Portugal or the islands for family visits in the summer, the height of *rancho* season, and they learn the latest dances, get costumes manufactured or repaired, interview elderly residents and hunt for authentic antique musical instruments to bring back to the United States. Another type of performance is that of Portuguese American bands that perform locally as well as, on occasion, tour Portugal. Katherine Brucher, a music

Figure 35
Provincetown decked out for its annual Portuguese festival at which rancho folclorico is performed.

professor at DePaul University, has written about the Lusitana Band of Cumberland, Rhode Island as an example of a *filarmónica,* a community-based amateur music organization.[239]

MONUMENTALIZATION OF THE LANDSCAPE

As Europeans, the Portuguese place a greater value on "grand monuments" in their semiotic glossary than do Americans. This monumentalization of the landscape as cultural expression, or monumental iconography,[240] is a conscious, deliberate effort to build monuments to celebrate and to preserve heritage. This cultural initiative is made possible by the increasing political power and growing affluence of the Portuguese American community. In particular, the accumulation of wealth by a few prominent Portuguese American social leaders who are willing to donate private funds makes much of this commemoration possible. In effect, the Portuguese Americans of New England have finally achieved a certain minimum level of affluence and political power that now allows them as a group to impact the public landscape. Increased political influence also helps as well as assistance from the Portuguese and Azorean governments.

Despite a sharp decline in immigration and in the proportion of Portuguese-only speakers, the monumentalization of the landscape is taking place at an increasing pace. Geographer Brian J. Godfrey refers to this stage of ethnic occupation as a consolidation phase. This phase occurs when an ethnic group dominates a district demographically and seeks to deliberately promote a coherent sense of place by building enduring monuments, landmarks and community institutions. Godfrey believes that the purposes of these actions are to build ethnic identity, to enhance collective memory and to reflect the enhanced status and political importance of the group.[241] One example is the monument to Mariano Bishop, a renowned local textile labor leader who was born in the Azores. While the monument is placed in a cemetery, its imposing presence (24-foot height) and acknowledgments to the Textile Workers Union of America, makes it clear that it is not just a grave marker.[242]

The first monument of substantial size and prominence in the Portuguese American communities of southeastern New England was a monument to Prince Henry the Navigator that has been in place in Fall River since World War II. The monument at the intersection of Eastern Avenue and Pleasant Street was erected in 1940 to coincide with the 800th anniversary of the founding of Portugal in 1140 and also with the 1940 Portuguese World's Fair. Not to be outdone, New Bedford dedicated its own monument to Prince Henry in 1996. In addition to a compass rose, wavy black and while tiles surround both statues, another Portuguese cultural symbol that is a common street and sidewalk tiling pattern in Lisbon and other cities including Rio de Janeiro in Brazil and Ponta Delgada in the Azores.

The Prince Henry monuments in Fall River and New Bedford and the Newport Explorers monument commemorate the seafaring and world exploration tradition of the Portuguese nation. Today there is great intellectual and political debate in Portugal and in the Portuguese

Figure 36
The monument to labor leader Mariano Bishop in Fall River's Notre Dame Cemetery was erected by the Textile Union Workers of America after Bishop's death in 1953.

American communities over the extent to which this era of Portuguese exploration in the fifteenth and sixteenth Centuries, collectively known as "The Discoveries," defines the heritage of the Portuguese nation. The Discoveries are based around not only the great explorers themselves, and Prince Henry who directed them (although he never left Portugal), but also the great national author Luís Vaz de Camões who wrote Portugal's great national epic poem, The Lusiads, (*Os Lusíadas*). This work has so come to define The Discoveries that *Dia de Portugal* is now celebrated internationally on the anniversary of Camões death. This view of the Portuguese nation, a popular one as evidenced by the themes of many of the great monuments constructed in the Portuguese American community, focuses the national image not only on exploration but on colonialism, the colonial wars and on overseas exploitation.[243]

A more modern trend, however, is a shift in the focus of monuments and celebrations to celebrate immigration rather than to celebrate exploration and colonialism. A prime example is the statue, "The Spirit of the Immigrant" that was unveiled in 1997 on the grounds of the Dartmouth public library, just outside of New Bedford. This shift is also evident in the dedicatory plaques on the two monuments to Prince Henry. The dedication text of the recently erected New Bedford statue is clearly focused on immigration in contrast to the traditional homage to exploration commemorated on the dedicatory plaques of the Fall River monument erected 57 years earlier. The deliberate facing of the New Bedford figure due East toward Portugal (recall that southeastern New England is about the latitude of northern Portugal) is reminiscent of two sculptures of a young Irish immigrant, Annie Moore, that face each other over thousands of miles of Atlantic Ocean between Ellis Island in New York and Cobn in County Cork, Ireland.[244] The contrast of the "great man" Portuguese monuments with the common young woman featured in the Irish statues is also instructive of two very different approaches to the commemoration.

The Statue to the Emigrant in Dartmouth, Massachusetts goes even further in its emphasis on immigration by expressing the Portuguese concept of *saudade*. The word *saudade* is inscribed in mosaic on the stature. *Saudade* is also the title of a novel written by Portuguese American author Katherine Vaz. She defined *saudade* in the preface to her novel as "A Portuguese word considered untranslatable. One definition: Yearning so intense for those who are missing, or for vanished times or places, that their absence is the most profound presence in one's life. A state of being, rather than merely a sentiment."[245] As we saw with Portuguese gardens, *saudade* is an emotion of such yearning for the homeland that the emotion becomes all-consuming. The sentiment is expressed figuratively in all monuments and, in the case of the Statue of the Spirit of the Immigrant, literally. It is also fitting that one of the most recent major monuments constructed is not to a famous male Portuguese explorer, but to the Portuguese immigrant.

The landscape of the islands and of the continental homeland back in Portugal is not full of monuments to the immigrants, so, within Portuguese

Figure 37
The Spirit of the Immigrant (left) was unveiled in South Dartmouth, a mile south of New Bedford, in 1997. The monument was a gift from the people of Povoação on São Miguel. The symbolism includes the American and Portuguese shields and speaks of saudade, longing for the homeland. The monument honoring Peter Francisco (right), whom George Washington called a "One-Man-Army," is located in downtown New Bedford.

culture, the evolution of such display is unique to the American landscape. Some monuments are similar in structure to those in Portugal and seem almost transplantations, such as the Newport monument to the Portuguese explorers, and both statues of Prince Henry. All the explorers' monuments are clearly modeled as local symbolic equivalents to Lisbon's great monument to the explorers at Belem.

Class distinctions within the Portuguese American community are evident in the landscape in the acknowledgments to donors whose contributions made the construction of various monuments possible. The lists of donors on the Newport Monument to the Explorers, on the Prince Henry statue in New Bedford and on other monuments, read like a "who's who" of the (mostly male) leadership of the Portuguese American community. The plaques acknowledge doctors, judges, elected political officials and business leaders. The names of the donors and their positions also illustrate how the Portuguese community has now established enough social and political weight to deliberately impress cultural symbolism upon the landscape and to deliberately "produce culture." Although this heritage so honored tends to be a traditional masculinized version of history (monuments to "great men," including the monument to Revolutionary War hero Pedro Francisco in New Bedford and the Mariano Bishop memorial in Fall River) these actions do create focal points in space and in time for the coming together of the community in a geographical and social sense.

Why all this monument building? Jackson reminds us that each of us needs something permanent in the world surrounding us, just as we need a permanent identity for ourselves. There is a fundamental human need to be part of something more lasting than we are; a part of a moral or ethical order that transcends our individual existence. No one wants to

Figure 38
The list of contributors to the Portuguese Discoveries Monument in Newport reads like a "who's who" of the Portuguese community, listing several doctors, judges and elected officials ("honorable"). These names illustrate how the Portuguese community now has enough social and political weight to deliberately impress cultural symbolism upon the landscape.

feel rootless without an identity linked to a particular place or places. We look to the landscape to reinforce our identity as political beings.[246] An increasing number of third-generation Portuguese who seek to renew and preserve their ancestral culture contribute to this interest and perhaps the decline of immigration and the fear of a culture slipping away contributes to the need to memorialize culture.

The origin of the word monument is related to monitor (as in the sense of reminding), commend, commemorate and memorialize. A monument is meant to remind us of a great public figure, a great public event or a great public declaration which the group is pledging itself to honor and remember. Monuments are more numerous where the inhabitants share a strong sense of a religious or political past, and where they are concerned with their beginnings. Jackson uses the term "Latin" to refer to the traditional "great man" type of monument and sees that as old-fashioned; abandoned by the average American community and replaced by a modern American style of celebration and commemoration such as that of the 1976 Bicentennial.[247]

Two other grand monuments reflect memorializations other than the traditional statues of great men. A reproduction of the "Gates of the City" in Ponta Delgada on the island of St. Michael's was constructed in Fall River in 2006. The idea for this monument dates to 1978 when Ponta Delgada and Fall River became sister cities. Fall River renamed a street Ponta Delgada Boulevard and the relationship evolved over the years with exchanges of visits by politicians. The mayors of the two cities participated in the dedication ceremony at which the mayor of Ponta Delgada, Berta Cabral, noted that the gates stand as a "symbolic gesture of our solidarity for our brothers and sisters who have immigrated." [248]

The Ponta Delgada Gates are part of a trend of copying buildings or structures that reflect or epitomize culture, such as building copies of the Great Sphinx and the Eifel Tower in Las Vegas.[249] Perhaps this tradition of reproducing cultural objects left behind began with religious statues, such as the creation of replicas of religious icons in churches, noted earlier. The second latest great monument is not yet constructed. This major effort in New Bedford, if completed, will be a "Monument to the Fisherman," which, while not officially intended to solely commemorate Portuguese fishermen, will inevitably emphasize Portuguese Americans as all the major proponents and the initial fund-raising efforts are connected to the Portuguese community. This proposed monument reflects the modern American tradition and modern academic historical tradition away from "great men" and toward the "common" man and woman. As of 2014, the monument has run into a variety of difficulties, not the least of which is that sufficient funds have not yet been raised for its construction. Although not an actual monument, the giant photographs of Portuguese women on a pier in Provincetown also represent this on-going shift toward greater equality in honoring Portuguese Americans regardless of gender.

Another category of monuments and statues is that commemorating Portuguese American war dead. These monuments are numerous and very visible in the landscape. In New Bedford and Fall River, many city parks have such a monument whether or not the park is located in the Portuguese communities of those cities. During World War II, Portugal was ruled by Salazar, a fascist dictator. While he never formally allied Portugal with the Axis powers, he was never fully supportive of the Allied cause. Salazar initially resisted, but finally allowed, Allied use of the Portuguese Atlantic islands for air bases. He made no secret of his admiration for the Italian dictator Mussolini. Salazar ordered Portuguese flags flown at half-staff after learning of the death of Hitler. By association, the loyalty of Portuguese Americans to the United States became somewhat suspect during World War II despite the large number of Portuguese Americans who fought and died in that war (as was the case with German, Japanese and Italian Americans).

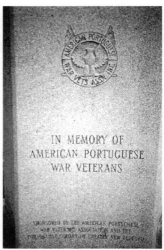

Figure 39
Due to the actions of Portugal's dictator Salazar, monuments erected during and shortly after WW II to Portuguese American war dead and to those who served, reversed the usual order of words to emphasize "American Portuguese" and "Loyalty" as on these monuments in Fall River (left) and New Bedford (right). The American eagle symbolism was used without the usual addition of Portuguese elements. Note also the use of the phrase "Portuguese colony" at the bottom of the New Bedford monument.

To counter this sentiment of unease in their affiliation, associations such as the Portuguese American Loyalty Association and the American Portuguese War Veterans Association were formed. Among other activities, they erected monuments to Portuguese Americans who had died in the war. Some monuments even reversed the usual order of the terminology and listed the name of the organization as the "American Portuguese Loyalty Association." Symbolism on these monuments often includes both the American eagle and the Portuguese shield. This severely pro-American attitude carried over even until the 1960s when a proposal by Azoreans and Madeirans to build a monument to Portuguese immigrants was opposed by the daily Portuguese newspaper in New Bedford as inappropriate. An editorial admonished the Portuguese to instead express their gratitude to this country for being here.[250] In the "monumental" landscape, there are also many markers designating small squares and plazas tucked into street corners and road intersections dedicated to Portuguese American war dead. These markers are often erected and maintained by Portuguese American social clubs or veterans' associations. A recent example is the Portuguese American Veterans monument erected by the Portuguese American Social Club of Pawtucket in 2012.

Monuments to war dead can incidentally reveal the ethnicity of veterans who fought in various conflicts. For example, a veterans' monument in Kennedy Park in Fall River honors city soldiers who died in all wars. While it is not specifically a "Portuguese monument" the list of names can be used to show the growth of the city's Portuguese population over time. The author's analysis of ethnic names in all conflicts indicates the percentage of Fall River's Portuguese American war dead as follows: Spanish American War, 0%; World War I, 9%; World War II, 26%; Korean War, 29%; Vietnam War 57%. Note that the percentage of the dead in Vietnam, 57%, exceeds the current percentage of the city's population that reports Portuguese ancestry (46%). Perhaps this reflects socio-economic class in that a larger proportion of Portuguese are less well-off than the general population and was more inclined to enlist or to be drafted, or less likely to gain deferments from the draft for educational or medical reasons.

One of the most intriguing Portuguese monuments is Dighton Rock, a rock deposited by the glaciers (termed a glacial erratic), which has evolved as a "Portuguese Rock" conceptually competing with Plymouth Rock. Dighton Rock is an automobile-sized rock with inscrutable inscriptions. It is housed in a small museum building located along the Taunton River in Dighton Massachusetts, about 15 miles north of Fall River. Like Plymouth Rock, the boulder was lifted from its original tidal location and placed in a new bed inside the museum to preserve the inscriptions. The history of this monument is complex due to the interplay of a number of cultural signifiers. Dighton Rock illustrates how an ethnic group can "appropriate" a monument. For example, the Alamo is not recognized as a special site of a victory by Mexican Americans because it has already been "appropriated" as a Texan American symbol.[251]

While scholars have advanced several explanations for the ancient inscriptions on the rock in addition to Portuguese explorers (Norse, Native

Figure 40
This monument in Fall River's Kennedy Park lists war dead by name allowing for an analysis of the ethnicity of the names of those who died in each war.

Figure 41
At left are the inscriptions on Dighton Rock shown before it was moved indoors into the museum. At right is an interpretation of the markings presented on a tile mural at the Museu da Marinha in Lisbon, attributing the markings to Portuguese explorer Miguel Corte-Real in 1511.

American and Phoenician, among others), the Portuguese believe that Miguel Corte Real, a Portuguese explorer who sailed along the New England coast in 1502, inscribed the rock. While all major theories are explained in the museum, it is clear that the visitor is encouraged to conclude that the predominance of evidence favors the Portuguese theory. The museum is, in effect, a "Portuguese shrine." One panel shows how some of the markings could represent St. John's crosses and how the markings resemble other inscriptions left by Portuguese explorers at other locations they explored in Africa. Two large ship models dominate the interior of the museum. They are models of ships of Portuguese explorers, sails decorated with Portuguese (St. John's) crosses, which were donated by the Portuguese government.

The southern European architectural style of the museum housing the rock, right down to its elaborately detailed door handles in the Portuguese Manuelian architectural style, leaves no doubt that this is a Portuguese cultural shrine. As such, it is a counterpart and counterpoint to the otherwise British colonial-dominated monumental landscape nearby honoring the Pilgrims as exemplified most notably by Plymouth Rock and Provincetown's Pilgrim Monument. The removal of Dighton Rock from its original tidal location in 1963 and its literal enshrinement in the museum in 1973 are parallels to the treatment of Plymouth Rock just 40 miles to the east. Local citizens have raised funds to send a cast of Dighton Rock to the Azores; a fitting exchange of reproductions considering the construction of the replica of the Ponta Delgada gates in Fall River.

Thus Dighton Rock is, in effect, a statement by Portuguese Americans that "We were here first." It is ironic that the Pilgrim Monument in Provincetown, dedicated in 1909, was built by the "Yankees" of that town, in part to commemorate and reinforce their status at a time when Portuguese made up 45% of the town's population and when the Portuguese had taken over control of the town's fishing industry.[252] In 1942, in another ironic twist, Depression-era photographer John Collier took a photograph of the "City Fathers of Provincetown" duly noting in

Figure 42
Above, the Dighton Rock Museum, 13 miles north of Fall River on the Taunton River, emphasizes the Portuguese interpretation of the inscriptions. Even the door handles (left) are in the Manuelian style.

the caption: "Provincetown, Massachusetts. City fathers of Provincetown, all of Portuguese descent, gathered in council, before a painting representing the signing of the Pilgrim compact in the bay of Provincetown upon the first landing of the Pilgrims on American soil." [253]

Figure 43
"City fathers of Provincetown, all of Portuguese descent, gathered in council, before a painting representing the signing of the Pilgrim compact in the bay of Provincetown upon the first landing of the Pilgrims on American soil." Photo by John Collier, Jr., 1942, from the collection U.S. Farm Security Administration/Office of War Information at the Library of Congress.

While the Portuguese American community as a whole supports these monument building efforts and contributes funds toward their design and erection, the monuments already constructed and others in the planning stages in New England are often the result of one individual's efforts amounting to a "crusade." The interpretation of Dighton Rock as a monument left by explorer Miguel Corte Real was the culmination of years of work by a linguist at New York University, Joseph Fragoso. His work was later popularized by a local medical doctor, Manuel da Silva, through books and websites. Significantly, da Silva's book was titled "Portuguese Pilgrims."

Arthur Raposo is another example of such an individual. Raposo carried on a campaign over many years to get the Portuguese Discovery Monument constructed in Newport, Rhode Island. He organized a committee of influential citizens of Portuguese American ancestry and worked with the local Portuguese Cultural Foundation, Rhode Island state legislators of Portuguese ancestry, and state and local officials to find a site and to obtain approval to construct the monument. Local donations and state funds from the Rhode Island Department of Environment were matched by money from the Portuguese government through its National Committee of the Commemorations of the Discoveries of Portugal. The monument was completed in 1988 at a total cost of about $250,000.[254] However, a few years later, deterioration of the concrete structures led to the removal of many of the individual monoliths making up the larger monument.

The fervor to plant monuments is even carried beyond the southeastern New England Portuguese cultural area. Edmund Dinis, former New Bedford politician, arranged for a monument honoring Portuguese explorer Estevan Gomez to be installed in Bangor, Maine in 1999 along the Penobscot River that Gomez explored in 1525. Dinis also was instrumental in establishing a monument honoring Portuguese explorer Alvares Fagundes in Halifax, Nova Scotia where Fagundes established a settlement in 1520, almost a century before the Acadian settlements. An Azorean businessman contributed funds for a statue of Portuguese soccer star, Eusebio, at Gillette Stadium in Foxboro where both the New England Patriots and New England Revolution, a professional soccer team, play.

NAMING AND RENAMING

Other aspects of monumentalization of the landscape include such things as the memorialization of Portuguese island names in the landscape and street naming (or more frequently, street renaming). This illustrates another aspect of the semiotics of the Portuguese landscape -- the memorializing in the landscape of the geographic places left behind. A very common type of memorialization in the landscape is the commemoration of geographic remembrances of the homeland and of island names. *Lusitano* or *Luso* and its Americanized form, Luzo, is a synonym for Portuguese often seen on business signs. These terms derive from Lusitania, the Roman name for the province that later evolved into Portugal. The term Luzo-American is frequently used to mean Portuguese American.

Pap notes that the association of Portuguese immigrants with their particular island of origin was so strong that early Portuguese were known by their islands: Fayals were those from Fayal in the Azores. Bravas were those from the Cape Verdean island of Brava and for a time this name was a general term for all Cape Verdeans. Sometimes self-ascribed and sometimes ascribed by others, neighborhoods took on the names of the origin of their inhabitants. In the early 1900s, the South End Portuguese neighborhood in New Bedford was called Fayal as was the Portuguese neighborhood on Martha's Vineyard.[255] Water Street in New Bedford's South End was once called "Fayal Street."[256]

Obviously, the home country, Portugal, is a favorite place-name carried to the United States. The *Portugalia* restaurant sign also sports the national colors, red and green. Lisbon, Portugal's capital, is a common name also, as seen on business signs such as the Lisbon Sausage Company. A Fall River restaurant is named Estoril for a coastal resort town near Lisbon. In southeastern New England, place names of the Portuguese Atlantic Islands abound on social clubs and businesses such as the Madeira Club, St. Michael's Club, Ponta Delgada Club, and the Acores Market. Place name adjectives such as *Madeirenses* (Madeiran), *Micaelenses*, and *Faialenses* are seen in restaurants, bakeries and other food stores. Brazilian places are featured on some Portuguese stores such as the San Paulo Restaurant (note the Anglicization of *São*) and Amazonia, a clothing store.

Street naming is another type of commemoration of geographic place. Yet there are not many streets named after Portuguese persons, places or cultural objects, largely because the southeastern New England streets were already established and named long before the arrival of the Portuguese. Because this area has been relatively economically depressed and has experienced only moderate population growth, it does not have the constantly expanding sprawl and concurrent street-naming opportunities of rapidly growing suburban areas expanding onto undeveloped land. Opportunities to add a street and give it a Portuguese name are rare.

Even so, there are streets with Portuguese names such as Fatima in Somerset, Warren, and Bristol; Lisbon in Fall River and Providence; Horta in West Warwick and Fayal in Taunton and Middletown, Rhode Island. More commonly, streets are renamed to honor the Portuguese. A six-block-long street in New Bedford, formerly Diman Street, was renamed Madeira Avenue in the 1970s in honor of the Madeira fairgrounds and the festival that takes place along it. In 1999 Fall River renamed a portion of Water Street in front of The Gates "Ponta Delgada Boulevard." A major thoroughfare in Fall River was renamed for Mariano Bishop, an important labor leader in the textile mills in the 1930s. Adding honorary street names to the formal name is also a common way of adding a Portuguese commemoration. Hartford, Connecticut added, "Father Jose da Silva Way" in honor of a popular civic-minded priest above the name Madison Avenue in that city's Parkville Portuguese neighborhood.

Murals are another way of recalling and paying homage to the homeland. In southeastern New England, some of these murals are on the interiors of restaurants and stores such as the Cinderella Restaurant in Fall River, and others are on building exteriors including that along the offices of *O Jornal* in Fall River, a weekly bilingual newspaper. In 2016 Fall River's Durfee High School students created a ceramic tile mural celebrating the city's history for the school system administrative building. It was made in the style of traditional Portuguese *azulejo* tiles.[257] An industrial mural in downtown Fall River has a quotation in English and Portuguese and Madeira Field in New Bedford recently added a mural of Madeira. One scholar states that exterior wall murals in the United States originated in Mexican ethnic neighborhoods in the Southwest in the 1960s, although their origin outside of the United States is much earlier in both Spain and in pre-Columbian Mexico.[258]

Figure 44
This mural of textile mills in downtown Fall River states in English and Portuguese, "The world is ours -- not to slave in but to own."

Finally, some important structures commemorating Portuguese Americans were not constructed as monuments as such. One example is naming schools or other buildings of note after Portuguese Americans of note. The naming of the central school administration building in New Bedford after Paul Rodrigues, a long-time high school principal and system superintendent of Portuguese descent, was considered quite an achievement for Portuguese Americans at the time (1972). Another significant example is the Braga Bridge that carries Interstate 195 across the Taunton River in Massachusetts from Somerset to Fall River. It is named for Charles M. Braga, a Portuguese American killed at Pearl Harbor.

7
PORTUGUESE CULTURE AND ASSIMILATION

What it means to "be Portuguese" is constantly shifting, as is the concept of what it means to be "Portuguese American."

THE CONTINUING CONSTRUCTION OF "PORTUGUESE AMERICAN" CULTURE

What is an ethnic group? A sociologist and historian provides a perspective. First, an ethnic group, like race or class, is not a scientific term but a socially constructed category used to designate groups of people. The ancestral distinctiveness may be claimed by the group or it may be imposed upon it by a politically more powerful group. Usually, the more powerful group does not claim ethnic distinctiveness. (Think of whites in the United States or the English in the United Kingdom; they are not referred to as an ethnic majority nor do they think of themselves as such.) In fact, the root of the word ethnic comes to us from the Greek *ethnos,* a word used to refer to a people, tribe or nation who were *not* Greeks. Only in the twentieth century did the phrase take on the meaning of nationality in the sense of a people from a particular political state. The group is set apart or sets itself apart on the basis of some combination of linguistic, cultural or racial characteristics. Often a common ancestry is presumed, even if it is a mythical ancestry. Minority status is not a numerical concept; it is based on the degree of social and political power; thus a large numerical majority can be a minority, as were blacks in South Africa for centuries. If we say that ethnic groups built America, we might also say that America built ethnic groups.[259]

"Portuguese culture" the cement holding the Portuguese ethnic group together, itself is a moving target. Scholars of culture tell us that culture is "produced" or "constructed" and it is constantly changing over time. To visualize constructed culture, think of the *Portas da Cidade* literally constructed in Fall River to replicate the gates back in Ponta Delgada, or the Holy Ghost feasts re-created in the United States or the very recent trend to hold *Romeiros* processions. What it means to "be Portuguese" is constantly shifting, as is the concept of what it means to be "Portuguese American." Bela Feldman-Bianco, a Brazilian anthropologist who has studied the Portuguese Americans in New England, writes that the situation of Portuguese Americans has changed just over the last decade for several reasons. These reasons include growing acceptance of the concept of the United States as a nation of immigrants; improvement in New Bedford's economic situation; the arrival of more diverse immigrants; the relative improvement of the situation for Portuguese Americans in New Bedford, and changes in how the Portuguese government views the responsibility of its overseas citizens: to assimilate and yet keep their Portuguese heritage alive.[260]

And what of the Portuguese subgroups? Williams, writing in 1982, noted that "only now," perhaps in part due to the influence of television, do Azoreans consider themselves to be Portuguese first and Azoreans second.[261] Although not evident in the landscape *per se*, the community is also knit together by numerous Portuguese radio stations and 24-hour cable television that provides a mixture of local, Portuguese and Brazilian television programming. Such a renaissance in Portuguese heritage is not limited to that of Portuguese culture with a "capital P" but also to Azorean, Madeiran and Cape Verdean heritage. Cultural heritage is overlapping and shared, sometimes even competing. Some scholars have referred to this as the multiple layering of place.[262] Think of the complexity of the place and cultural loyalties of the New England Portuguese Americans who, to some extent, feel themselves to be simultaneously persons of Portuguese heritage as well as, for example, Azoreans, *Micaelenses*, Americans and New Englanders.

Look at changes in "Portuguese culture" itself. Consider that over the lifetime of a 70-year old Portuguese national currently living in Portugal, he or she has seen a much radical change in Portugal as in any other nation on earth. If you are that 70-year old person, you were born around 1945, right at the end of World War II. When you were about 30, the fascist dictator, Antonio Salazar, died and his vestigial government was overthrown in a bloodless revolution in 1974. The colonial wars ceased and Portugal finally relinquished its African colonies, the last European power to do so.

These included Angola and Mozambique, São Tomé and Príncipe, Cape Verde Islands and Guinea-Bissau. Employment in agriculture in Portugal, a critical measure of economic development, dropped from 45% to 10% during your lifetime; the latter figure a percentage that had been reached in the United States in 1955. Portugal joined the European Union in 1986 when you were about 40. When you were about 50, the *escudo* was phased out and replaced by the euro (1999-2002).

In your lifetime, you have seen so much emigration that Portugal is second only to Ireland among European nations in having the largest proportion of its citizens living abroad. And that emigration has not been just to the United States (where Portuguese are now the largest immigrant group in New England) but to France, Switzerland, Spain, the United Kingdom, Germany, Canada, Brazil and elsewhere. Lisbon's smaller rivals today are not just Porto in Portugal, but Paris, Brussels, Toronto, New Bedford and Fall River and Newark, New Jersey. You have seen Lisbon, like many other national capitals, become a multiethnic hub with its attendant displacements and racial tensions. Indeed by some measures, Lisbon is now the most African city in Europe due to massive immigration from the Cape Verde Islands and the former Portuguese African colonies.[263]

But the American Portuguese are used to dealing with cultural complexity. The early Portuguese in southeastern New England settled into a complex ethnic and sociological network. While, in theory, the new nation they arrived in may have been dominated by Anglos, on a day-to-day basis most Portuguese did not deal with Anglos. They dealt with Irish cops and school teachers; Jewish and Lebanese merchants; French-Canadian landlords; Norwegian fishing boat captains and Polish auto mechanics. By simple geometry, a large proportion of Portuguese lived on the edge of the Portuguese neighborhoods and thus frequently came into contact with people not from the dominant Anglo culture, but from other ethnic groups. And common ethnicity itself was no guarantee of friendliness. Perhaps the person who gave the immigrant a hard time in the mill was a Portuguese foreman or co-worker. Modern scholars would say that America did not build the Portuguese ethnic group, but the American culture sharpened or honed Portuguese awareness of their shared ancestry in competition and in comparison with other ethnic and religious groups in ways that did not exist in the more insular world of the Portuguese islands.[264]

THE COMPLEXITIES OF ASSIMILATION

We are all familiar with the concept of the American "melting pot," but, like other everyday concepts, there is a lot more complexity to cultural assimilation than simplistic models such as the melting pot can explain. Given the urban environment that surrounds the Portuguese Americans of New England, the concept of segmented assimilation as developed by sociologists can help describe what actually happens during the assimilation process and the possible futures for individuals in this group.[265] Briefly, the concept of segmented assimilation recognizes that "assimilation" means different things to different people and the assimilation process may result in three very different kinds of outcomes based on the predilections of individuals and their social environments, family structures, economic circumstances, levels of education, and other variables.

The first outcome of assimilation is the traditional simplistic and optimistic view of assimilation, often characterized as the "melting pot" blended with upward mobility. This outcome assumes that ethnic groups in the United States will experience upward mobility and will eventually assimilate into the generic "middle class" of American culture. They and their descendants, usually by the third generation, will choose non-ethnic partners as mates, lose the ability to speak the language, move out of the ethnic neighborhoods, and in effect, lose their ethnic identity. They may only retain their Portuguese surname as a tie to their ethnic group. For women especially, even that tie may be lost through marriage. However, the basic assumption is that children of immigrants are bound for the middle class as they and their children get better jobs and move up the socio-economic ladder.

The second outcome of segmented assimilation, sometimes called the structuralist view, recognizes that the outcome of immigration for the immigrants and their children depends upon the nature of their interaction with the social and economic structure of the host culture. This view recognizes the possibility of what might be called "downward" assimilation. Assimilation will take place, but which economic class will the immigrant assimilate into? Given the prevalence of social dysfunction that is at hand in the economically depressed former New England textile cities, one outcome is that some Portuguese American children might adopt values that spurn education and hard work. They may drop out of school, have children out of wedlock, join gangs, become drug users, turn to crime and prostitution, become HIV/AIDS victims and perhaps serve time in prison.

Even if the outcomes are not that extreme, they and their descendants may be trapped in lifetimes of work in low-end service or minimum wage jobs and thus experience sequential rounds of unemployment and dependence upon social services. To some extent these outcomes appear to be associated with a pattern of the children revolting against parental values and their "Old World" culture, turning against their parent's native language and abandoning parental values in adopting too quickly the values "on the street" in their community.

The third perspective offered by segmented assimilation, the multiculturalist view, suggests that Portuguese Americans can retain ethnic connections for many generations. Rather than a "melting pot," their experience is better characterized as a "lumpy stew" or an "ethnic salad." (Why do scholars of assimilation prefer food analogies?) They may lose the ability to speak Portuguese but still live in the neighborhood, actively attend Portuguese festivals and a Portuguese church. They will retain exposure to the culture through food and connections with neighbors and relatives who immigrated to nearby locations. They will probably marry someone of Portuguese ancestry. In this model immigrant parents and their second generation, children learn English after arrival at about the same rate and the children do not revolt against parental authority and the "old ways." Both parents and children remain involved with and appreciative of the surrounding ethnic culture. This approach describes a kind of "slow but steady" path to assimilation for both parents and children. And immigrants may no longer simply become Americans; they may fully Americanize by becoming *ethnic* Americans like everyone else.[266]

The concept of modes of incorporation (paths to assimilation) adds another dimension to the process of assimilation.[267] Paths to assimilation are complex and dependent upon the class of origin of the immigrant, ranging from manual laborer to entrepreneur. The concept also takes into account the context of how the immigrant group is received by the host society, which can vary from handicapped to advantaged. While most Portuguese clearly arrived in the laborer category, the earliest arrivals were disadvantaged and discriminated against. Those immigrating after the volcanic disturbances in the 1960s were indeed arriving under great hardship but they were also welcomed and assisted by local governments and the established Portuguese American community and may fall into the advantaged category.

All assimilation theories recognize the value of educational attainment. Education is such an important factor in the assimilation process that it has been shown that children of highly educated recent immigrants fare better than third and fourth generation children of immigrants with lesser levels of education.[268] Thus the Portuguese Americans of New England need to continue to strive to overcome their initial very strong disadvantage on this factor of educational attainment as we will discuss in detail in the next chapter. In comparing levels of assimilation among groups of immigrants, geographer Caroline Nagel states that the important measures are language use, employment patterns, intermarriage rates, naturalization rates and residential location. On all of these measures, except perhaps intermarriage, research has shown that the Portuguese are still less assimilated than other groups that have been in the country the same amount of time or longer.[269]

Where an immigrant group lives shapes the environment where assimilation will take place. The tendency for Portuguese to cluster in the same residential neighborhoods after many years is still particularly strong compared to other ethnic groups. In fact, ethnic neighborhoods seem to be such an assumed fact of immigrant location that we seldom think it could be otherwise. Yet scholars have shown that some groups in some areas, such as Cubans in Washington DC, Estonians in suburban New Jersey, Danish in Seattle, Barbadians in London, and other groups, have not clustered in ethnic neighborhoods, but have dispersed around metropolitan areas and yet interact with each other just as other immigrant groups do. They use the term "heterolocalism" to describe this phenomenon.[270] True assimilation is a two-stage process. Outward aspects of assimilation may inevitably take place. If you followed second and third generation immigrants and tracked where they go -- work, schools, shopping, recreation -- their travel patterns may appear identical to the general population. But assimilation into the inner spheres of their surrounding society, such as social cliques and clubs, is not inevitable and may not take place.[271]

Many Portuguese Americans indeed assimilate and for many their relationship to the Old World culture becomes that of symbolic ethnicity, an outcome near the end of the assimilation process. According to scholars, symbolic ethnicity is the voluntary retention of the "good things" of the old world culture such as food, festivals and museums, without having to really live in, invest in, or be involved with that culture on a daily basis. Certainly, these Portuguese Americans adopting symbolic ethnicity do not suffer any of the disadvantages or discrimination that might be felt by some members of that culture.[272] Symbolic ethnicity is most often adopted by third and later generations.

Almost all American immigrant groups eventually assimilate but, especially by the third generation, they still feel an attachment to the heritage of their ancestors. Children of immigrants, especially by the third generation, become very selective in their ethnic behavior, symbols, and interactions.[273] People of third and later generations are seen to be more concerned with maintaining a sense of ethnic identity and discovering how to express that identity in ways that bear little or no social cost to them.[274] Those means of expressing identity are of a voluntary and symbolic variety: taking part in holiday festivals, eating ethnic food, visiting places, and museums associated with one's ancestry. This idea has also been called "voluntary ethnicity"[275] and "convenience ethnicity."[276] There are also third generation and later "converts" who deliberately proselytize the old culture.

Some reasons for the renewed interest in the old culture are that by the third generation, people forget the traumas and the structural constraints imposed upon their parents and grandparents. They are free to selectively remember only the good things about the cultural differences they experienced. Often they now live in the suburbs or have moved to areas where their primary social groups are not others of the same ancestry. Ethnic occupational specialization has largely disappeared and the third generation does not rely on its ethnic ties to get a good job or to find decent housing. They aren't courted by ethnic politicians for votes. They perhaps have married someone of a different ancestry, and perhaps because of marriage, they may also have drifted away from the dominant religion of the group. Their ethnicity is very watered-down and that of their children even more so. Children may have a hybrid ancestry due to the spouse being of a different ethnic group.

In brief, the idea of symbolic ethnicity means the third generation can like the "feeling" of being Portuguese (or Irish or Polish or Italian) and can have these feelings without social or economic costs. Symbolic ethnicity is basically a nostalgic allegiance to the culture and the old country of the immigrant generation, and a love for a tradition that can be admired without having to be incorporated into everyday behavior.[277] This revival of ethnicity can explain the apparent paradox associated with the renewed interest in ancestry from groups once considered to be fully assimilated such as the Swiss in New Glarus, Wisconsin or the Swedes in Cambridge, Minnesota.[278] The Cajuns in Louisiana revitalized interest in their ethnicity *after* it was discovered by tourists.[279] This perspective suggests that ethnicity can be a factor in people's lives if they want it to be and, indeed, many people have pursued such a connection.[280]

A historian who first seriously questioned the melting pot concept summarized these ideas by writing that ethnicity is fluid; it can wax and wane if the cultural, economic and political context encourages it. Ethnic revivals are to be expected. If one generation finds little use for its ethnic roots, that hardly means its interest in its ancestry is dead; rather the stage is set for the next generation to rediscover its roots.[281] These factors also remind us that the ancestry surveys are "pliable" to say the least with census-to-census variation based on people "rediscovering" their Portuguese heritage, their American Indian heritage or their Italian heritage or even deciding that they will list a heritage simply as "American."[282]

PORTUGUESE AMERICAN CULTURE IN THE CONTEXT OF ASSIMILATION

The concept of what it means to be Portuguese American is informed by many aspects of both modern American and modern Portuguese life. Religion, food, language, landscape, and cultural symbols are a few of the obvious major signs (signifiers) of Portuguese culture in terms of semiotics. There are many nuances in Portuguese American culture and this chapter touches on some of the major ones which include politics, patriarchy, and prejudice.

How does one preserve the culture and national identity amidst such rapid change in the cultural hearth and while one is a transplanted emigrant? While culture is complex and defies all simplistic generalizations, one summary is worth noting. Hans Leder's book is dated (it was written in 1968) and it concerns Portuguese Americans in California, but it is of interest in a variety of ways, particularly for what it tells us about Portuguese culture as it was transplanted to the United States.[283] This work focused on a community of Azorean Portuguese in the fictitious community of Bayside (which Pap identified as San Jose).[284]

Leder was writing his doctoral dissertation for an anthropology degree at Stanford University and apparently set out to examine the cultural distress produced by the emigration process within an immigrant group. What he found instead was a community of transplanted Portuguese who had adapted well to American culture, and in fact, had in some ways "out-Angloed" the Anglos (as he called the non-Portuguese Americans). The Portuguese American immigrant culture he describes tempts one to characterize the community, not only as not under duress but just short of idyllic: a poster child for the "American Dream." Rather than finding symptoms of societal distress, the typical academic expectation of response to emigration, the anthropologist found a community with few such symptoms; a well-adapted community almost totally lacking in indications of societal disorganization such as juvenile delinquency, dependence on welfare, unemployment, psychoses, alcoholism or school disciplinary problems.

Indeed, on all these measures of societal distress, the Portuguese Americans were in better shape than the Anglos, with the exception of the school dropout rate and the almost total lack of young Portuguese Americans going on to college.[285] Leder used the term "benign acculturation" to describe a situation that he felt described a transition in the new country that enabled *Portuguese* cultural ideals (not Anglo or American ideals) to be realized. For example, *independência* in the sense of land ownership and family economic management, could be achieved in the United States, as could the idea of having extended family members live nearby without living in the home, a situation almost impossible in the islands where the system of land tenure resulted in widely dispersed family-owned or family-worked parcels worked from a central residence.[286]

A similar situation was discovered by Gilbert in her 1989. Once again, that study began as an effort to identify problems with the Portuguese Americans and their negotiation of the American system of health care. Like Leder, she had expected to find that the immigration experience was likely to be disintegrative and generally negative.[287] After some initial investigation, Gilbert instead changed her focus to look at how poor agrarian immigrants to an American industrial city should become relatively economically successful in a relatively short period of time. She measured economic success as meaning the immigrants achieved approximately the same median household income as other inhabitants of Fall River.[288] Gilbert ended up finding that the Fall River immigrants contradicted the expectations other scholars who wrote of anomie and social disorganization such as drunkenness, crime, insanity, prostitution, and abandonment of wives and children found in some immigrant groups in Boston.[289] Instead the Portuguese adapted well to the societal stresses listed by Pap including individualism, the democratization of the family, freer choice of marriage partners, separation of workplace and home, increasing job opportunities for women, and compulsory schooling for the young. On the other hand, Pap was concerned about the increase in divorce, which, while legal in Portugal since the 1910 revolution, was very much discouraged by the still-dominant Catholic influence. His opinion as he wrote in 1981 was that divorce had become "an epidemic" among Portuguese Americans in the United States.[290]

And yet there is a social environment in the East Coast cities in which the Portuguese settled that can foster "downward assimilation." While crime, drug use and gang membership data specific to Portuguese Americans are not available, the area has a high rate of births to children and to unwed mothers compared to the Massachusetts average which was, fortunately, relatively low among the fifty states.[291] Hard drug use is prevalent, fueled in part by ties between the fishing industry and illegal drug smuggling and the use of heroin on fishing voyages. A tradition of sharing needles on fishing boats contributes to high rates of HIV/AIDS[292] exacerbated by an urban environment in which sex workers openly ply their trade. About a dozen gangs are prevalent in both cities, half of which are affiliated with major national groups such as the Latin Kings and Folk Nation, so much so, that both New Bedford and Fall River received special state funding, as recently as 2015, to help combat gangs.[293] Nationally affiliated gangs in the area tend to be comprised of Asians, African Americans or Hispanics whereas Portuguese youths may belong to unaffiliated neighborhood gangs. In 2014 New Bedford had the highest rate of violent crime of all Massachusetts cities and Fall River was second. New Bedford's rate was about three times that of the national and Massachusetts rates. New Bedford also had the highest rate of property crime, about double that of the national rate, but Fall River's rate was much lower.[294]

None of these measures of social dysfunction imply that the Portuguese Americans *per se* as individuals or as a group are more prone to these types of behaviors. Indeed, what evidence there is specifically related to the Portuguese, such as Leder's 1980 study of Portuguese Americans in the San Jose area of California in the 1960s, which was noted earlier, showed them to be assimilating into an almost idyllic or model citizen role with extremely low rates on almost any measure of social dysfunction. Still, Portuguese Americans are not immune to these aberrant paths. Police departments do not collect arrest records by ancestry but one measure shows that more than a thousand Portuguese citizens have been deported from the United States since 1996 for offenses such as drug use and related larcenies, drug-dealing and prostitution. There were 151 deportations of Portuguese citizens in 2012 and 91 in 2013.[295]

One issue the Portuguese Americans do face in adapting to and assimilating into American culture relates to their cultural attitudes toward health care. Traditional folkways, what some might call superstition, as discussed by Taft and others, continue to impact Portuguese Americans. Superstitions are common among the Islanders and those from rural areas and small towns of Continental Portugal. These folk traditions include things such as a belief in the evil eye, evil air (vapors that cause sickness), the *figa*, and attribution of illness to the devil (*diabo*). There is also a belief that people (mainly women), who are old and unattractive, or young and exceptionally beautiful, have supernatural powers that can be used for either good or evil and for healing.[296]

As recently as 2005 a study found that among Azorean immigrants as many as 58% used some type of traditional healing system (religion or some combination of herbalist medium or healer), either solely, or in combination with the medical system, to help with their medical problems. Some illnesses appear to American eyes as psychosomatic, such as the *agonias* experienced by about two-thirds of Azorean women. These "agonies" are a combination of physical and mental ailments experienced during times of great stress whose symptoms range from shortness of breath and heart palpitations to premonitions of death.[297]

Of course acquiring the American dream did not always occur under the idyllic scenario presented by some researchers. The Portuguese struggled to accept and to be accepted into American culture. Charles Reis Felix, a Portuguese American author, exemplifies this struggle in his semi-autobiographical works, especially in *Through a Portagee Gate*.[298] The son of a cobbler from the Azores, Felix grew up in New Bedford's North End in the era just before World War II. He eloquently describes his feelings of exclusion from American culture, even as a second-generation Portuguese American. In his work he describes how he later moved to California as a teacher and led people to believe he was of French ethnicity. Felix relates how uncomfortable he was with the school's Portuguese janitor who, knowing the teacher was Portuguese, always ascribed stinginess to Felix's motives. As a youth, Felix grew up in poverty eating kale soup every single day and never had a nickel to buy a Coca-Cola. Felix writes that he knew that even if he had a Coca-Cola someday, it would not taste as good to him as it did to Americans (again, Felix was second generation) because he was "not supposed to drink it."[299]

POLITICS AND CITIZENSHIP

In the Portuguese community of southeastern New England, there have been many studies and much discussion about obtaining citizenship and participating in politics. Nationally, in 2013, according to the ACS 2011-2013 3-year survey, about 30% of the American population reporting Portuguese ancestry does not hold American citizenship. But that is a figure in constant decline as the population ages and fewer new immigrants arrive. Many

Portuguese do not vote or otherwise engage in American politics not only because of their lack of American citizenship but also because of their educational levels, given the well-documented interconnections among political participation, income, education, and literacy. Studies have shown that the Portuguese are much less likely than other European ethnic groups in the region to learn English and to obtain American citizenship. It also appears that among the New England Portuguese, even those who become citizens are less likely to vote, and are, in general, less likely to be politically and civically active.[300]

The Portuguese Americans in southeastern New England tend to be "blue collar" or "lunch bucket" Democrats. Surveys showed that of those who voted, more than 90% voted for Clinton as opposed to Bush in the 1992 election. Attitudes of Portuguese Americans on various issues tend to be similar to those of the average American but a bit more liberal in support for gay rights and less support for the death penalty, and yet a slightly more conservative view of women's traditional roles in the home.[301]

Hard data on whether or not Portuguese Americans who hold citizenship actually vote are seldom collected but there certainly are impressionistic data suggesting that they are less likely to participate in politics which would again confirm the well-known associations among lower levels of education, lower levels of income and lower levels of participation in political activity. The Luso-American Foundation's "Portuguese American Citizenship Project"[302] begins with the assumption that Portuguese Americans are less likely to become citizens and even when they hold citizenship, less likely to register to vote, and in general, are reluctant to become involved in civic affairs. Perhaps some of this is related to the findings of one study that feelings of powerlessness among Portuguese American women remain high even after a considerable time living in the United States.[303]

A study from the Center for Policy Analysis at the University of Massachusetts Dartmouth examined ethnic stereotypes about Portuguese Americans and politics. These stereotypes include that they are less politically active than other ethnic groups; that they have low levels of political knowledge; that they have a high level of distrust of government; that they do not have a distinct political identity compared to other groups, and that part of this lack of political activity stems from their experiences under the long-lived Portuguese dictatorship. Generally, the study found that the majority of these stereotypes are indeed just that, and when Portuguese become citizens, they are generally as active and as knowledgeable as other ethnic groups. However, they still suffer the disadvantages of lesser levels of income and educational attainment that act as barriers to obtaining citizenship in the first place. The study also noted that the generally disadvantaged economic situation in the cities of southeastern Massachusetts tends to prevent all groups from "moving up" and therefore tends to keep the Portuguese in a disadvantaged political position.[304]

The process of obtaining American citizenship also appears more difficult when we compare the process with that of Portuguese obtaining citizenship in Canada. The largest concentration of Portuguese in Canada is in Toronto, Ontario. One Canadian sociologist characterized the difference between Portuguese in Ontario obtaining Canadian citizenship and Massachusetts Portuguese obtaining American citizenship as "enormous." Figures showed that 62% of Ontario Portuguese obtained Canadian citizenship within ten years compared to 17% of American Portuguese. Perhaps the largest difference between the two countries related to national and private group support to encourage the acquisition of citizenship by new immigrants.[305]

The persistence of usage of the Portuguese language and the strength and tenacity of Portuguese culture is a major factor in voting and politics. It is striking that according to 2014 ACS 1-year data, there are 681,000 United States residents who speak Portuguese at home, almost exactly half of all those who report any Portuguese ancestry. Undoubtedly that figure includes some Brazilians and Cape Verdeans who report their home language as Portuguese. In any case, of those who converse in Portuguese in the household, about two-thirds report that they speak English very well, and one-third report that they speak English less than very well. The one-third who speak Portuguese at home and who do not speak English very well is higher than the corresponding numbers for those who use other European languages including French, Italian, and Greek, all groups with around 20% to 25% speaking their language at home. But as time progresses and generations change, English language speaking ability improves. A study in 2005 noted that of Portuguese born in the United States only 5% did not speak English well, whether or not they spoke Portuguese in the household.[306]

Because Portuguese immigration has slowed almost to a stop and because many Portuguese immigrants mainly now arrive in areas other than the southeastern New England core, 86% of foreign-born Portuguese living in the Providence metro area immigrated prior to 1990 as did 75% of those in Massachusetts. Yet despite the longer length of their residence, Massachusetts and metropolitan Providence foreign-born Portuguese are still more likely to speak their native language at home (35% and 32%

respectively) than foreign-born Portuguese nationally (27%). Thus they are also more likely to report that they "speak English less than well" -- 17% in Massachusetts and 14% in Providence – compared to the national figure for foreign-born Portuguese, 10%.

The proportion of Portuguese who were born abroad is obviously a factor in the use of language and obtaining citizenship. Among Portuguese Americans, the percentage born abroad varies by state and metropolitan area reflecting how recently immigrants arrived. Returning to the standard definition used in this book (*any* Portuguese ancestry, not *primary* Portuguese ancestry) nationally, by 2007, 19% of those reporting any Portuguese ancestry had been foreign-born. Proportions of foreign-born Portuguese were higher than that national average in Massachusetts (24%) and in the Providence metro area (21%).

Nationally, foreign-born Portuguese had higher rates of citizenship (56%) compared to all foreign-born Americans (41%) although this largely reflects the fact that the Portuguese, while a more recent *European* group of immigrants, are an older immigrant group compared to *all* American immigrants. Nationally, 71% Portuguese foreign-born immigrated prior to 1990 whereas only 44% of all foreign-born Americans immigrated that long ago.

Comparing the Portuguese to five other major European ethnic groups in southeastern New England (French Canadians, Greeks, Irish, Italians, and Poles), the Portuguese are indeed less likely to obtain citizenship, although this characteristic may be lessening among more recent immigrants. For example, among Portuguese Americans who immigrated to Rhode Island prior to 1965, 76% have become American citizens compared to rates of 89% to 94% for the other five groups. Figures for Massachusetts are similar. For post-1965 immigrants, however, 34% of the Portuguese have become citizens and that is in the middle of the range among the six groups: greater than the French Canadians, Irish and Poles, but less than the numbers for Greeks and Italians.

As with other American immigrant groups, it has taken the Portuguese several generations to work their way up the socio-economic ladder and into "stepladder" public service positions such as teachers, police, and firefighters. But it has taken even longer for Portuguese Americans to enter the political process and to gain access to major political positions. Undoubtedly their delay in English language acquisition has been a handicap as well as lower levels of educational attainment. Only within the last 25 years has it not been unusual, although it is still not common, for either New Bedford or Fall River to have a mayor of Portuguese ancestry, despite the fact that half of each city is of Portuguese ancestry. And consider that perhaps another 25% of the population in each city is related to someone of Portuguese background by marriage and connections with in-laws. Yet the Portuguese are far from "dominating" local politics as their numbers might suggest should be the case.[307]

Ethnic traditions and stereotypes die hard. Old timers can be found in both cities who think along traditional ethnic lines. Some French Canadians, Irish or Poles, for example, will not vote for Portuguese candidates. The first Portuguese mayor of New Bedford in the 1960s was an individual with an anglicized name who would not speak Portuguese in public, even though his parents were immigrants and he could speak the language. The same name change issue cropped up again in the Fall River mayoral election as recently as 2009. The winning candidate had changed his name from Sylvia to Flanagan but kept the support of most Portuguese, according to one newspaper columnist, because his wife emigrated from Portugal and he promoted his Portuguese heritage.[308]

However, the days of the ethnic politician, running as an ethnic, as described by Felix in his book, *Da Gama, Carry Grant, and the Election of 1934*, are over.[309] Even so, the Portuguese Americans in southeastern New England never developed the ethnic voting base that allowed them to control city wards and patronage as did the Irish in Boston or the Italians in New York. Again, perhaps this was due to the low levels of English language literacy and the low rates of obtaining citizenship that characterized the group until the turn of the century. As noted by scholar Rita Duarte Marinho, otherwise New Bedford and Fall River would have Portuguese American mayors more frequently.[310] A study by the Center for Portuguese Studies and Culture found that only 17% of local decision-making positions were held by Portuguese, a "50% underrepresentation." Yet, the same study showed that two-thirds of Portuguese Americans felt they were well-represented politically and three-fourths disagreed that people were best represented by members of their own racial/ethnic background. (Although that means that one-third did feel the nationality of the candidate was important.) The study also found the community "deeply fractured" over whether Portuguese ethnicity is a political identity or a cultural one.[311]

But Portuguese Americans are savvy enough to realize that voting for a Portuguese person, *per se*, while symbolic, means little compared to voting for a person who will represent their perceived interests regardless of the nationality of the political candidate.[312] Portuguese Americans hold this noble sentiment more than other ethnic groups, a fact that contributes to their lack of representation. (On the other hand, in matters of personal interaction, one study found that Portuguese, at least in Canada, were more likely to use a Portuguese real estate agent than other ethnic groups.[313])

Further, the Portuguese community itself is still somewhat culturally and, in turn, politically factionalized. For example, it is not uncommon for someone from Madeira to say privately that he or she will not vote for a Portuguese candidate who is from the Azores (or vice-versa). Some Azorean residents protested the renaming of Diman Street in New Bedford to "Madeira Avenue." One researcher found that these patterns persisted among women in an electronics factory where women from rural and urban communities did not socialize with each other; nor did continentals and islanders, and even the islanders subdivided socially by the island of origin.[314] In the old days, these within-group rivalries could have serious repercussions. Pap claimed that the rivalry between Portuguese immigrants originating from two neighboring provinces in northern Portugal in Ludlow, Massachusetts was of such intensity that one group eventually migrated to Connecticut.[315]

Figure 45
The Ponta Delgada social club in New Bedford, for those from St. Michaels, sports the city's gates logo and the Portuguese and American flags.

Today, while these cultural distinctions are most often preserved in social clubs organized by geographic origin and by some churches focused on parishioners from a single island or region, all those of Portuguese origin regularly come together to celebrate their common Portuguese heritage at the major festivals, even those ostensibly focused on geographic origin. Today, all of the Portuguese groups attend and celebrate major community events such as the Feast of the Holy Ghost in Fall River, initiated by Azoreans, and the Feast of the Blessed Sacrament in New Bedford, initiated by Madeirans.

One form of American politics that the Portuguese appeared to have learned from their American neighbors is the willingness to demonstrate and protest. There certainly were few, if any, protests allowed in Portugal during Salazar's regime. The earliest Portuguese demonstrations in the United States were labor protests involving large numbers of Portuguese who worked in textiles or fish processing. There were massive textile strikes in 1904, 1922 and 1928. In 1924, six thousand Portuguese rallied in New Bedford against publication of the book *Two Portuguese Communities in New England*, by sociologist Donald Taft of Columbia University. According to scholar Cristiana Bastos, the crowd protested his racialist premises and conclusions regarding the non-whiteness of the Portuguese and what they saw as his eugenic premises.[316] Then, after the infamous "Big Dan's" pool table rape case, more than 10,000 Portuguese turned out in a misguided protest of the trial of the accused rapists in 1984, arguing that the media had targeted them for being Portuguese. (All of the assailants and the victim were of Portuguese ancestry.) Onésimo Almeida, a professor of Portuguese and Brazilian Studies at Brown University has analyzed the publicity surrounding the case that drew national attentional and was one of the first nationally-televised court trials with gavel-to-gavel coverage.[317]

Portuguese protesters again captured national headlines when thousands returned television cable boxes to protest additional charges aimed at Portuguese cable television subscribers. In this demonstration, more than 10,000 Portuguese protested in Taunton, Massachusetts, selected because it was central to Portuguese in Fall River, New Bedford and other cities in Bristol County. During the protest, the crowd played the song made famous as a symbol of Portugal's "Carnation Revolution" that overthrew the Portuguese dictatorship in 1974.[318] In 2000, more than 200 Portuguese women in New Bedford gathered to protest deportation laws.[319] In 2007, Portuguese rallied in several venues to protest the proposed closure of several local Portuguese consular offices by the Portuguese government. The protests garnered the support of then-Massachusetts Senator Ted Kennedy, Rhode Island Senator Jack Reed, Massachusetts Congressman Barney Frank, and many state legislators and mayors, and successfully prevented the consolidation from taking place. Smaller local protests have occurred such as when the Sacred Heart of Jesus church in Pawtucket ceased its weekly Portuguese language mass in 2006.

THE ROLE OF THE PORTUGUESE NATIONAL GOVERNMENT

An additional factor that impacts American political participation by Portuguese is the continued role of the Portuguese national government in the life of the immigrant. The Portuguese government promotes the involvement of American Portuguese in Portuguese national affairs because of the large proportion of its citizenry overseas. The importance of Portugal's overseas citizens in numerous countries to the national government is illustrated by the fact that the Secretary of State to the Portuguese Overseas Communities is a cabinet-level position. In fact, until two generations ago, many Portuguese in both Portugal and the United States regularly referred to the American Portuguese settlements as "colonies." The Portuguese government maintains an active interaction with its overseas citizens, frequently attempting to involve them in mainland Portugal's concerns or to involve them in political activities in the United States to assist Portugal. The Azorean Autonomous Regional Government is also active in a similar way. The relatively low percentage of Portuguese who become American citizens, is, in part, related these trans-Atlantic nationalistic ties which can be seen as both a cause and an effect of Portuguese citizens pulled back to the homeland culture.

Portuguese officials promoting their national culture are frequent visitors to the Portuguese American community in New England. In 2007 the President of Portugal, Anibal Cavaco Silva, visited New Bedford to speak of deepening the relationship between American emigrants and their mother country, to remind them of their role in the Portuguese nation, and yet to encourage them to simultaneously become more involved in American civic affairs to promote the good name of Portugal.[320] Cape Verdean nationals resident in southeastern New England represented the swing vote in the closely contested Cape Verdean national presidential election in 2001.

More recently the Portuguese national government has been promoting a single national Portugal Day (*Dia de Portugal*) as a "Day of Portuguese Communities" specifically to promote the ties of overseas Portuguese back to their homeland. After the Revolution of 1974, the government officially appended the phrase *de Camões e das Comunidades Portuguesas*. Camões is the author of the great Portuguese epic of exploration, the Lusiads, written in 1572. The last part of the phrase refers to the overseas Portuguese Communities. This action tries to officially recognize the overseas Portuguese and to encourage their involvement with the homeland. Simultaneously the phrasing is an attempt to redefine their history as emigrants and explorers rather than as colonizers.[321] So far the effort to promote a single day has not had much success because the Portuguese Americans understandably prefer to celebrate multiple times in neighboring communities. So in 2017, for example, New Bedford held its celebrations from June 9-11; Providence and East Providence on June 10-11; Fall River on June 15-18 and Provincetown on June 22-25.

There is some support for a more focused and secular "national day" as a celebration of arts and "high culture" by some of the more educated Portuguese American elite who worry about the broader community's perception of their culture engendered by this more-or-less continuous public exhibition of what some have called "peasant pageantry."[322] It remains to be seen to what extent this national endorsement and promotion of the celebration and its officially expanded context will supplement rather than replace these island-focused events. But it is likely that the on-going decline in immigration and the concern that the community is diminishing will continue to bring the subgroups within the Portuguese community closer together.[323]

The Portuguese government financially supports classes in the Portuguese language and in Portuguese culture at area universities, such as at the University of Massachusetts at Dartmouth, and activities such as student exchanges, athletic competitions, and cultural displays. The Portuguese national government and the Azoreans Autonomous government are frequent contributors to monument and museum construction. As noted earlier, two large ship models donated by the Portuguese government dominate the interior of the Dighton Rock Museum. The Portuguese government, the Azorean Autonomous Regional government and the City of Ponta Delgada are major contributors to monument construction including Fall River's recreation of Ponta Delgada's Gates. The Portuguese government provided $500,000 toward construction of the Azorean exhibit at the New Bedford Whaling Museum[324] and the Azorean government contributed substantially to the publication of the book, *Community, Culture and the Makings of Identity: Portuguese Americans Along the Eastern Seaboard* by the Center for Portuguese Studies at the University of Massachusetts Dartmouth in 2009.[325]

While official Portuguese government promotion of continued involvement by immigrants in Portuguese national politics and support for cultural activities certainly helps preserve Portuguese national culture, it is uncertain if these actions further delay immigrant assimilation into

American life. Traditional assimilation theory recognizes that the creation of ethnic communities provides a safe haven for immigrants which, in the long run, facilitates their assimilation into American culture. It is interesting to speculate on the extent to which strong ethnic communities promote or retard assimilation into American society. One could argue that retaining your own culture leads to the security to absorb the new ways of the society around you (as bilingualists argue) or that it slows assimilation into American culture. This has been called the ethnic paradox.[326] Whether or not a strong community and a strong heritage lead to delays in the assumption of traditional stepladder occupations, or to delays in the assumption of political and economic power by the Portuguese in this country, is another question that deserves further study.

PATRIARCHY

Patriarchy, a societal condition where fathers, or males in general, are dominant is an important aspect of Portuguese culture. Patriarchy implies restrictions upon women and limits on opportunities for them. Aspects of patriarchy are, of course, found worldwide and in all Southern European cultures but the situation is of greater concern in Portuguese culture because there is a long history of institutionalized prejudice against women under Portuguese law. Until the new Portuguese Constitution of 1976 was adopted women were legally on a par with children. They could not travel abroad without permission of their husbands nor could they legally practice a profession, contract debts, sell property, or hold major political office. Island customs, often transplanted to the United States, expected women to stay home and live with parents until they were married. If for some reason they traveled away from home, arrangements had to be made for them to stay with relatives or in a convent. There was no such thing as single women living alone or even together in an apartment setting.

Education for women suffered. Until the 1950s girls in Portugal were not legally required to attend school at all. Public school on the Azorean island of Sao Jorge, for example, only went to 4th grade because that was all that was offered. Better-off families might send girls for additional education to Catholic school.[327] A Portuguese American woman relates that in 1956 she had to join a convent to get an education. She left the convent in 1968 and then emigrated to the United States.[328]

While patriarchal influence and "double standards" are also common in the United States, they appear stronger in Portuguese culture. Leder reports that a Portuguese American woman who managed to become a lawyer found Portuguese male clients did not respect her. Her father was disappointed that she was a lawyer rather than in a "feminine occupation" as he felt it meant she could never marry or stay home with children. Young women are often overly protected. One Portuguese woman tells a story of finally getting permission to go to a high school dance and finds her mother there before her; the only parent who attended the event in the whole school. Even in the United States, a woman might be allowed out with a man only if a sibling accompanies her.[329] Another woman tells of not being allowed to speak English at home because her father only allowed Portuguese to be spoken in the home. Nor was her mother allowed to teach her daughter English even though her mother knew English. She dropped out of school in 8th grade because her parents needed her to work at home.

Yet Portuguese women have found strength despite cultural obstacles imported to the new world from Portuguese ways back in the old country. Sue Fagalde Lick interviewed a number of older California Portuguese American women in her book *Stories Grandma Never Told* and relates many stories of the way patriarchy limited opportunities for females but also how Portuguese females developed numerous strengths.[330] Lick quotes Estellie Smith in her work *The Portuguese Female Immigrant: The Marginal Man* that the women were often the ones to spur the move to America; in 85% of migrations to the United States they either spurred the move or gave it strong support. In only 15 % of households did migration occur with the opposition of the female. Women did most of the planning and arranging to make the move.[331] Women go to church more frequently than men and thus shape the religious outlook of the family. One father would walk the family to the church door but not go in.[332]

Women were also sometimes discouraged by men from working outside the home because in the islands it was a sign of a man's success that his wife could stay at home; a sign of his failure if she had to work. However, that outlook often changed with the family's arrival in the United States.[333] Even when men were the ostensible head of the family, many Portuguese admit that the woman runs the household --decorating, choosing foods, directing the children's education and conducting the family's social life. If the mother is Portuguese and the father is not, more of the Portuguese cultural traditions are carried forward than if the father is Portuguese and the woman is not. Leder even describes some characteristics of Island Portuguese culture that are more matriarchal and where the position of women is equal to or even economically superior to that of men.[334] Perhaps the strength of Portuguese women from the Atlantic Islands and from coastal cultures in Portugal derives in part from the tradition of wives whose husbands spent long periods at sea while they fended for themselves and their children.[335] Among the earliest immigrants to New England, this tradition of women fending for themselves certainly continued among whaling families as whaling voyages usually lasted at least two years and sometimes even three years.

Despite the cultural influence of patriarchy, in general, parents of both sexes are respected. Leder noted that in the Portuguese American culture he studied, parents were always consulted in major decisions, whether or not their opinions were actually followed, and even parental siblings were treated deferentially and with great respect.[336] The godparent relationship (*padrinho* and *madrinha*) is close and extends to the parents to whom the godparents are *compadre* and *comadre*, (literally, co-father and co-mother). Unlike in Spain and Latin America, the *compadre* relationship is not as layered with the advantage of economic protection. Asking one's boss to be a godparent, for example, is common in Latin America, but in Portuguese culture, the prospective godparents often offer to serve in that role rather than being asked by the family of the godchild. Once their relationship is established, the *compadre* will serve to assist the godchild economically and with advice and influence.[337]

Patriarchy, like other aspects of culture, is reflected in the landscape. Geographers refer to these male-female differences in the landscape as gendered geographies. Social clubs are an example. During weekdays, only men, usually those from a certain island or even a certain island neighborhood, frequent the bar. The men will drink, shoot pool, watch televised Portuguese soccer games, and play cards and dominos. The club probably also supports a soccer team, or perhaps two teams: one for men and one for youths. As in Hispanic American immigrant culture, as discussed by Price and Whitworth, soccer players are usually exclusively men. Men drink and therefore some women don't like the soccer games. Women and children participate only as fans and vendors, although an exception is soccer games for youths. Games on Sunday are a break from the routine of work and a chance to socialize, including socialization with people coming and going back to the islands.[338]

Social clubs and soccer games are a regular form of social exchange about jobs, housing, ridesharing, and used cars. Since these interactions link people with similar levels of social status and information, they help people survive but these interactions may not help them improve their social status. For many men, a soccer league or social club may be the only immigrant organization to which they belong. Team names and uniforms are often those of the home communities or that of the national team. The club may also sponsor activities for youths besides soccer such as a drum and bugle corps. On the weekend, women and children may attend events such as a wedding reception held in the club hall. Women are usually responsible for the organization and the cooking and cleaning at such events.

In traditional Portuguese American culture, there are still male-only places such as bars that women are not expected to frequent. These issues received national publicity through the infamous "pool table" rape case that took place in New Bedford in 1983. Even Portuguese grave markers reflect the patriarchal structure of Portuguese culture. Many stones are labeled with the man's name and "his wife;" none that the author has encountered are labeled with the woman's name and "her husband." Among the fifty *festeiros* who direct the Madeira feast in New Bedford, only male descendants of the original founders have formal input. The annual *Romeiros* religious procession in Fall River was initially established as an all-male event, but now includes women.

Earlier in this book, the construction of monuments was discussed. Patriarchy plays a role in the on-going movement to construct monuments, often monuments to great men, although that may be changing. One scholar notes that among European immigrant groups in the United States, as was the case in Europe, national commemorations were largely the preserve of elite males. These males were traditionally seen by their societies, and they saw themselves, as the appointed carriers of progress. But due to ongoing changes in gender roles, they feel the past slipping away from them much faster than women.[339] Societal changes strengthening the roles

Figure 46
The installation "They Also Faced the Sea" in Provincetown by artists Ewa Nogiec and Norma Holt honors five Portuguese American women: Eva Silva, Almeda Segura, Mary Jason, Bea Cabral and Frances Raymond. (Mrs. Segura's picture has been destroyed by weather.)

of women and in effect, weakening the patriarchal structure, gives men a profound sense of losing touch with the past resulting in an insistence that it be restored and preserved. Do Portuguese men ban together to form committees to construct these monuments because they see both the historic past and the traditional male roles eroding? Until very recently they were also the only ones commemorated. Perhaps the five larger-than-life black and white photos of Portuguese women on MacMillan Wharf in Provincetown is the start of a new trend.

PREJUDICE

Another factor in the Portuguese American community and the concept of being Portuguese American is prejudice. There is prejudice against the community and within the community. The Portuguese of mainland Portugal, like all the European peoples, were a great mix of races and tribes reflecting many waves of population mixing over generations. Like other southern European peoples, the Portuguese had some ancient African ancestry. Then in the Eighth century, Portugal experienced even more population mixing from the Moorish invasion from northern Africa. This was particularly true in the southern half of Portugal. In addition, as the Portuguese were instrumental in beginning the system of using Africans as slaves on Atlantic island plantations, and in its colonies around the world, very early even Lisbon had large numbers of Africans who eventually merged into the general population especially after slaves were freed in 1775. (Note that Portugal ended slavery almost a century before the United States.) The greater population mixture of southern Portugal was important because it was primarily people from southern Portugal who colonized the Atlantic Islands and Brazil in greatest numbers.[340]

While the Continental Portuguese have diverse backgrounds, each Atlantic Island is even more diverse and each Portuguese Atlantic island has a unique population and settlement history. St. Michael's, where many of the Fall River Portuguese originated, was initially settled mainly from Extremadura and Algarve provinces in southern Portugal and had more slaves than European population in the 1530s. In the case of the Cape Verde Islands, the African population eventually predominated and that population is considered "African" by modern American standards. There were other racial influences on the islands as well, as when 1500 Flemish settlers from what is now Belgium arrived on Terceira in the fifteenth century. They too eventually merged into the general population.

One outcome of this mixing was that the Portuguese were noted for their racial tolerance and willingness to intermarry with Africans and Amerindians more so than any other European colonizers, including the Spanish. Taft cited a study that showed the Portuguese were the most likely of 55 ethnic groups in New York City to marry outside their group. As noted earlier, a relatively large number of Portuguese men married Irish women in New Bedford as early as the 1840s. In theory, these attitudes toward racial and ethnic mixing partly explain why Brazil has become known as such a racially mixed society, although this is not to say that there is a lack of racial prejudice in Brazil or that Cape Verdeans have not suffered racial prejudice at the hands of their own linguistic compatriots.

Like southern Italians, the Portuguese were considered non-white or "lesser whites" by many Americans especially during the main period of early mass immigration from the 1880s to the early 1920s.[341] Racist attitudes against southern Europeans predominated to the extent that immigration quotas were imposed to stem the influx of people from places other than northern Europe. Miguel Moniz, an anthropologist at the University of Lisbon has compiled numerous references to the Portuguese as non-white in literature through the mid-twentieth century including references from Jack London and many other popular authors.[342] In the 1920 novel *The Portygee* by Joseph Lincoln, that term was a general derogatory label used for all dark-skinned foreigners. Carolyn Karcher has analyzed Herman Melville's short story "The 'Gees'" (short for Portugees) as an example of such racism.[343] Reinaldo Francisco Silva analyzed Mark Twain's *The Innocents Abroad* as a slight against Azoreans.[344] A 1937 short story by Benedict Thielen in *Harper's Monthly*, "This is My Own, My Native Land," is a story of Yankee prejudice against the Portuguese in Provincetown.[345]

Taft's work, whose statistical findings are cited several times in this book, is indeed an example of prejudice written in the language and with the pejorative attitudes of its time (1923).[346] He writes or cites earlier works referring to traces of African ancestry in many Portuguese not in a scientific sense, but in a pejorative way. He writes of the "so-called white Portuguese" and quotes an unidentified Fall River "prominent businessman" as saying the Portuguese are "half-negroes anyhow." Portuguese from Madeira and from St. Michaels receive the most criticism. He writes of their "good-natured ugly faces," their "shambling gait" and their "ill-knit frames." Their intelligence is not of a "high order" Women on the islands are "half-clad," "idle" and "inane," with a look of "despair." Naked babies crawl across floors and "brutal and savage children" beg visitors for money. Homes of the islanders are variously described as "miserable," "squalid" and "hovels." He quotes a writer who says they do not seek religious freedom, political liberty or educational opportunity. Mothers are indifferent to their children and they have low-grade intelligence and too-frequent pregnancies. A visitor to a Portuguese home will be impressed with the intellectual bareness of their lives and (in regard to infant mortality) "It is not surprising that people so ignorant are unable to keep their babies alive." We can clearly see why the Portuguese demonstrated against Taft's book.

Needless to say, the Portuguese as a group experienced prejudice in their new homeland. In an environment of discrimination and in ignorance of American laws and customs, immigrants are subject to misinformation and exploitation. The immigrant or the second-generation Portuguese American who speaks with an accent or who "dresses," "looks," or "acts" Portuguese, quickly learns terms such as "Portugee," "Port," "Geese," "Greenhorn" or "Greenie." A famous basketball star of the 1950s, Florindo "Porky" Vieira was given his nickname as a derivative of "Portagee." [347] A collection of squatter and fishing shacks near the New Bedford docks until the 1950s was derisively called the "Portugee Navy Yard" – a double

Figure 47
As late as World War II some Portuguese fishermen and dockworkers lived in a shanty settlement along the New Bedford waterfront. The area was derisively referred to by some as the "Portugee navy yard." Photo "Fisherman's shacks" by Jack Delano, 1941, from the collection U.S. Farm Security Administration/Office of War Information at the Library of Congress.

slur on the ethnic name and the quality of the settlement. The Gloucester Portuguese community was known as "Portagee Hill." [348] Portuguese American teacher and New Bedford community leader, Laurinda Andrade, writes in her autobiography of bias she personally experienced and she wrote of "English" prejudice against Portuguese factory workers, particularly Portuguese women.[349] Joseph's Conforti's memoir of growing up as the son of immigrants (Italian father and Portuguese mother) in Fall River in the 1950s and 1960s is replete with stories of prejudice against Portuguese. He commonly heard the term "Black Portagee" and essentially grew up thinking of himself as a "Portagee-Wop." [350] One scholar noted not just the frequency, but the vehemence with which the term "Greenhorn" was used.[351] Another scholar wrote of the bias against Portuguese students she found in a survey and interviews with local teachers and guidance counselors around 1990.[352] A 1999 survey of 400 Portuguese Americans found that about one-third responded that they had experienced prejudice at some point because of their ethnicity.[353]

In his quasi-autobiographical writings, Felix tells how his father reminisced about how before World War II he was told that there was "no room in the public high school for Portuguese" so he legally changed his surname so his son could attend. During the massive textile strike of 1928, the Portuguese, along with other recently-arrived ethnic groups such as the Polish and the French Canadians, affiliated with the newly-formed Textile Mill Committee, a branch of the Communist Party, largely because the traditional union, primarily made up of English and Irish members, would not allow Portuguese to participate.[354]

With increased Brazilian and Cape Verdean immigration, racial distinctiveness is added to the differentiating factors that contribute variety to the Portuguese community. Although skin color of both Cape Verdean and Brazilian immigrants ranges from white to black, in the context of American culture the majority of Cape Verdeans would be characterized as African Portuguese Americans (or Portuguese African Americans) and many Brazilians might be considered black by white Americans. As such, members of both groups are on occasion subject to discrimination within the broader American society as well as within the Portuguese community. Within the ethnic community are also found both black and white Portuguese from other former Portuguese colonies such as Angola and Mozambique, although in New England these groups are relatively small in number compared to the numbers that have immigrated to the Newark, New Jersey Portuguese community.[355]

The Portuguese women in the true-life stories of Lick's book experienced prejudice and fought it or adapted to it in a variety of ways. Some related hiding their heritage, as the young girl who tells her relatives not to speak so loudly in public so people would not know they are Portuguese. Another young Portuguese woman tells people she is Filipino. Some young people disassociate themselves from the ethnic festivals so they cannot be identified as Portuguese. Some refer to "passing for white" and being "just like white people." Some take pains to dissociate themselves from Cape Verdeans who were considered non-white.[356]

Although Hawaii is outside the scope of this book, the assimilation experience of the Portuguese in Hawaii is instructive in the context of the discussion of prejudice against the Portuguese. In the years 1878-1887, 12,000 Portuguese were contracted to come to Hawaii, mostly from Madeira but also from the Azores. An additional 13,000 arrived between 1906 and 1913. The Portuguese came as sugar cane cutters, the same occupation many practiced back on their islands. The recruiting corporations paid for entire families to migrate because the plantation owners had learned that single male workers without local family left the hard, low-paid farm labor as soon as they could to make more money elsewhere. As studied by sociologists, the Portuguese did well as cane cutters and lower level plantation supervisors, but they never assimilated into the middle class. Despite their Caucasian appearance, due to their class of labor (almost *caste* of labor), the Portuguese came to be thought of as "locals" by those in power, along with native Hawaiians, Samoans, and Filipinos. They were not considered Haoles, non-native Hawaiians, who were mainly non-Catholic Europeans, Chinese and Japanese. The Portuguese sent their children to public school with the locals; the Haoles sent their children to private schools.[357]

Unlike their East Coast urban cousins, the Hawaiian Portuguese were primarily a rural people. As mechanization increased and the need for plantation labor decreased, the Portuguese were unprepared for the new economy. They were more rural than other European groups, with much less formal education and lower incomes. While some took up other agricultural pursuits such as coffee-growing and contract sugarcane production, and some step-migrated to California, most moved to urban areas in Hawaii where many quickly lost their Portuguese culture and where their lesser economic status persists today.[358] (Census Bureau figures for 2010 show that Hawaiians reporting Portuguese ancestry have per capita incomes about 11% less than the average for all state residents.) Williams attributes this swift loss of Portuguese identity among Hawaiians to the outright discrimination that rural Hawaiian Portuguese experienced, although he saw signs of a revival of ethnicity among the Portuguese in the 1980s.³⁵⁹ It remains to be seen to what extent the Hawaiian Portuguese have experienced "de-ethnicization" as Pap states,³⁶⁰ or are experiencing an ethnic revival as Williams states, or if they are simply engaged in enjoying symbolic ethnicity.

Another recent example of prejudice was evidenced in Newport, Rhode Island, where a large sprawling monument, a tribute to Portuguese navigators and explorers, was constructed in a park along the waterfront. However, once the monument was completed, local non-Portuguese citizens waged a concerted effort including a petition to have it removed because it was unsightly and took up too much of the waterfront; the sculptures looked like "phallic symbols" and that it had been "snuck in behind Newport's back." ³⁶¹ Many Portuguese considered the failed attempt to remove the monument a sign of anti-Portuguese sentiment. Brazilians in Framingham have been "stalked" by an anti-immigrant group making videotapes of them.³⁶²

Not all prejudice is external to the ethnic group. Like other ethnic groups, such as the Mexicans Americans as documented by Vila,³⁶³ the Portuguese include some among their group who are not immune to anti-Portuguese sentiment themselves. Some abandoned or attempted to hide their Portuguese heritage,³⁶⁴ anglicizing their names, or "put-down" first-generation immigrants as "greenhorns." Some individuals of Portuguese American ancestry transfer the general societal prejudice against Portuguese towards "continentals" or "Islanders" or even toward members of their own subgroup. In an author interview, Gaspar noted that the Lisbons vs. Islanders factionalism in Provincetown was aggravated by class. The latecomers in Provincetown's case, "the Lisbons," more recent immigrants from Continental Portugal, looked down upon the earlier arrivals from the Islands because they were fisherman and dockworkers of lower socio-economic status and lesser education.³⁶⁵ Pap states that, in turn, the Azoreans in Provincetown called the newer, olive-skinned arrivals from the southern province of Algarve, "Guineas" in reference to the black inhabitants of Portugal's African colonies. Gilbert mentions the within-group prejudice of the older Portuguese immigrants toward the newer arrivals who "have it easy" and "don't even have to learn English" and have never had to "stand with their hat in hand."³⁶⁶

Another example of within-group prejudice was illustrated by The Portuguese Continental Union, the largest fraternal organization among East Coast Portuguese. That society excluded Azoreans and Madeirans until 1931 and Cape Verdeans until 1959. Those from the Azorean island of Fayal thought the "Migueis" (Islanders from St. Michael) were "coarse" and that they used "improper" Portuguese. The longer settled Hawaiian

Portuguese called the new wave of Madeiran cane-cutters Kanakas, likening them to Hawaii's indigenous dark-skinned people. Some Cape Verdeans referred to the Azoreans as "nhambobo" (yam-growers) and occasionally darker skinned Cape Verdeans referred to their lighter-skinned cousins as "batateiros," potato-growers. In turn, some African Americans in the San Francisco Bay area called Cape Verdeans who tried to socialize with them "whites."[367]

But Portuguese Americans now actively challenge these slurs and blatant prejudice using techniques of public outcry that they have learned in their new land. The protest of Taft's book cited earlier is an early example. To cite a more recent example, in 1998 a sports reporter for a Fall River newspaper used the term "greenhorns" to refer to new players on a high school hockey team, many of whom were Portuguese. The newspaper was flooded with indignant calls, emails, and letters. The consensus was that while the writer may have intended to use the term in the traditional sports jargon sense of "unseasoned players" he should not have been, and could not have been, ignorant of its broader pejorative context in the Portuguese community.[368] The reinvigorated battle against prejudice is assisted by two groups of actors, the social elite of the Portuguese American community, and officials of the Portuguese national government. And surely the fight against prejudice and the desire for respect from the larger community is in part responsible for the renaissance in the promotion of Portuguese heritage.

A LARGE COMMUNITY WITH A LOW PROFILE

Despite the increasing promotion of the community, the Portuguese community in southeastern New England still maintains a relatively low profile. Because large numbers of Portuguese arrived more recently than other European groups, the national numbers of Americans with Portuguese ancestry are smaller than for many other groups. But that is not the case with the number of foreign-born, as shown in Table 7. How many Americans would realize that among European groups, only the Germans, Poles, Italians and English outnumber the Portuguese foreign-born in the United States? Few realize that there are more foreign-born Portuguese living in the United States than any of the following European groups: French, Greeks, Irish, Spanish, Dutch, Hungarians, Scots and all the Scandinavian countries combined.[369] The "Second Wave" of immigration from 1958 through 1990 made the Portuguese one of the most populous modern European immigrant groups.

Despite these numbers, several scholars have referred to the Portuguese as an "invisible minority" that is relatively unknown to the general public and even to other scholars.[370] As early as 1917 one researcher wrote that the Portuguese seemed to have almost entirely escaped the notice of the public.[371] Hans Leder's book about Portuguese in California written in 1968 described them as a virtually unstudied group,[372] while as recently as 2005, a study stated that Portuguese immigrants remain virtually ignored.[373] Repeatedly, modern scholars characterize the Portuguese and the Cape Verdean communities, (and Portuguese-speaking Brazilians) separately and collectively with terms such as "invisible minorities" despite their greater numbers of recent immigrants than many other European groups.[374] Undoubtedly, the geographic concentration of the group, or, expressed differently -- their lack of dispersal, discussed above -- contributes to the relative lack of awareness of the group to Americans outside of southern New England.

	Birth Country	Number		Birth Country	Number
1	Germany	595,502	16	Bulgaria	65,766
2	Poland	445,821	17	Scotland	64,367
3	Italy	360,042	18	Belarus	54,056
4	England	338,237	19	Sweden	46,878
5	**PORTUGAL***	**183,485**	20	Austria	46,868
6	France	163,260	21	Croatia	42,800
7	Romania	159,028	22	Switzerland	39,717
8	Greece	135,269	23	Moldova	37,241
9	Ireland	128,301	24	Lithuania	36,164
10	Bosnia and Herzegov.	118,090	25	Serbia	33,073
11	Spain	94,949	26	Belgium	32,506
12	Netherland	83,318	27	Denmark	28,990
13	Albania	80,695	28	Norway	26,148
14	Hungary	72,903	29	Macedonia	24,825
15	(Ck. Rep. and Slovakia)	69,083	30	**AZORES ISLANDS***	**23,229**
			31	Latvia	23,087

Source: US Bureau of Census, Place of Birth for the Foreign-Born Population in the US; 2010-2014 American Community Survey 5-Year Estimates

*Total for Portugal and the Azores is 206,714. Many more Portuguese than listed were born in the Azores because in earlier years Azoreans were listed as born in Portugal.

Table 7. Number of Foreign-Born US Residents from European Countries

Perhaps "low profile" is a more accurate phrase than invisibility. The Portuguese are industrious with low crime statistics and a record of the limited use of social services, so they do not attract much media attention. Their concentration in a few states and in a few cities within those states contributes to this low profile. Often Americans get to know ethnic groups by their cuisine; but compared to Italian, Mexican, Chinese and Greek restaurants, how many Portuguese restaurants can be found in American cities outside of the Portuguese core areas?

8

THE ECONOMIC GEOGRAPHY OF THE PORTUGUESE AMERICAN COMMUNITY

Given the tendency of the Portuguese Americans to stay in place and not migrate out of the area, compared to other American ethnic groups, "geography has been destiny" for the Portuguese Americans of New England.

In this chapter, we will examine the many economic geographical forces including some socio-economic factors that help shape the experience of the Portuguese American community and their landscape in southern New England. Specifically, we will look at the historical conditions of income, and to some extent, poverty, facing the Portuguese in the region; the connections between educational attainment, income and poverty, and the economic geography of the region including some peculiarities of the local economy. Given the tendency of the Portuguese Americans to stay in place and not migrate out of the area, to an extent, geography has been destiny for the Portuguese Americans of New England.

HISTORICAL CONDITIONS OF THE ECONOMY IN THE NEW ENGLAND COMMUNITY

The conditions under which the Portuguese immigrants lived in the early 1900s, especially those from the Atlantic Islands, were documented by Taft who wrote about the "notoriously excessive mortality" and "shockingly high" rate of infant mortality among Portuguese Americans in 1920.[375]

Some of his findings, particularly those about infant mortality, were so startling that many Portuguese considered his work a racist and eugenic attack on their culture. As noted earlier, 6,000 Portuguese protested his book in a street demonstration in New Bedford in 1924. Taft's reporting echoed the racialist attitudes of the time but there is no evidence that his data were inaccurately reported. While not all of his explanations of conditions and behaviors of the immigrants would be accepted today as contributing factors to that exceptionally high mortality rate (for example, pregnant women working outside the home) it is worth reviewing his explanations, written in 1923, for what they tell us about living conditions and customs at the time.

In Fall River and New Bedford, the earliest immigrants lived in apartments and three-decker tenements of extreme density. This experience of density was common to most American urban immigrants at the time, but conditions for the Portuguese may have been even worse than those for other immigrant groups. The infant mortality rate among the Portuguese in New Bedford was twice that of any other American immigrant group. As might be expected, infant mortality was higher for immigrants than for native-born Portuguese. For infants born to mothers of Portuguese and Azorean descent, 30% died before the age of one year, a figure equivalent to the approximately one-third infant mortality that had afflicted the densest Italian immigrant slums of Mulberry Street in New York City thirty years earlier.[376] To give an idea of the magnitude of this mortality rate compared to current world conditions, the very highest national infant mortality rate is 12% in Afghanistan (2014), about one-third the rate suffered by Portuguese American infants in the early 1920s.[377]

Among the numerous reasons for this excessive infant mortality rate, according to Taft, were overcrowded housing and poor hygiene, of which he cited detailed examples, earning the ire of an entire ethnic group. Poverty, the illiteracy of mothers and their inability to speak or understand English were cited as barriers to seeking help from doctors and following and understanding instructions even when doctors were summoned. The Portuguese had a higher rate of the use of only midwives at childbirth (rather than doctors assisted by midwives) as compared to other immigrant groups at the time. The high proportion of mothers working in mills during pregnancy (twice as many as other immigrant groups), the immigration of the mother while pregnant, and the general ill health of mothers were cited by Taft as contributing causes to the high infant mortality rate.

Other factors Taft cited included the high percentage of mothers working outside of the home, the lack of breastfeeding, improper methods of formula feeding and the custom of offering a bread and milk paste on mothers' fingers to week old babies. Portuguese families had fewer children at home, undoubtedly due to the higher infant mortality rate. An attitude of folk fatalism was also cited as a cause of infant deaths. Why summon a doctor? If the infant is really sick, he or she will probably die anyway; if not, the baby will get better without the doctor's help. On the positive side, Taft noted that the Portuguese had lower rates of alcoholism among parents and a lesser rate of desertion of families by fathers compared to other immigrant groups at the time.[378]

There is other scholarly evidence of dire conditions among the Portuguese in the early 1900s. In 1971 a scholar exhumed a multi-volume US government survey by the Immigration Commission undertaken in 1909. It was an extensive survey of half-million mining and manufacturing workers, about two-thirds of whom were foreign-born. Of the 35 foreign-born ethnic groups analyzed, 3,125 Portuguese were surveyed. About 58% of the Portuguese had been in the United States at least five years at that time, placing them in the middle of the groups. In terms of average weekly earnings, the Portuguese ranked second to last; only Turkish immigrants had lower earnings. The Portuguese were ranked 26th in terms of the percentage speaking English (45% speaking English) and the Portuguese were lowest of the 35 groups in literacy (48% literate).[379]

Poverty among the newly arrived Portuguese immigrants was often stark and "Latin Americanesque." An example is the collection of squatter shanties adjacent to the New Bedford docks, mentioned earlier, and derisively called "the Portugee Navy Yard." While the wages and opportunities available in the United States were better than those in Portugal, the occupations in which the Portuguese were employed paid relatively low wages by American standards.

An important reason why the Portuguese were employed in low-wage occupations was that the industries in which the Portuguese were employed were already in decline and therefore offered low wages, marginal economic advancement, and uncertain economic futures. A labor economist might argue that it was precisely when these industries were in decline that they failed to pay sufficient wages to attract native American workers, and thus the need for immigrant labor became most critical. To cite an example, the whaling industry, made obsolete by petroleum products, was drawing to a close and operating semi-derelict ships by the early 1900s.[380] American crews could not be found at wages that the industry would pay. The ships sailed from New Bedford with skeleton crews intending to fill out the crew with willing deckhands in the Cape Verde and Azores islands.

Figure 48
"Bringing home some salvaged firewood in a slum area in New Bedford, Massachusetts." Photo by Jack Delano, 1941, from the collection U.S. Farm Security Administration/Office of War Information at the Library of Congress.

The condition of poverty on the islands and in the United States is illustrated by the writings of most Portuguese American novelists, poets, biographers and autobiographers including Katherine Vaz, Frank Gaspar, Charles Reis Felix, Alfred Lewis, Sue Fagalde Lick and Laurinda Andrade.

Much of Gaspar's work, whether in his poems or in his novel, *Leaving Pico*, gives us glimpses of this poverty by showing us a lifestyle that seems incongruent with the chronological era of the poems. They are pictures of poverty in a post-World War II world that are reminiscent of life in the early 1900s. Wood stoves, kerosene space heaters, and coal chutes are commonplace after most of the nation had progressed to central heating using electricity or natural gas. Only cold water flows from Portuguese American taps while the vast majority of the American urban population has only to turn a faucet to receive steaming hot water. Hanging laundry and dishpans abound when clothes dryers and dishwashers are common elsewhere. Rotten linoleum covers the floor while others change wall-to-wall carpeting every few years. Fittingly, Gaspar's first collection of poems, *The Holyoke*,[381] takes its name from an ancient, broken water heater that the boy in the poem is able to get working In *Reliquary*,[382] the family sells its heirlooms to survive. The poverty can be startling, aggravated by the bitter disappointment and disillusionment of those who came seeking better material lives. The women, more eloquently than the men, express these sentiments. In *Kapital*,[383] the wife of an injured fisherman asks: "What will we eat? How will we live?" In *The Old Country*, a boy remembers his mother's rage: "*I'll burn this God-dammed house down. We never came from the old country to live like this.*"[384] In the poem *February*, a boy remembers his step-father sending him down to the docks with a bucket to beg for fish from the boats.[385]

But what were the feelings of the immigrants who arrived during years around the Great Depression when black banner newspaper headlines announced the closing of textile mills and the loss of thousands of local jobs? It surely was a shock to the new immigrant to discover they were not an asset to the labor force of the extended family but suddenly an additional burden: one more eating from the soup pot. One wonders as the immigrants must have wondered if they would not have been better off economically if they had remained in their rural island environment during those years of the Great Depression. Many did indeed stay at home and the numbers of Portuguese immigrants declined drastically between 1930 and 1940.

Estimates of the number of textile mills in New England shrank from 153 to 30 between 1923 and 1937 while employment in those mills declined from 34,000 workers to 12,000. New Bedford alone lost more than 21,000 textile jobs between 1927 and 1938. With job losses and declining wages came labor unrest. In Fall River, there had been a series of strikes as early as 1879, a six-month strike in 1904, a year-long wave of strikes across New England in 1922 and a six-month strike in New Bedford in 1928.[386]

Pictures taken of the Portuguese neighborhoods during the Depression such as those in the collections of the US Farm Security Administration and the Office of War Information are devastating.[387] After the economic bust in the textile industry, the apparel industry was encouraged to decentralize from metropolitan New York by the pool of unemployed and underemployed Portuguese labor in the old textile towns.[388] The lack of employment in New Bedford and Fall River also encouraged step migration to some small Connecticut cities like Danbury and Bridgeport and even to metropolitan New York and to Newark, New Jersey. In Newark, unemployed textile workers, mainly from New Bedford, formed a core of Portuguese settlement that later attracted more immigrants from continental Portugal, especially from Murtosa, Chaves and other towns in the northern Minho region of Portugal.[389] The Portuguese community in

Minneola, New York (in Nassau County, Long Island) began with unemployed men from New Bedford coming to find construction jobs in New York.[390]

Figure 49
Little girl in New Bedford, Massachusetts. Photo by Jack Delano, 1941, from the collection U.S. Farm Security Administration/Office of War Information at the Library of Congress.

Pap quotes a scholar as writing that that up to a third of New Bedford's Portuguese population drifted away during the economic crises of the 1920s.[391] However, most returned as such permanent step-migration was a relatively rare occurrence because we have seen how the New England Portuguese have tended to stay in place. Williams even faults the devastating unemployment that hit New England mill towns in the 1920s and 1930s as a contributing factor in some individuals turning away from their Portuguese heritage during this time. Being Portuguese became synonymous with being unemployed and some thought if only they could somehow become "more American" things might improve.[392]

Eventually, the devastation of the Depression finally lessened. A few textile jobs returned but most were lost forever. Apparel jobs replaced some textile work and for a few decades electronic assembly, plastics manufacturing, and seafood processing expanded for a time. But, as is the case throughout most of the United States, manufacturing jobs are continuously being shed through automation and through overseas competition. Inevitably the population of the two core cities declined. New Bedford and Fall River fell from their peaks of about 120,000 in 1920 in both cities to about 95,000 and 89,000, respectively, in 2015.

THE PORTUGUESE COMMUNITY WITHIN ITS LOCAL ECONOMIC GEOGRAPHICAL SETTING

There is little reason to believe that the Portuguese arrived in southeastern New England with terribly incorrect stereotypes about what they would encounter. They were not expecting streets paved with gold, just a better life. That being said, there is always some element of exaggeration as described by one writer in the context of the on-going increases in Brazilian immigration. He writes about "….the myth – spread through rumors – that everyone has a high living standard, that it is easy to find a job as well as to receive welfare, buy property, and own more than one car. Rumors make many Brazilians believe that the United States pays high salaries, even for simple jobs such as delivering pizza and newspapers, house cleaning and yard care." [393] But in reality return migration streams, visits, letters, phone calls and emails back and forth to relatives and neighbors remaining at home give a constant and fairly reliable flow of information. What the immigrants could not predict were the fluxes that were on the horizon for the New England and the American economy, such as the Great Depression and the general decline in manufacturing jobs in which most Portuguese Americans were historically employed since the disappearance of the whaling industry.

The milieu in which the arriving Portuguese immigrants and the already-resident Portuguese Americans find themselves affects their livelihoods and their landscape. Even without its distinctive Portuguese American community, one might ask, how typical an American landscape is that of the former textile towns of southeastern New England? These cities have been essentially economically depressed for close to a century, since the decline of the textile industry. To an extent, "geography has been destiny" for the Portuguese in southeastern New England. This group of immigrants tied its economic future to the economy of this area of the country, often with uncertain results. Like all ethnic groups, the areas to which the Portuguese chose to migrate influenced their economic outcomes. This is especially true in the case of the Portuguese because they have remained relatively place-bound compared to other ancestry groups.

This place-boundedness of the Portuguese is true at the macro-scale (southern New England) as well as at the micro-scale (the seven-or-so largest Portuguese neighborhoods in New Bedford and Fall River). In short, a great number of Portuguese hitched their economic wagon to the unique booms and busts of the economy of these two medium-sized southeastern New England cities. Their long-range economic futures have reflected this choice. Had they migrated to the rural life of dairying and fruit- and nut-growing in northern and central California, these long-range outcomes would have been different as we see from the income and educational levels of the Portuguese in California. West Coast Portuguese Americans have measures on socio-economic factors close to or even above the mean for the United States. These East Coast-West Coast economic differences even show up in Portuguese American literature. Felix's main character in *Through a Portugee Gate* flees New Bedford and writes of his surprise in learning of the prosperity of the Portuguese Americans in California. These differences in socioeconomic status between Portuguese on the two coasts existed long before the age of electronic media, although the proximity of many Portuguese to Silicon Valley undoubtedly played a role.[394] Almeida notes how this experience forced the character in Felix's novel to reconsider his views of the Portuguese American experience.[395]

EMPLOYMENT AND UNEMPLOYMENT

The core urban areas in this region, New Bedford, Fall River, Providence and East Providence, might be described by a term that, while non-technical, is apt: tough cities. Consider that in 2009 *Forbes* magazine placed the Providence-Fall River metropolitan area first among hundreds of metropolitan areas in a category of "Hardest Cities to Get By In" based on a combination of measures of average income, unemployment and cost of living.[396] Although *Forbes* did not update that specific listing, in 2016 Forbes cited Providence among the five worst cities to find a job in among the 150 largest metropolitan areas. The ranking was based on an index developed by *WalletHub* that looked at job opportunities, employment growth, monthly median starting salary, median annual income, time spent working and commuting, and housing affordability.[397]

The economic situation in New Bedford and Fall River may be even worse than the Providence metropolitan area as a whole. In some ways, these two cities never fully recovered from the Great Depression and have maintained unemployment rates often double that of the Massachusetts figure. In contrasting New Bedford's situation to another former textile city in

Massachusetts, Lowell, one economist describes New Bedford's situation as one of "extended decline."[398] In 2009 during the economic recession when the national unemployment rate was 9.4%, the unemployment rates in the two cities were 16.0% in Fall River and 14.7% in New Bedford. By May of 2013, the national figure had improved to 7.6% and that of Massachusetts to 6.9% but the rate in New Bedford was 13.0% and in Fall River, 12.6%. In March of 2017, the national percentage of unemployed was 4.5 [399] and the figure in Massachusetts had improved to 3.9% but in Fall River and New Bedford, the rates were still among the very highest of Massachusetts cities; 7.9% and 7.2%, respectively.[400] However, we should note that Portuguese Americans actually have a lower unemployment rate than their neighbors. For example, based on the 2011-2013 3-year American Community Survey data, those with Portuguese ancestry in Bristol County, Massachusetts had an unemployment rate of 6.4% compared to the overall county rate of 6.8%. But, as we will see, Portuguese Americans simply do not earn as much for their hard work.

INCOME

In the analysis of data in this book, the reader will see in several places a repeating pattern. At the national level, Portuguese Americans are at or near national averages on income and educational attainment. However, in southern New England, and then in metropolitan Providence, the group falls further behind these national averages. Portuguese Americans fall even further behind national averages in the two cities in which they are most concentrated, Fall River and New Bedford.

Like many American immigrant groups, most Portuguese fled great poverty and arrived in the new nation hopeful of better economic opportunities, but still in poverty. Because of the lateness of their arrival compared to most other European immigrant groups, the Portuguese were also poor relative not only to the established English and northern European groups but also to the other immigrant groups around them including the French Canadians and Irish who had arrived one or two generations earlier.

Some of the reasons for this relative poverty include the fact that Portugal has traditionally been one of the poorer nations of Europe based on per capita and other measures of income. Thus the Portuguese were economically disadvantaged when they arrived, more so than other European groups. Throughout much of the period of earliest substantial Portuguese immigration, roughly 1870 to 1916, the only European nation with a lower per capita income than Portugal was Albania. The Portuguese Atlantic islands, from which most immigrants came, had even lower earnings than those in continental Portugal. The lower income status of Portugal relative to other nations of the European Union continued through the more recent wave of immigration from the Azores in the 1960s and 1970s. Even in 2010 GDP per capita in Portugal was only $22,539, about 69% of earnings in the European Union and about 47% of that of the United States. The Azores were poorer, at only 94% of Portugal's income and at 73% of the European Union's average in 2011.[401] One contrasting bright spot was Madeira where the average income was actually higher than Portugal's (130%) and even above the EU average (105%).[402]

As we examine data in detail, at first glance we see that those reporting Portuguese ancestry nationally appear very close to or even above some national income averages. (We will use liberal rounding in the text to discuss trends more simply; exact data are available in Table 8 (Population, Income and Poverty Data for Portuguese Americans by Area). Nationally, Portuguese American household income in 2010 was about $60,000, substantially higher than the national average for all American households, about $52,000. However, among the Portuguese in Massachusetts, the amount drops to $57,000; in metropolitan Providence, to $52,000, and in Fall River to $36,000. Using exact figures, median household income in 2010 among those of Portuguese ancestry in the City of Fall River, the single location with the largest number of Portuguese Americans in the United States, is dramatically below national income for those with Portuguese ancestry (40% less) and below the median for all American households (31% less). Portuguese in neighboring New Bedford are somewhat better off than in Fall River but still far below national household averages -- 28% less, and 17% less, respectively.

Figures for per capita income, rather than household income, show even stronger differentials in southeastern New England. The national per capita amount for Portuguese Americans in 2010 was about $29,000, above the national average of $27,000. Those of Portuguese ancestry in Massachusetts have a per capita income of about $500 less than the national amount. However, in metropolitan Providence, the per capita figure drops to less than $25,000, and in the City of Fall River, the figure for the Portuguese is less than $20,000. Again, the Portuguese in that core city have a per capita income about 27% below the national average and about 31% below the average for those with Portuguese ancestry nationally. Portuguese Americans in New Bedford are again slightly better off than their neighbors in Fall River.

THE ECONOMIC GEOGRAPHY OF THE PORTUGUESE AMERICAN COMMUNITY

	Population	No. of Households	Avg. HH size	Avg. Fam size	Median HH Income	Per Capita Income	% in poverty
UNITED STATES							
Portuguese	1,426,121	532,818	2.62	3.14	$60,251	$29,129	9.1
All	303,965,272	114,235,996	2.59	3.17	$51,914	$27,334	13.8
CALIFORNIA							
Portuguese	374,602	141,427	2.57	3.11	$64,436	$31,917	8.2
All	36,637,290	12,392,852	2.89	3.48	$60,883	$29,188	13.7
CONNECTICUT							
Portuguese	54,477	20,022	2.64	3.17	$69,129	$29,251	6.0
All	3,545,837	1,359,218	2.52	3.09	$67,740	$36,775	9.2
MASSACHUSETTS							
Portuguese	311,767	116,410	2.57	3.08	$56,744	$26,776	9.4
All	6,477,096	2,512,552	2.48	3.09	$64,509	$33,966	10.5
RHODE ISLAND							
Portuguese	101,095	37,058	2.51	3.08	$52,913	$24,817	9.4
All	1,056,389	410,305	2.47	3.11	$54,902	$28,707	12.2
PROVIDENCE							
Portuguese	265,512	99,823	2.52	3.05	$51,647	$24,640	10.4
All	1,602,822	621,094	2.49	3.09	$54,920	$28,376	11.9
FALL RIVER							
Portuguese	41,443	16,926	2.39	3.08	$35,893	$19,989	16.3
All	89,482	38,140	2.30	3.01	$34,236	$20,337	20.2
NEW BEDFORD							
Portuguese	38,603	15,631	2.40	2.98	$43,123	$21,642	16.1
All	94,945	38,729	2.40	3.03	$36,172	$20,447	22.7
BRISTOL COUNTY							
Portuguese	164,417	62,765	2.52	3.04	$50,684	$24,531	11.0
All	546,433	210,789	2.52	3.07	$54,955	$27,736	11.3

Source: US Census Bureau, American Community Survey 2006-2010

Table 8. Population, Income and Poverty Data for Portuguese Americans by Area

Income differentials for Portuguese Americans are also evident when the ancestry group is compared to other major European groups in southern New England. Table 9 (Selected Massachusetts Ancestry Groups: Income, Poverty, and Education) shows earnings for all groups with European heritage in Massachusetts that include more than 40,000 persons, as well as for a few other groups of interest for comparison. Like the Portuguese, those of English, French/French Canadian, German, Irish, Italian or Polish ancestry all have per capita incomes above the national average. But per capita income for the Portuguese in Massachusetts trails all of these other European groups ranging from 39% less than those of German heritage to 16% less than those with French/French Canadian heritage. The Portuguese do have higher incomes than some other groups shown for comparison, ranging from 35% more than Brazilians to 71% more than Hispanic/Latinos.

Ancestry Group	Population over 16	Per Capita Income	% Below Poverty	Bachelor's Degree or higher
German	353,819	$43,960	6.0	53.9
English	625,697	$40,477	5.7	44.3
Polish	277,642	$37,419	6.4	42.2
Irish	1,193,519	$36,814	6.0	42.6
Italian	699,321	$34,073	7.0	37.1
French or French Canadian	659,547	$31,862	7.4	28.1
Portuguese	**249,698**	**$26,776**	**9.4**	**19.1**
Brazilian	51,058	$19,896	10.0	14.4
Black or African American	364,614	$19,215	21.7	22.0
Cape Verdean	37,825	$17,832	19.7	13.9
Hispanic or Latino	408,976	$15,688	29.6	16.0

Source: US Census Bureau, American Community Survey 2006-2010

Table 9. Selected Massachusetts Ancestry Groups: Income, Poverty and Education

Despite lower household and per capita income than their neighbors, the Portuguese Americans have a lesser poverty rate in all geographic units shown in Table 9. Nationally, the ethnic group has 9.1% of individuals in poverty compared to 13.8% for the nation as a whole. In the city of Fall River, 16% of Portuguese are in poverty compared to 20% of all residents. In New Bedford, 16% of Portuguese are in poverty compared to 23% of all residents. Note however that these are dramatic levels of poverty in both cities for Portuguese and non-Portuguese alike.

It is not a contradiction for Portuguese Americans to have relatively lower household and per capita income than the surrounding population in their geographic unit and yet have lower levels of poverty. As low as the per capita figure seems of $20,000 in Fall River, for example, it is still substantially above the federal poverty level for one person of $11,137. If the comparison is limited to other European ancestry groups in Massachusetts, however, Portuguese Americans do have higher poverty rates as was shown in Table 9. The poverty rate of 9.4% for the Portuguese is higher than that for all other European immigrant groups which range from a low of 6.0% for Germans to 7.4% for French/French Canadians. The Portuguese do have lower poverty rates than the other four comparison groups which range as high as 30% for Hispanics/Latinos.

Before continuing with an analysis of data on educational attainment, it is worth stepping back and taking a look at what these data for income tell us so far. First, income levels among Americans of Portuguese ancestry are complex and vary by region. In some regions of the country figures for the Portuguese may be above the national average; in another part, they may be much lower. Specifically, the 375,000 Portuguese Americans have done very well in California.

These higher-than-average figures for income among the Portuguese in California inflate national income statistics for all Portuguese Americans. Scholars can correctly study Portuguese Americans as a whole and come away with the impression that the Portuguese are doing fine nationally, maybe just a bit behind the average American on education, but they are catching up and assimilating just fine.[403] And of course, the situation of the Portuguese in California is generally very different than that in urban New England. Even this last statement is a rough generalization because as Table 8 showed, at the state level, Portuguese Americans in Connecticut have higher median household incomes than non-Portuguese residents of that state (although lower per capita figures). Perhaps the Portuguese in Connecticut are doing slightly better because they are located mainly in areas outside of the Portuguese American core in metropolitan Providence; namely, in Fairfield County, adjacent to New York City, and in the New Haven and Hartford metropolitan areas.

Second, showing that the Portuguese Americans nationally have higher-than-average measures on income is not really saying a lot. Just about all European ancestry groups have higher incomes than the general population in the United States in large part because self-identification as a member of a European ancestry group largely excludes from that calculation African Americans, Hispanics, American Indians and individuals of other minority status, groups that often have substantially lower levels of income compared to the national population.

Third, being aware of the higher-than-average achievements of Portuguese Americans in California helps us understand that differences in economic and social outcomes have evolved between the urban New

England Portuguese Americans and the more rural California Portuguese Americans. Understanding how these differences in economic and social outcomes evolved is important because it demonstrates that the lower incomes and lower levels of educational attainment of the Portuguese Americans in New England are not a function of cultural traits or personal attributes of the Portuguese themselves. Nothing could be further from the truth. As Maria Gloria de Sa, sociology professor,[404] and David Borges,[405] a research director at the University of Massachusetts Dartmouth, have noted, some researchers and reporters on statistical studies sometimes "blame the Portuguese" and Portuguese culture for what they see as a "Portuguese problem," whereas, as de Sa and Borges note, Portuguese Americans very much understand and appreciate the value of education and show that support through contributions to scholarships and museums. And understanding this distinction is important because ever since Taft, (and perhaps because of Taft), many in the Portuguese community, including some in leadership positions, have taken the tone that discussion of statistical portrayals of conditions of the Portuguese Americans are to be objected to as criticism of the Portuguese themselves or of their cultural values.

With their characteristic outlook on life, it is fascinating to note that Portuguese Americans help deal with many of these difficult issues with humor. "Portuguese Problem" is the name of the most widely subscribed Facebook site for Portuguese Americans. And a group of four young Portuguese American men in Fall River has created a popular comedy act titled "Out of the Gutter."

EDUCATIONAL ATTAINMENT

In addition to low rates of relative income upon arrival, we saw a persistence of relatively lower earnings among Portuguese Americans in southern New England. Why such a persistent income deficit? A well-established fact in social science is that income and the level of poverty are directly connected to levels of educational attainment. Portugal only recently started requiring an eighth-grade education before allowing students to drop out of school. Generally, only three years of formal schooling were compulsory in Portugal until 1956; four years in 1957; six years in 1964 and nine years in the mid-1980s.[406]

Because of the rural and agricultural nature of the islands, educational opportunities and attainment were even less than on the mainland. A local college education was unavailable until 1976 when the University of the Azores was founded. Thus the Atlantic Island populations were both less educated and poorer than Portuguese on the mainland. When many recent immigrants were children in Portugal, they may have completed compulsory schooling at age eleven or twelve. It must feel very odd for a young person to come to the United States and be required by law to leave the workforce to return to school. This phenomenon undoubtedly contributes to the high dropout rate among young Portuguese people.[407] As with income levels, the Portuguese were disadvantaged in terms of their level of educational attainment upon arrival, and that disadvantage has been carried forward to the present.

On measures of educational attainment, the Portuguese immigrants, even as late as the 1990s, had educational traits making them statistically more similar to Mexican immigrants than to other European immigrants, even those immigrants from other southern European nations such as Italy, Spain, and Greece. In fact, of the 34 OECD nations (Organization for Economic Development and Cooperation), which generally consists of all the European nations, the United States and the British Commonwealth nations (Canada, Australia, New Zealand) and a few outliers (Mexico, Brazil, Chile), in chart after chart, Portugal does not fare well on measures of education even as recently as 2011. Portugal is clustered with Mexico, Brazil, and Turkey among the nations with the lowest levels of educational attainment and below other southern European nations with historically low levels of educational attainment such as Spain, Italy, and Greece.[408] In 2011 *The Wall Street Journal* ran an article about Portugal titled "A Nation of Dropouts Shakes Europe."[409]

Lesser levels of educational attainment impact the Portuguese compared to others when they arrive in the United States A study by the Center for Portuguese Studies and Culture at the University of Massachusetts, Dartmouth in 2005, based on 2000 data, gave a snapshot of socioeconomic characteristics of the Portuguese in the southeastern New England region compared to Massachusetts and national figures.[410] The study noted that about 67% of the area's foreign-born Portuguese had immigrated between 1960 and 1980 when Portugal only required four to six years of formal education. Education in southeastern Massachusetts, an area the study labeled the "Portuguese Archipelago," continued to lag behind the remainder of the state.

Income and educational attainment are so closely correlated that we expect these two categories of measures to be similarly connected for those of Portuguese American ancestry. Nationally, as of 2010, about 6% of Americans have less than a ninth-grade education (Table 10, Educational

Attainment for Portuguese Americans by Area). For those with Portuguese American ancestry that statistic is 9%. In metropolitan Providence the figure rises to 17% and in Fall River and New Bedford it is 26% and 27%, respectively. Therefore, in these two Massachusetts cities, the population of Portuguese Americans with less than a ninth-grade education is at least four times the national average. We know the unfortunate situation of education for many Atlantic Islanders and for rural Portuguese continentals, but some statistics are still startling to see in print: among the Portuguese Americans in the Providence metropolitan area are approximately 5,000 individuals, one assumes of the oldest generation, who have never received a single year of formal schooling.

	Population	Less than 9th grade	High School Graduate Only	Bachelor's Degree	Graduate or Prof degree	High School Graduate or Higher	Bachelor's Degree or Higher
UNITED STATES							
Portuguese	1,426,121	8.8	30.1	15.2	7.3	82.0	22.6
All	303,965,272	6.2	29.0	17.6	10.3	85.0	27.9
CALIFORNIA							
Portuguese	374,602	4.9	28.9	15.6	6.4	87.0	22.0
All	36,637,290	10.4	21.5	19.2	10.8	80.7	30.1
CONNECTICUT							
Portuguese	54,477	13.4	32.2	14.3	8.0	75.9	22.3
All	3,545,837	4.7	28.6	19.9	15.3	88.4	35.2
MASSACHUSETTS							
Portuguese	311,767	14.3	32.9	13.4	5.7	73.9	19.1
All	6,477,096	4.9	26.7	21.9	16.4	88.7	38.3
RHODE ISLAND							
Portuguese	101,095	13.9	32.3	12.4	4.9	73.9	17.3
All	1,056,389	7.0	28.2	18.5	11.9	83.7	30.3
METRO PROVIDENCE							
Portuguese	265,512	17.0	31.9	11.4	4.3	70.2	15.7
All	1,602,822	7.9	28.9	17.8	10.6	82.4	28.4
FALL RIVER							
Portuguese	41,443	26.0	29.4	6.8	2.7	58.5	9.5
All	89,482	17.4	30.3	9.6	4.5	67.6	14.1
NEW BEDFORD							
Portuguese	41,443	26.7	30.8	8.1	3.0	59.3	11.1
All	89,482	19.1	31.9	9.3	4.3	65.9	13.7

BRISTOL COUNTY							
Portuguese	164,417	18.8	31.6	10.9	3.9	68.1	14.8
All	546,433	9.7	30.3	16.7	8.1	80.1	24.7

Source: US Census Bureau, American Community Survey 2006-2010

Table 10. Selected Massachusetts Ancestry Groups: Income, Poverty and Education

A basic measure commonly used in discussions of educational attainment is the percentage of persons 25 years of age and over who have graduated from high school or who have an equivalent credential (such as the GED). As shown in Table 10, for the United States population as a whole the high school graduation rate is 85% and for Portuguese Americans nationally, the figure is only slightly less, 82%. However, that rate falls to 70% for the Portuguese of metropolitan Providence and to 59% in both Fall River and New Bedford. Not only is this last percentage substantially lower than in other areas, it is exceptionally low compared to the very high achievement level for graduation from high school for all residents of Massachusetts which is 89%.

The education gap widens as we look at educational attainment in 2010 beyond high school graduation. For the population 25 years of age or older, of those holding a bachelor's degree or higher credential, the national average for those of Portuguese ancestry is 23%, which is less than 28% for the national population. This measure falls to 16% for those with Portuguese ancestry in metropolitan Providence, 11% among Portuguese in New Bedford and 10% in Fall River. The southeastern New England figures are dramatically lower than the national average and in the case of Fall River and New Bedford, close to one-third of the national percentage. Educational attainment for the Portuguese in the two cities cited is even lower compared to others in the metropolitan region or state: about 28% of persons in metropolitan Providence have a bachelor's degree or higher (a 12% gap for Portuguese Americans) and in Massachusetts 38% of residents hold at least a 4-year college degree (a 19% gap for Portuguese Americans). Expressed another way, the rate of college completion among Portuguese Americans in Fall River and New Bedford is about one-fourth that of the Massachusetts state average.

The educational gap widens even further when we look at graduate and professional degrees. Here we can easily see the connection between education and income. Individuals with advanced degrees are almost always high-income earners in positions including those of professors, doctors, dentists, and lawyers. Nationally, about 10% of Americans over age 25 have such an advanced degree, but the rate for Portuguese nationally is lower at 7%. Among those with Portuguese ancestry in metropolitan Providence and in Fall River and New Bedford, less than 4% have an advanced degree; this is less than half the national figure and only about one-fourth of the rate for all Massachusetts residents, 16%.

As was the case with income, educational achievement for persons of Portuguese ancestry is less than that of other European groups. Returning to Table 9 shows us that the percentage of persons of Portuguese ancestry in Massachusetts holding a bachelor's degree or higher is 19.1% in 2010. Those of German ancestry have a rate almost three times that of the Portuguese (54%). College completion rates for those of English, Polish, Irish and Italian ancestry are all about double that of the Portuguese. For comparison, data for some minority groups are included and it can be seen that those with African American ancestry have a slightly higher rate than the Portuguese. Only Brazilians, Cape Verdeans and the Hispanic/Latino groups have lower rates of baccalaureate completion than the Portuguese. These 2010 figures update and confirm findings in a 2005 study by the Center for Portuguese Studies, based on 2000 Census data, that showed that the Portuguese had the lowest levels of attainment among ethnic groups in southeastern Massachusetts. That study noted that these lower levels of educational attainment among the Portuguese are undoubtedly related to the low levels of education in the Atlantic Islands.[411]

While many Portuguese have some catching up to do, it is important to note that the situation back in Portugal is constantly improving. Many of the charts in the 2005 study mentioned above note that Portugal is making strides in achieving equality over time with the other OECD nations, particularly among younger people and women, and those improvements are undoubtedly reflected in the levels of educational attainment among more recent immigrants.

EMPLOYMENT AND OCCUPATIONAL SPECIALIZATION

While some Portuguese, particularly some members of the second and third generations, have achieved economic comfort and even affluence, the majority of the Portuguese in southeastern New England today do not fully partake in these middle-class material benefits. Although middle- and upper-income migrants arrive occasionally from Portugal, many immigrants still arrive in relative poverty. In terms of socio-economic status, the Portuguese occupy many of the lower occupational levels and specialties cast off by the dominant cultural groups. In addition to the few remaining manufacturing jobs, these include positions such as waitpersons, maintenance workers, healthcare support workers, gardeners, and maids. Livable family incomes are achieved by holding multiple jobs, one or more of which may be part-time, at minimum wage, and without benefits.

Many Portuguese Americans follow the custom of pooling the incomes of all family members, including children. The tradition of adult children living at home and contributing to household income and expenses is still strong among recently arrived and first-generation Portuguese Americans. With the strong family structure of the Portuguese, working children of the first and second generation often turn over much or most of their paychecks to their families to help pay off the mortgage on the parental homes before they marry and start their own households. The custom often means children drop out of school to enter the workforce. Among American-born Portuguese, this tradition gradually declines over time.

After arriving at the bottom of the American socio-economic ladder, the vast majority of Portuguese immigrants remained for considerable periods of time in lower socio-economic class status eventually working themselves up to what some have called "Catholic working class." In discussing employment opportunities, the distinction between "step jobs" and "trap jobs" made by some scholars is helpful.[412] Step jobs allow for genuine career advancement and improvement of living conditions; trap jobs provide only modest monetary increments as a worker progresses through life.

In New England, the vast majority of Portuguese entered and remained in trap jobs, such as those in textile and apparel mills as noted by De Sa and Borges.[413] In California, on the other hand, many Portuguese who started as day laborers on farms accumulated enough capital to buy their own farms and prosper, eventually dominating the entire state's dairy industry and some fruit and nut specialties. Near San Diego, Portuguese deck hands eventually bought their own boats and dominated the area's tuna fishing industry by the 1970s.

On the East Coast, whaling was a trap job. Ownership of whaling vessels was entirely beyond the Portuguese and the industry eventually disappeared; although some, such as the Cape Verdeans, bought derelict whaling ships for cargo and passenger business. East Coast fishermen, catching fish in over-exploited waters, did not fare as well as their West

Coast counterparts. Portuguese in Hawaii moved out of the trapping job of sugar cutting, an "ethnic mobility trap" that appeared to pay off to the collective ethnic group at first but collapsed when times changed.[414] Most Portuguese left rural agriculture to live in Honolulu. Back in New England the majority of the New England Portuguese population remained trapped in low-paying manufacturing jobs with attendant layoffs, strikes, factory closings and unemployment.[415]

As one 2002 study noted, Portuguese Americans were still exceptionally dependent upon the shrinking pool of manufacturing jobs as 25% worked in this category compared to 15% of the non-Portuguese in the Archipelago.[416] That 25% figure was higher than even the national percentage of all foreign-born workers, where about 19% worked as manufacturing operators, fabricators, and laborers in 2002.[417] This was a bad sign because of the continuing loss of such jobs. Only about 9% to 10% of the American workforce is employed in manufacturing in 2015 compared to nearly 30% in 1950 and 20% to 25% when the largest recent wave of Portuguese arrived in 1960 to 1980. Further loss of the remaining manufacturing jobs can be expected, but the number of such jobs is still highly significant for the area. In 2014 there were still almost 31,000 manufacturing jobs in the Bristol County workforce area of Massachusetts.[418]

Census data allow a comparison of types of occupations between those who list Portuguese ancestry and those who do not. Table 11 shows data in detail for the workers of metropolitan Providence, which includes the cities of Fall River and New Bedford. Table 12 gives national salary data for selected occupations. Then in Table 13, we will examine the occupations of Portuguese Americans in different geographical regions. All three tables give detailed data, allowing the use of rounded numbers in the text.

The Census Bureau divides occupations into five major categories. It is worth discussing these categories in detail because they tell us much about the employment situation of the Portuguese Americans compared to jobs held by all workers. The five occupational categories are: 1) Management, Engineering, Sciences, Education, Law, Arts, Business, Human Resources, Finance and Health Professionals; 2) Services, including health care workers in support roles, police and security workers, food workers, custodians, personal care and childcare workers; 3) Sales and Office Workers, including secretaries, clerks, and cashiers; 4) Natural Resource Workers, including all construction and building trades as well as farmers, fishermen, forestry workers, miners, mechanics and maintenance personnel, and 5) Production, Transportation and Material Movement including all factory line jobs.

Based on the 2010 census, there were roughly 776,000 workers age 16 or over in metropolitan Providence and 17% of those (about 131,000) listed Portuguese ancestry. Roughly 81,000 were in the Massachusetts portion of the metropolitan area, that is, Bristol County, which includes New Bedford and Fall River. About 50,000 of these Portuguese American workers were in the Rhode Island portion of the metropolitan area, many in and around the small cities within the eastern Providence metropolitan area such as Pawtucket, Central Falls, and East Providence, just 15 miles from Fall River.

As shown in Table 11 (Workers in Metropolitan Providence by Occupational Category), the categories of employment of Portuguese Americans are substantially different from that of all workers in the Providence area. While the numbers of Portuguese Americans in the two categories of Services and Sales and Office employees are about the same as that for all workers in the metropolitan area (shown at the bottom of the Table), Portuguese Americans are substantially under-represented in the Management category (by about 32%) and over-represented in the two categories of Natural Resources (about 34%) and Production and Transportation (about 24%). In brief, the data show that Portuguese Americans hold too many blue collar jobs and not enough white collar jobs. Undoubtedly this is related to lesser levels of educational attainment by Portuguese Americans.

	ALL WORKERS		PORTUGUESE AMERICAN WORKERS		% OF TOTAL WORKERS, PORTUGUESE AMERICANS
	Number	%	Number	%	%
Workers Over 16	776,247		131,218		16.9%
OCCUPATIONAL CAT:					
Management	275,153	35.4%	35,339	26.9%	12.8%
Services	153,852	19.8%	26,496	20.2%	17.2%
Sales and Office	194,800	25.1%	33,501	25.5%	17.2%
Natural Resources	61,372	7.9%	15,615	11.9%	25.4%
Prod. and Transp.	91,070	11.7%	20,267	15.4%	22.3%

Source: US Census Bureau, American Community Survey 2006-2010

	ALL MALE WORKERS		PORTUGUESE AMERICAN MALE WORKERS		% OF TOTAL MALE WORKERS, PORTUGUESE AMERICANS
	Number	%	Number	%	%
Male Workers	392,052		65,224		16.6%
OCCUPATIONAL CAT:					
Management	123,430	31.5%	13,902	21.3%	11.3%
Services	68,928	17.6%	10,449	16.0%	15.2%
Sales and Office	72,163	18.4%	11,193	17.2%	15.5%
Natural Resources	59,162	15.1%	15,230	23.4%	25.7%
Prod. and Transp.	68,369	17.4%	14,450	22.2%	21.1%

Source: US Census Bureau, American Community Survey 2006-2010

	ALL FEMALE WORKERS		PORTUGUESE AMERICAN FEMALE WORKERS		% OF TOTAL FEMALE WORKERS, PORTUGUESE AMERICANS
	Number	%	Number	%	%
Female Workers	384,195		65,994		17.2%
OCCUPATIONAL CAT:					
Management	151,723	39.5%	21,437	32.5%	14.1%
Services	84,924	22.1%	16,047	24.3%	18.9%
Sales and Office	122,637	31.9%	22,308	33.8%	18.2%
Natural Resources	2,210	0.6%	385	0.6%	17.4%
Prod. and Transp.	22,701	5.9%	5,817	8.8%	25.6%

Source: US Census Bureau, American Community Survey 2006-2010

	ALL	MALE	FEMALE
Management	-11,173	-6,633	-4,541
Services	489	-1,018	1,507
Sales and Office	572	-812	1,384
Natural Resources	5,241	5,387	-147
Prod. and Transp.	4,872	3,076	1,797

Source: US Census Bureau, American Community Survey 2006-2010

Table 11. Workers in Metropolitan Providence by Occupational Category

If we probe further and look at the occupational categories of men and women, we see that Portuguese American women are underrepresented in Management by about 22% while men are extremely underrepresented in that category, by about 48%. Men are also underrepresented in the Sales and Service and Office Worker categories (compared to other men) but overrepresented by about 35% in Natural Resources and by 22% in Production and Transportation jobs.

It is worth detailing exactly what these numbers mean. We can calculate from Table 11 that if Portuguese American men had the identical profile as the area's workers as a whole, there would be about 6,600 more Portuguese American males in managerial, business, sciences, and art positions. There would also be 1,800 more men in the two categories of Services and Sales and Office work. In turn, there would be 8,500 *fewer* Portuguese American male fishermen, mechanics, construction workers, factory workers, and tradesmen. Thus more than 8,500 Portuguese American men would need to acquire additional education and perhaps also improve their English language skills to obtain higher-level and much better-paying jobs. More simply put, about one of every eight Portuguese American men would have to make such a substantial change in career. Men who obtained such education could move from the $35,000 to $45,000 range as truck drivers and manufacturing and construction workers to fields paying more than $70,000 annually. Such higher-paying fields include positions in business and finance, management, sciences and the legal field. To illustrate the types of positions available and the salary differentials, national average salaries for selected occupational categories are shown in Table 12 (Representative Salaries by Occupational Category).

Portuguese American women likewise illustrate an imbalance, although, as noted by other scholars, women are closer to the norm than Portuguese men.[419] While their numbers in Sales, Services and Office work and Natural Resources are within 10% of the population as a whole, Portuguese American women are underrepresented in Management (by about 22%) and overrepresented in Production (mainly factory workers), by about 33%. In the case of Portuguese American females, they lack proportionally about 4,500 Management jobs that would be made up from shifting out of excess positions they hold in the Services and Production categories. Women who obtained education and made this transition could move from the $25,000 salary range as waitresses, healthcare support workers, and hairdressers to fields paying $70,000 annually. About one in fourteen Portuguese American women would have to make such a change in their career.

Occupational Salary	Annual Salary
MANAGEMENT, BUSINESS, SCIENCE, ARTS	
Managers	$110,550
Scientists	$69,400
Business and Financial	$71,020
Architects and Engineers	$80,100
Legal Professionals	$99,620
SERVICES	
Counselors and Social Workers	$44,710
Healthcare Support Workers	$28,300
Protective Services	$43,510
Food Preparation and Handlers	$21,580
Custodians and Groundskeepers	$26,010
Personal Care Professionals	$24,710
SALES	
Retail	$38,200
Office Workers	$34,900
NATURAL RESOURCES	
Fishermen, Farmers	$24,330
Construction Trades	$45,630
Maintainence and Repair	$44,420
PRODUCTION AND TRANSPORT	
Production Workers	$34,930
Transportation Workers	$33,860

Source: Bureau of Labor Statistics 2013

Table 12. Representative Salaries by Occupational Category

Table 13 (Portuguese American Occupational Categories by Area) compares the percentage of Portuguese American workers by occupational categories nationally, as well as in California, where the Portuguese have done well, and in the three states of southern New England as well as in metropolitan Providence, Bristol County, Fall River and New Bedford. As we shall see, the regional figures repeat the patterns we saw in income, which would be expected because the type of occupation category is closely related to income. Nationally, almost 33% of Portuguese Americans are in the highest-paying category of Management, very close to the national figure of 35% for all workers. In California, 35% of Portuguese are in Management, which comes even closer to the California average for all workers, 36%. These two comparisons are important because it demonstrates again that Portuguese Americans are fully capable of achieving such goals and it is not something in Portuguese culture that holds back Portuguese Americans in New England.

	Population	Management, Business, Sciences, Education, Art, & Health	Services	Sales and Office Work	Natural Resources, Construction, Maintenance	Production, Transport., Materials
UNITED STATES						
Portuguese	1,426,121	32.7	18.2	26.2	11.8	11.0
All	303,965,272	35.3	17.1	25.4	9.8	12.4
CALIFORNIA						
Portuguese	374,602	35.1	15.9	28.7	10.8	9.5
All	36,637,290	36.2	17.4	25.4	9.9	11.1
CONNECTICUT						
Portuguese	54,477	31.3	20.4	22.3	12.2	13.8
All	3,545,837	40.0	16.8	25.0	8.0	10.2
MASSACHUSETTS						
Portuguese	311,767	28.6	20.7	24.3	12.3	14.2
All	6,477,096	42.8	16.6	24.2	7.4	9.1
RHODE ISLAND						
Portuguese	101,095	28.5	20.5	26.2	10.5	14.2
All	1,056,389	36.2	18.7	25.2	7.7	12.2
PROVIDENCE						
Portuguese	265,512	26.9	20.2	25.5	11.9	15.4
All	1,602,822	35.3	18.5	25.4	8.3	12.5
FALL RIVER						
Portuguese	41,443	19.8	21.1	26.2	13.4	19.6
All	89,482	23.8	20.9	26.9	10.5	17.8
NEW BEDFORD						
Portuguese	41,443	23.5	22.0	21.5	15.3	17.7
All	89,482	25.0	23.2	21.8	11.9	18.2
BRISTOL COUNTY						
Portuguese	164,417	26.0	20.0	25.1	12.7	16.2
All	546,433	33.4	18.2	25.8	9.5	13.1

Source: American Community Survey, 2006-2010

Table 13. Portuguese American Occupational Categories by Area

Looking now at occupational categories by state, rather than in the Providence metropolitan area, we continue to see similar patterns: substantially lesser percentages of Portuguese Americans in southern New England are in the higher-paying job categories and substantially more in the lesser-paying categories. Portuguese Americans hold proportionally fewer Management jobs compared to the overall state populations in Rhode Island (29% vs. 36%), Connecticut (31% vs. 40%) and especially in Massachusetts (29% vs. 43%). The converse is true, of course, that Portuguese Americans hold proportionally more jobs in the lowest-paying occupational categories. For example, in New Bedford and Fall River, respectively, about 18% and 20% of Portuguese Americans hold jobs in Production (mainly manufacturing), whereas only 9% of all Massachusetts residents hold such jobs and only 10% do so in Connecticut.

Only in New Bedford and Fall River do Portuguese Americans come close to equaling the averages for all workers in Management jobs. In New Bedford, the figures for Portuguese Americans is 24% vs. 25% for the general population, and in Fall River the percentages are 20% vs. 24%, respectively. This is because management jobs are so scarce in those two cities: recall that for Massachusetts as a whole, 43% of workers hold management jobs.

As we did with income, it is worth comparing the situation of Portuguese Americans in New England with those in California. In California, there is no significant gap between the Portuguese Americans and all Californians in terms of occupational categories. Portuguese Americans hold 35% of the jobs in Management, a figure almost identical to the 36% of all workers in the state. Portuguese Americans are even less likely to hold jobs in Production (10%) compared to 11% of all California workers. As we know, income and level of occupational category are closely connected, so these statistics go a long way toward explaining why California Portuguese Americans are better off in a material way than their kindred in New England.

Again, education is the key for Portuguese Americans to move into these higher paying occupational categories, for men, and for women. Of course, obtaining the education necessary for such higher-level jobs does not guarantee that jobs will be available. The Portuguese Americans are caught in the cause-and-effect or chicken-and-egg cycle in the occupational structure of the local economy. In New Bedford, for example, only 20% of the city's jobs are in the management cluster compared to 43% of all jobs in Massachusetts. But metropolitan Providence offers plenty of opportunities. In fact, the proportion of Management jobs for all workers in metropolitan Providence is 35.3%, a figure identical to the national average.

Yet there is an opportunity. Much of the Providence-Boston corridor is now effectively a single commuting field within reach of all Portuguese Americans in southeastern New England. Gilbert's concern expressed in 1989 about individuals going to college running the risk of outpacing the area's capacity to employ them is no longer true.[420] Those with the required educational level will be able to obtain better jobs, even if those jobs are not in the immediate area. But one thing is certain: the level of occupations and salaries for Portuguese Americans will not improve without greater levels of educational attainment for individuals and for the Portuguese American community as a whole. Aiming for an occupational profile equivalent to what is already available in the region is within reach of Portuguese Americans in New England just as demonstrated by the Portuguese in California.

THE FISHING INDUSTRY

One particular industry, fishing, is worth looking at in detail because of its importance to the Portuguese, in myth and in reality. Since the decline of the whaling industry that started the Portuguese migration, maritime-related industries never employed the great numbers of Portuguese that the textile and apparel industries did. Despite common stereotypes, most Portuguese who migrated to New England had not been fishermen in Portugal or the Atlantic Islands; rather, they acquired fishing skills after their arrival in the United States, just as they acquired factory production skills.

A considerable amount of time elapsed between the arrival of the Portuguese and their control of any part of the maritime industry. The white Anglo captain and the darker-skinned Cape Verdean deckhands shown in many whaling photos typified the situation. While small one- and two-man boats, like those of Provincetown, were within easy economic reach of the Portuguese, it was not until the 1970s that deep-sea diesel-powered vessels capable of reaching the Grand Banks or Georges Banks were owned and operated by Portuguese. Generally, until that time, Portuguese were hands on ships owned by Anglo and Norwegian captains. Portuguese men found work on the vessels, while women worked on the land in fish processing plants.

But just when Portuguese ownership of vessels in the New Bedford fleet became common or predominant, (one estimate put Portuguese ownership at 65% of the fleet of about 320 vessels in the 1980s), the New England fishing industry went into deep decline. The decline is cataloged in a non-fiction work, *Down at the Docks* by Rory Nugent.[421] Indeed, the declining value of these aging vessels and their lesser productivity in hard economic times were factors that brought their prices within reach of Portuguese Americans. This repeats the situation that occurred within the dying whaling industry. By the late 1800s and early 1900s, when the whaling industry was in terminal decline, ownership of the ships had passed almost entirely into the hands of Azoreans and Cape Verdeans.[422] Many whaling ships were used as cargo vessels to transport goods and immigrants between the Atlantic Islands and New Bedford.

New Bedford was and remains dominant in the New England fishing industry, just as it was in whaling. This is true even though the picturesque fishing communities in Gloucester and Provincetown received the most publicity perhaps because the fishing vocation fits the American stereotype of Portuguese, just as the small town nature of those two communities fit the stereotype of what a fishing town should be. But the Portuguese communities in both Gloucester and Provincetown were never very large. In 1905 when New Bedford and Fall River each had more than 7,000 Portuguese, Gloucester and Provincetown each had about 1,000 Portuguese-born residents.[423] Today the two small cities have about 3,200 and 800 persons of Portuguese ancestry, representing about 11% and 23% of their respective populations.

The small two- and three-man boats of lesser ports like Gloucester and Provincetown were put out of business by the larger scale operations of New Bedford. Gaspar's prose and poetry are dotted with symbols of this maritime decline: derelict seafood freezer storehouses and the stark ribs of abandoned vessels littering the shore. He notes that in the Provincetown landscape since his youth, the number of Portuguese-owned boats in the fleet has declined from 80 to 15; the old cold storage plants and bars are gone; the condos have spread like psoriasis, and he worries that the yuppification could lead to a Disneyland environment.[424] But, in turn, New Bedford's fishing fleet went into decline due to over-fishing and competition from Alaskan, Canadian and overseas factory fishing vessels. The adoption of the 200-mile exclusive economic zone by nations in the late 1970s and early 1980s forced American fishermen out of traditional fishing grounds that now came under Canadian jurisdiction.

Today, while the New Bedford fishing industry *per se* is still in decline, the scallop industry is booming. Scallops, not fish, have always made up the largest portion of the New Bedford catch.[425] Scallops are harvested by dragging weighted nets across the floor of the ocean and the boats are called draggers. Fishing in New Bedford is a billion dollar annual operation that employs directly or indirectly about 4,500 workers, many of them Portuguese Americans, on boats and in local processing and distribution plants. Between 1993 and 2012, the volume of scallop landings quadrupled while the price of scallops doubled from about $6 per pound to $10 and occasionally rose as high as $15 per pound. European demand for American wild-caught scallops is constantly growing. New Bedford remains the leading fishing port in the nation by far, not in terms of tonnage, but in terms of value, producing more than $400 million a year of catch, about double that of the value of the second-leading port, Dutch Harbor, Alaska, famous from the television show *Deadliest Catch*. Fortunately, scallops develop profusely on areas of the ocean floor banned from trawler fishing, so when areas are declared over-fished, scalloping can compensate somewhat.

Figure 50
Fishing boats, mainly scallopers (draggers) in New Bedford harbor. Photo "Fogged in Redux" by Gerry "twoblueday" on Flickr Creative Commons, license 2.0.

In the last few decades, the nature of the industry has completely changed. Privately owned boats have given way to corporate fleets of vessels. The National Marine Fisheries Service, a division of NOAA, regulates the fishing industry not only in terms of zones where fishing is prohibited or limited but by vessel licensing and by regulation of the number of trips, hours per year and volume of catch allowed in total and per boat. While fishermen can still make good money ($2,200 a week on average in 2011) these limitations allow fishermen to work only for 90 days a year, effectively making the occupation a part-time job. The free-wheeling wild-west atmosphere on the docks and on the privately-owned boats in days of old, colorfully described in Nugent's book, has been replaced by OSHA paperwork, green cards, criminal background checks and drug tests. Another burden very recently added to the trials of Portuguese workers is enforcement of the Jones Act, a 1920s law that limits the number of foreign-born fishermen to 25% of a boat's crew regardless of whether or not the foreign-born individual has obtained citizenship. This is a devastating challenge to Portuguese-born or naturalized fishermen. This law is a remnant from the era of quotas and discrimination against immigrants and it had been allowed to lie dormant. However, concern about national security after 9/11 led to a resurgence in the enforcement of this law in 2007.[426]

Today, the still-vibrant docks of New Bedford add a colorful landscape component to the economic geography of the Portuguese American community, as do the many still-standing four- and five-story brick mills surrounded by a sea of three-decker tenements. It is fascinating how remnants of each industrial era in the economic geography of the community have been preserved in the landscape.

9
FUTURES

The Portuguese communities of this region are still vibrant despite the decline in immigration seen over the last three decades. What happens next?

Given the long history of the Portuguese community in southeastern New England, and given the factors of poverty, patriarchy, politics, and prejudice that we have discussed, what are possible futures of the community and what might be the most likely outcomes over the next two generations? Will it die out like so many other American urban ethnic communities have? One sociologist describes futures for "Little Italies" in a series of not very optimistic but self-explanatory phrases: oblivion, ruination, ethnic theme parks, immigration museums and anthropological gardens. [427] Other scholars have speculated on these possible futures for the Portuguese and the pace with which inevitable assimilation will take place. [428]

With decreased immigration, the decline in some indications of Portuguese culture can be rapid. In 1999, out of 23 school districts in Massachusetts where Portuguese language classes had been offered, only in New Bedford, Fall River and Seekonk were more than 25% of high school students taking Portuguese as their foreign language. In most districts, less than 10% were taking Portuguese, far outnumbered by the percentages taking Spanish or French. [429] Just between 2002 and 2009 the number of children in Fall River public schools who reported their language at home as Portuguese declined from about 18% to 11%. The latter figure is just about equal to the 10% (and growing) number of students in the city who report Spanish as their home language. This decline in the use of Portuguese language has already had an impact on the school system which has been decreasing the number of Portuguese language classes and increasing those of Spanish. [430] There are occasional conversations and news reports about the danger of the community "losing its identity." But with almost 40% of the populations in the cities of Fall River and New Bedford reporting some Portuguese ancestry, some officials, paraphrasing Mark Twain, note that the "demise of the community is greatly exaggerated."[431]

Portuguese American landscape of southeastern New England is a work in progress. Unlike the ethnic neighborhood landscapes of so many European groups in urban areas of the United States, where ethnic populations have declined and communities have shrunk or even been abandoned, the Portuguese communities of this region are generally still vibrant despite the decline in immigration seen over the last three decades. So far, the local experience contradicts one geographer, Michael Reibel, who writes that ethnic enclaves tend to lose their identity three decades after significant immigration ends, and as the third generation children relocate to the suburbs.[432] Indeed, with the slower pace of assimilation experienced by the Portuguese in southeastern New England due to their levels of income and education, many third and later generations of Portuguese still live in three-deckers in Portuguese neighborhoods. In some cases, movement into the suburbs of New Bedford and Fall River has been a movement into three-decker and two-decker neighborhoods that adjoin these cities where the political boundaries are often indistinguishable in the landscape. This is the case in neighborhoods immediately adjacent to New Bedford in the suburbs of South Dartmouth and Acushnet and in Fall River's suburb Tiverton, Rhode Island. Yet their numbers are so great that many Portuguese residents, born in Portugal and speaking Portuguese at home, live in single-family suburban neighborhoods in southeastern New England outside of the traditional urban Portuguese neighborhoods.

The plural, "futures," is used above because there are a variety of possible outcomes for the southeastern New England Portuguese community: growth, decline or the maintenance of a more-or-less steady state. The Portuguese have always been attracted to job opportunities. In recent years the economic situation in Portugal has not been good. In 2014, when unemployment averaged 10% in the European Union, unemployment in Portugal was 14%, 15% in Madeira, and 16% in the Azores.[433] Substantial emigration still continues from Portugal but migrating to southeastern New England, with cycles of high unemployment, is not as attractive as migrating to closer European countries such as France, Switzerland, Spain, the United Kingdom or Germany, or to the former Portuguese colonies of Angola and Mozambique. Recall that the unemployment rates in Fall River and New Bedford are still close to double the state's average of 3.9% in 2017. Portugal's plummeting birthrate, the lowest of all nations in Europe in 2015, also does not bode well for a revival in the numbers of immigrants heading to the United States.[434] While the birthrate in the Azores is slightly higher than that in continental Portugal, it is still substantially below what is called the "replacement level," meaning, barring a great increase in immigration into Portugal or the Azores, the population will continue to decline.[435]

But who knows if an economic boom in southeastern New England might renew the economic attractions of the area? Casinos, currently on the horizon, could add some job opportunities as might various proposed off-shore wind generation proposals, for which the staging area for one was to be based in New Bedford. More than $100 million was spent on improvement of port facilities for the wind project. With or without wind projects, perhaps the completed improvements to the harbor could take advantage of larger container ships now using the expanded Panama Canal. Exploitation for offshore oil may present possibilities for economic expansion. A future natural disaster in Portugal or the Azores, such as a volcano or earthquake, as occurred in 1957-1958, could generate another generation of refugees such as the *Capelinhos* immigrants. As we discuss futures in this chapter, while we maintain our focus on southeastern New England, we will continue to make some references to Portuguese Americans in other regions of the United States for comparison.

CONCENTRATION, DISPERSAL AND ETHNIC VITALITY

In the end, while no one can predict the future, we can make educated guesses to frame speculation within the context of what has been discussed about the maintenance of ethnic neighborhoods. There are literally dozens of factors involved in maintaining an ethnic group so we will focus on the more geographical ones. We need to temper these general observations with an awareness of the distinctive factors of the Portuguese community that have been described in this book. Some of the factors shaping the maintenance of the community that we will look at in this section include the amount of continuing migration as well as return migration, dispersal vs. continued concentration of the community, and the role of various actors in promoting Portuguese culture including the role of the Portuguese national government.

As we have seen, studies have shown that the more clustered or concentrated the ethnic community, the greater is its chance of surviving. The Portuguese have remained one of the most concentrated American ethnic groups, as discussed earlier. This context works in favor of the preservation of a strong community. Yet there is no doubt that on any measure the Portuguese are becoming less concentrated over time. Earlier it was noted that the Portuguese are one of the most spatially concentrated of American immigrant groups. We know that this concentration was reinforced by the massive wave of immigration in the 1960s and 1970s which was mainly targeted toward the East Coast Portuguese communities. As late as 1978, with the exception of a generalized drift toward very large metropolitan areas, there was very little change in the relative distribution of Portuguese settlement among states since the 1930s.[436] Five of the six counties in Massachusetts where most Portuguese lived in 1978 were the very same counties where the Portuguese had been most clustered in 1900. Specifically, Bristol County, where New Bedford and Fall River are located was the most favored destination in both eras. In California, the same three counties in the Bay Area and Tulare County in the San Joaquin Valley (the center of the Portuguese dairying industry) the counties that had the heaviest concentrations of Portuguese in 1900 were the same counties with the largest numbers of new arrivals in 1978.

Yet, change occurs. In 1960 the Portuguese population was distributed as follows: 48% in the three states of southern New England, 35% in California, 7% in New York and New Jersey and 3% in Hawaii.[437] We should note that these figures were compiled using a measure of first-ancestry: those born in Portugal as well as Americans born of Portuguese-born parents. In any case, 93% of Portuguese Americans lived in those seven states. By 2010 the Portuguese were finally "spreading out" as another study noted in 2000.[438]

By comparing 2010 statistics to those of Pap fifty years earlier, all areas showed declines in the concentration of Portuguese Americans except Hawaii, where those declaring Portuguese ancestry increased by 1%. (Since few Portuguese immigrants or mainland residents with Portuguese ancestry are migrating to Hawaii, this may reflect the ethnic revival in Hawaii that Williams writes of. More people are simply taking pride in and listing their Portuguese ancestry.) By 2010 32% of persons with Portuguese ancestry lived in southern New England; 26% in California; 6% in New Jersey and 4% in New York. Thus the top 7 states in 2010 were home to 72% of the Portuguese population, a decline from 93% in 1960. Even if we take into account that state rankings had changed, with Florida replacing New York on that list, the top 7 states housed only 73% of American Portuguese, so they are finally spreading out or deconcentrating somewhat. This phenomenon is a relative deconcentration because the actual number of people reporting Portuguese as one of the multiple ancestries is still increasing each year. In 1990 the Census Bureau reported approximately 1,150,000 Americans listing Portuguese among multiple ancestries, a figure that increased to 1,200,000 in 2000 and to 1,400,000 in 2010.[439] This increase of 26% from 1990 to 2010 makes sense, despite greatly reduced immigration, as more people with Portuguese ancestry intermarry and have children.

In all regions of traditional Portuguese settlement, there are increasing numbers of Portuguese leaving the old established small metropolitan areas in New England and migrating to larger regional metropolitan areas, as happened generations ago in Hawaii.[440] In the Northeast, Portuguese are going to Boston, Providence, and New York-New Jersey from smaller cities in New England. In California, they are leaving rural areas to go, San Francisco, Los Angeles, and San Diego. After all, the largest traditional areas of Portuguese settlement on both the East and West coasts face huge challenges in terms of employment. In the East, we have seen the decline of traditional manufacturing jobs in southeastern New England. In California, there is an on-going loss of agricultural jobs where, even by 1980, the possibility of an immigrant starting from scratch as a laborer and owning a family farm no longer existed in that state because of the increased cost of land and the vast scale necessary to start economically successful agricultural operations.[441]

The gross national figures above tell us where Portuguese Americans are located but they do not tell us where the newest immigrants have been going. From 2010 to 2013 these new immigrants, those with a permanent resident or "Green Card," have gone, in order, to New Jersey, Massachusetts, New York, California, Florida, Rhode Island and Connecticut. Many final destinations are actually unknown because these data are compiled for "intended state of residence." The three states of southern New England were the destination of 30% of new Portuguese permanent residents, almost identical to the distribution a decade earlier when southern New England received 31% of new residents. When analyzed by metropolitan area, New York, which includes Newark and several other cities in New Jersey, is now the leading metropolitan area attracting Portuguese, with Providence second and Boston third.

GROWTH, DECLINE, OR STEADY-STATE?

The extent to which an ethnic group maintains its identity over time has been referred to as ethnic tenacity or ethnic vitality. By some measures, the Portuguese American community in New England is still in good shape: especially in terms of the size of the community, the degree of geographic concentration and strength of the culture. Where the community is weakest is in the flow of new immigrants to keep the culture renewed. It is still too early to say to what extent this might happen in southeastern New England, but despite the fact that it has been three decades since significant immigration ended, clearly, the southeastern New England community remains vibrant.

Three scenarios relating to ethnic tenacity have been described.[442] An American ethnic group can merge or dissolve into the overall surrounding culture and essentially lose its identity through submergence and dissolution. This is akin to the traditional idea of the "melting pot" and perhaps it is best illustrated by what has happened to the Portuguese in Hawaii. A second scenario is cultural pluralism, the continued independent survival of the group but often with very modified ethnic or cultural traits. A third possibility is that of ethnic revival. We have seen that attachment to ancestral heritage is a bit like a pendulum. The first generation is truly oriented to its ethnic roots; the second generation is uncertain and insecure and wants to comply with demands of Americanizers and may even actively shed its heritage. The third generation does not have these insecurities and can explore its heritage with confidence, a phenomenon sometimes called the "ethnic return" or the "third generation return." If the community is large enough, many essential and even peripheral elements of the group's culture can survive.[443] One psychological study of young Portuguese in Newark, New Jersey found that the greater the density of Portuguese contacts, that is, the larger the Portuguese community and the more likely an individual interacts with other Portuguese persons, and the more emphasis parents placed on a Portuguese marriage partner, the greater was the young person's commitment to "being Portuguese." This was especially true for women, who, as noted earlier, are often more active carriers of the ancestral culture than are men.[444]

Several factors maximize the vitality of ethnic groups in an urban area: the absolute size of the ethnic population, the proportion of the overall population made up of that ethnic group and their geographical concentration. The absolute number of people of the same ancestry is probably of greatest importance but the geographical concentration in certain neighborhoods may be especially important for groups that are smaller in size.[445] The size of the ethnic group, the extent of settlement, the recency of their arrival, their relative geographical isolation, and cultural values favoring tradition over change, all contribute to the survival of an ethnic landscape. The single most important factor in establishing an ethnic imprint is the volume of immigration in relation to time and place; that is how many immigrants come over how long a period of time.[446] Not surprisingly, there is a correlation between the landscape vitality of an ancestry group with its language or linguistic vitality. Although the following example relates to Brazilian Portuguese, it could apply to the Portuguese language as well. In the potential ethnolinguistic vitality of Brazilian Portuguese, both group and individual factors play important roles. Group factors include size and distribution of the community, rates of immigration and emigration, and the status that people of that ancestry occupy within the community. Individual factors include gender, age, birthplace, marriage patterns, reasons for migrating, ability to speak English and level of education or professional status.[447]

Also important is the economic distinctiveness of the ethnic group – either at the higher end on the economic scale that allowed housing elaboration like the great German timbered homes or at the lower economic end, such as the Scots-Irish log houses on the fringe of the Appalachian frontier. Isolation can also preserve an ethnic cluster. The strength of shared values, especially shared religious values, can help preserve an ethnic group. Think of the well-preserved Amish culture over many generations as an example of many of these variables. Least likely to produce a lasting ethnic imprint are heterogeneous migrant streams; dispersed destinations; little tendency to cluster, unsuccessful colonization (and thus great mobility) and the very strong pull of the new culture.[448] Fortunately, many of these negative aspects do not apply to the Portuguese community. The concentration of Portuguese migrants in a small number of locations facilitated the continued use of their native language, provided young people a pool of potential spouses, and allowed the Portuguese to continue their tradition of self-reliance rather than utilizing American social services.[449]

An important additional factor is the large infusion of Brazilians and Cape Verdeans into the southern New England communities. As we have seen, Portuguese immigration has greatly slackened since 1990. With the great decline in Portuguese immigration, these two groups are basically replacing the Portuguese as the main source of new immigrants. Table 14 (Recent Portuguese, Brazilian and Cape Verdean Immigrant Arrivals by State) shows the destination states for Portuguese, Brazilians and Cape Verdeans over approximately the last decade; specifically comparing 2002-2004 figures with those for 2011-2013 using a three-year average to smooth out annual fluctuations.

	2011-2013		2002-2004	
	Annual Number (3-year average)	% going to that state	Annual Number (3-year average)	% going to that state
PORTUGUESE				
New Jersey	192	22.6%	306	28.7%
Massachusetts	176	20.7%	219	20.5%
New York	93	10.9%	126	11.8%
California	84	9.9%	92	8.6%
Florida	56	6.5%	68	6.4%
Rhode Island	42	5.0%	44	4.1%
Connecticut	33	3.9%	44	4.1%
US Total	850		1,069	
MA, RI, CT	252	29.6%	331	30.9%
BRAZILIANS				
Florida	2,583	22.6%	1,688	19.3%
Massachusetts	1,720	15.1%	1,683	19.2%
California	1,181	10.3%	1,188	13.5%
New Jersey	918	8.0%	788	9.0%
New York	845	7.4%	578	6.6%
Connecticut	384		282	
Rhode Island	46		43	
US Total	11,412		8,770	
MA, RI, CT	1,348	11.8%	2,008	22.9%
CAPE VERDEAN				
Massachusetts	1,357	78.8%	640	72.7%
Rhode Island	276	16.0%	161	18.3%
Connecticut	32	1.9%	37	4.2%
US Total	1,722		880	
MA, RI, CT	1,665	96.7%	838	95.2%

Source: Yearbook of Immigration Statistics; US Department of Homeland Security, various years 2002-2013

Table 14. Recent Portuguese, Brazilian, and Cape Verdean Immigrant Arrivals by State 2011-2013 compared to 2002-2004

Most newly arriving Portuguese now go to New Jersey, but the total for the three southern New England states is still larger than that for any single state. Southern New England still accounts for about the same percentage in 2013 as it did in 2004, about 30%, but the annual number has declined to about 250 annually from 330 a decade earlier. The figures are tiny compared the thousands per *month* at peak times of immigration in the 1960s. New York has replaced California as the third most popular destination state.

Nationally, Brazilian immigration now averages about 11,000 annually, up from 9,000 a decade earlier. Brazilian immigration is now more than ten times the current average annual arrival of new Portuguese immigrants in the United States, while annual Brazilian immigration into southern New England is five times that of the Portuguese (about 1,350 annually compared to 250). Annual averages for the top five destination states for Brazilians are shown in Table 14. The top five states in 2011-13 are Florida, Massachusetts, California, New Jersey and New York, essentially the same states as for 2002-04 with the exception that Florida has replaced Massachusetts as the primary destination.

Figure 51
This Brazilian store in Fall River illustrates the growing Brazilian influence in the area.

Massachusetts receives an average of almost 1,700 Brazilian immigrants annually and, although Connecticut and Rhode Island are not among the top five destination states, in comparison to the small number of recent Portuguese immigrants, the numbers are not insignificant. An annual average of about 400 Brazilians arrives in Connecticut and 50 in Rhode Island over the most recent three-year interval. Immigration figures place the total number of Brazilian immigrants in Massachusetts at 60,000 in 2013[450] but some estimates are as high as 336,000.[451] With the increase in the popularity of Florida as a destination, the proportion of Brazilians arriving in the three states of southern New England is now 12% compared to 23% a decade earlier. When analyzed by metropolitan area, Brazilians immigrate first to the Miami-Ft. Lauderdale metropolitan area, then to New York-New Jersey, and third to Boston. This metropolitan ranking is the same in 2011-13 as it was in 2002-04. Clearly, with the exception of the attraction of Miami, Brazilian immigrants remain drawn to states and metropolitan areas that have large communities of Portuguese.[452] Major Brazilian settlements in Massachusetts include Framingham, Boston, and Hyannis (on Cape Cod), but Brazilians reach southeastern Massachusetts through step-migration often because of lesser rents in these areas.

Immigration by Cape Verdeans is increasing and remains extremely concentrated in Massachusetts and Rhode Island. Annual immigration has doubled for the 3-year average between 2002-2004 (880) and 2011-2013 (1,722). For both decades 95% or more of Cape Verdeans have arrived in these two states with about 5 times as many going to Massachusetts as to Rhode Island. When analyzed by metropolitan area the major destinations are Boston and Providence in about a three-to-one ratio. Like Brazilian immigration, what is striking is that the numbers of Cape Verdean immigrants into the three states of southern New England is about seven times that of Portuguese immigration in the period 2011-2013. Unlike, Brazilians, Cape Verdeans remain extremely concentrated in just a few destinations. In 2009, about one-third of the students in Brockton High School, the largest high school in the state of Massachusetts was Cape Verdean immigrants or of Cape Verdean ancestry.[453]

We should also note that some illegal immigration occurs, as demonstrated by an immigration raid on a factory in New Bedford that made national news in 2007. More than 500 federal agents assembled to arrest 361 employees, the entire workforce of a factory making backpacks for the U. S. military.[454] All were undocumented workers from Portugal, Brazil, Cape Verde and Central America. Illegal immigration often entails the simple process of overstaying a 90-day tourist visitation permit. Numbers can be significant. As noted earlier, some estimate the number of Brazilians in the state, including undocumented immigrants, at 200,000 or 336,000 rather than the official number of 60,000. In 2015 Homeland Security estimated that of 165,000 visitors from Portugal, about 3,300 stayed on in the United States; quite a significant figure since that exceeds by almost four times the annual number of legal immigrants from Portugal. Overstays by Cape Verdeans were about 300 annually and by Brazilians about 36,000. These are significant numbers.[455]

How the Portuguese community will change with the changing composition of the community remains to be seen but the situation presents numerous possibilities for researchers to explore. Brazilians and Portuguese have a common language, albeit with a distinct dialect and some differences in vocabulary, but different cultures. The Cape Verdean *criolo* language, based in Portuguese, is also a dialect with many differences from standard Portuguese. How does one ethnic group co-mingle with another based on language similarities but not nationality? One study showed that local Portuguese are comfortable with Brazilian music and televised soap operas and that Brazilian idioms are working their way into Portuguese spoken by non-Brazilians.[456] Perhaps the Hispanic experience in the United States, where Hispanics speak Spanish but represent many different nations and cultures (Mexicans, Cubans, Colombians, Ecuadoreans, etc.), can offer a basis for comparison.

THE GROWTH OF TRANSNATIONALISM, RETURN MIGRATION AND IMPACT ON BOTH COMMUNITIES

The slowing of immigration is a major factor in the preservation of the Portuguese community as we have seen. The phenomenon of return migration is an additional important factor. Obviously, the numerical size of the Portuguese community is largely a question of math dependent upon the number of incoming migrants, the number of those who are born into the community and who retain their Portuguese culture minus the number of migrants returning permanently to continental Portugal or to the islands. The pull of the homeland is strong enough that many Portuguese Americans do eventually return to Portugal. Some dream of returning home to die and be buried as in Gaspar's poem *Chronicle*, the tale of an old man returning to the old country to a house filled with servants, happy to anticipate rest in a grave in the soil where he was born.[457]

Return migration is an increasingly important issue to the long-term continuation of the Portuguese community in New England. There has always been a return migration stream among Portuguese immigrants, as with every other immigrant group. Studies of Portuguese emigrants to Brazil over several decades from the mid-nineteenth century to the early twentieth century showed that between 30% and 50% of emigrants from northern Portugal to Brazil eventually returned.[458] As early as 1908 when 6,809 Portuguese entered the United States legally, 898 (13%) of those, or others, returned to Portugal that same year. Immigration statistics show that return migration averaged about 14% of Portuguese immigration annually between 1908 and 1919, and, indeed, in 1919, when a literacy test for immigrants had been implemented, immigration fell to 3,525 and emigration back to Portugal rose to 1,574.[459]

Williams reviews the wide variety of different life paths chosen or experienced by immigrants. Some intended to emigrate permanently and did so. Others were disappointed in their search for employment and/or disappointed in the new land and returned. Some men who returned to Portugal did so intending to marry and return to the United States but sometimes the spouse did not want to leave her family and village, so the couple stayed in Portugal. Some men acquired their bankroll and returned to Portugal intending to stay but saw their money dwindle due to adverse economic circumstances and decided to return to the United States once again. Some worked in the United States for twenty or more years, cherishing the idea of returning home, only to do so and to return again to the United States because they found that their native village had changed dramatically. Often they were now a stranger in their old neighborhood. Friends and family had died or moved away, and the traditional culture they grew up with and idealized had disappeared.[460] In any case, gone are the days experienced by the first wave of immigrants who very likely never again saw those they left behind and when the only regular contacts were monthly letters; the ones arriving from the United States containing *vinte dólares no envelope*. Some scholars have even written of the idea of virtual citizenship, the general decline of commitment to traditional nationhood and to a national society, and the concurrent rise of social circles of dual and multiple national loyalties that circumvent the state.[461]

Taft noted return migration in his study, and although he did not specifically state this, his statistics appear to demonstrate what geographers would call a distance decay function. Simply put, return migration is less the farther the distance traveled by the emigrant. This makes sense due to the cost of the emigration voyage and the potential cost of the return trip. For example, fewer than 100 Portuguese returned from Hawaii annually from 1908-1919, which is about one out of every ten immigrants. During the same time period, about one of every eight Portuguese immigrants returned from California but one of every five from Massachusetts did so. Return migration was proportionately less from California not only because of distance but because farming provided for more steady work than did mill labor on the East Coast.[462] About two-thirds of those who returned did so within the first five years, so it appears that some emigrants decided relatively quickly that they did not like living in the new land. Conversely, the longer an immigrant stays in the United States the less likely he or she is to return.[463] Williams also discussed this phenomenon noting that the longer the length of residence has been, the less likely the Portuguese are to return. Of one decade he studied, 69% of those who returned to Portugal had been in the United States for less than five years; 25% returning had been here for between five and ten years, and only 2% of those returning had been in the United States for more than twenty years.[464]

There were gender differences among return migrants too. Often those leaving the United States were men returning for a period of time to get married, sometimes with the intention of re-immigrating. Once in the United States, women were much less likely to return to their native land compared to men who might emigrate temporarily to accumulate funds before returning home to marry.[465] In any case, gone are the days experienced by the first wave of immigrants who very likely never again saw those they left behind and when the only regular contacts were monthly letters; the ones arriving from the United States containing *vinte dólares no envelope*. Jacobson has even written of the idea of virtual citizenship, the general decline of commitment to traditional nationhood and to a national society, and the concurrent rise of social circles of dual and multiple national loyalties that circumvent the state.[466]

Return migration impacts the home country as well. This is particularly true of the Azores where a huge proportion of the population has left. Amazingly, Pap cites various sources to note that as early as 1933 the 7,000 Portuguese American expatriates living in the Azores, who were former American residents, constituted the largest American expatriate community outside of London and Paris. In Portugal and the islands the transplanted Portuguese Americans impacted everything from clothing styles to vocabulary. They introduced ideas of democracy to a dictatorship, and increased concern for literacy, schools and farming methods.[467] Undoubtedly Portuguese emigrants in democratic countries around the world helped introduce ideas and expectations that led to the 1974 "Carnation Revolution" that resulted in the overthrow of dictatorship in

Portugal. Even architecture was affected and *"casa do emigrante"* became the common name for a large American-style single family home in Portugal. So much out-migration from the islands created a labor shortage back home, thus improving opportunities for those back in the islands and an additional incentive for emigrants to return.

Interaction also increases with tourism which is on the rise on the islands and in mainland Portugal as Portuguese Americans fly in for family visits and vacations from Boston and Providence.[468] The Azores are much closer than we think: the flight distance from Boston's Logan airport to Ponta Delgada (2400 miles) is less than that from Boston to Phoenix. European and American tourism is also on the rise as cruise ships increasingly make stops at Ponta Delgada on St. Michael's and at the islands of Horta and Terceira. The islands have become a favorite second home and vacation spot for Britons who have always also had a special fondness for vacationing, buying second homes and retiring in Portugal.

Perhaps the best geographical analogy to study the comparative impact on the Azores of massive migration and return migration resulting in a steady state of the population at both ends of the migration stream might be Puerto Rico, where a similar situation prevails. Visitation back and forth and temporary stays with relatives is so common that, like the Mexicans studied by Smith in New York, it may be helpful to think of the Azorean population within the concept of terms such as transnational or translocal or bilocal.[469] This concept has also been referred to as a "two-legged existence," one in the home country and one in the country of immigration. This lifestyle is made possible by telecommunications and ever-cheapening airfare that allows periodic return by the immigrant and frequent visitation by relatives.[470]

Portugal's allowance of dual citizenship helps the transnational process. Continued close contact is made possible by cheap telecommunications and declining airfare prices that allow frequent return by the immigrant and regular visits to the United States by relatives. Cell phones, email, and Skype allow daily contact if desired. Remittances sent by American Portuguese (and by Portuguese in all the other nations with large immigrant communities) is an important part of the economy of Portugal and the Atlantic islands as is the accumulated life savings or returning immigrants and a monthly flow of American social security or pension funds.

All that being said, we are remiss if we do not note that some of this transnational interaction can have an adverse impact on the island culture. The Portuguese were not coming from idyllic pre-modern island societies. Increasingly the islands have been subject to global influences including such unfortunate aspects of modern global culture as violence, HIV/AIDS, and drugs. Indeed, in the case of the Portuguese Atlantic Islands, some of the intrusion of these modern societal ills can be traced directly back to the connections between the islands and southeastern New England. These connections exist through return migration steams and the American legal practice of deporting Portuguese citizens who are convicted of drug use or prostitution in the United States.[471] Frequently these individuals are still drug-addicted and often have HIV/AIDS and hepatitis C as an associated characteristic. New Bedford, in particular, has a high rate of HIV/AIDS infection, the fifth highest in Massachusetts because intravenous drug use (especially heroin) is not an uncommon practice to relieve boredom among fishermen on week-long fishing voyages.[472] The practice of sharing needles is not uncommon. Of all Massachusetts cities, New Bedford has, by far, the highest percentage of those who contracted the disease via needles.[473]

The policy of deporting non-citizens who are convicted of crimes such as drug use, drug dealing or prostitution, even if the deportee does not speak Portuguese, has helped create a high level of HIV/AIDS and hepatitis C in the Portuguese islands. (Portugal itself has the highest rate of HIV/AIDS in Europe.) In 2001 an infamous case of the suicide of a New Bedford teenager who was deported to the Azores even though he did not speak Portuguese, made the deportation practice notorious. Another individual, an HIV/AIDS sufferer deported from Providence, was featured in a 2007 *New York Times* article on Cape Verdean emigration.[474] When President Clinton visited Portugal in 2000, the impact of American deportees on the Azorean islands was a specific item of discussion with the Portuguese President.[475] Deportation figures vary annually and most recent data show 151 Portuguese deportations in 2012 and 91 in 2013.[476] Most are deported to the Azores, a large number in proportion to the small populations of the islands.[477] American legal policy has not changed since the Clinton visit and the Azores has launched a program to inform Azoreans citizens who emigrate of the consequences of breaking American law and to encourage them to become American citizens if they do emigrate.[478]

CULTURAL PROMOTION

Heritage tourism is what geographers and economists call the use of the cultural landscape to attract tourists. Geographers Graham, Ashworth, and Tunbridge note that ethnic identity, a major motive for the creation of heritage, is the main way that distinctive local representations of place can be shaped and then exploited for external promotion. But such promotion can also strengthen the identification of the inhabitants with their localities.[479] Heritage tourism can extend beyond the simple economic motive. Heritage tourism can revitalize an ethnic group, and extend an ethnic group's time of domination in a region. The fact that tourists show an interest in an ethnic culture can serve as an impetus to maintain and even intensify that culture.[480] And of course, as has been amply demonstrated by the Portuguese, heritage can serve as a reason for international tourism as members of the ethnic group cross and re-cross the Atlantic to attend festivals, visit family and renew acquaintance with family and friends.

Heritage tourism is based on cultural and historical attractions rather than natural and recreational amenities. Successful heritage tourism features the identification and promotion of a distinctive image of urban personality.[481] Geographer Charles Stansfield states that among those ethnic neighborhoods long famous as tourist attractions in their own right are the "Chinatowns" of many cities and Manhattan's "Little Italy" all of which deliberately display and promote ethnic cultural landscapes and are conscious of their role in serving tourists. These districts feature food and beverage service, entertainment, and "fun shopping" (souvenirs, crafts, decorative items and jewelry stores). Stansfield calls these areas "ethnic epitome districts" and includes Newark, New Jersey's Ironbound Portuguese district as an emerging district.[482] He writes that in our latter-day Chinatowns, whatever their historical origins, we have created a "fantasy made tangible," a make-believe China as tourists like to imagine it; "…a China that works best at separating visitors from their money." [483]

The very successful commercial development of River Walk ("Paseo del Rio") and La Villita ("Little Town") in San Antonio, Texas has been described as a tourist landscape so artificial that it is nothing like the downtown area that has been shaped and sustained by the local Mexican population." [484] Instead, a "contrived, exotic, romantic, ideal landscape" was created, as were festivals and culture, and the whole idea was conceived of and carried out by non-Hispanics.[485] So we see that a line can be crossed in the ethnic promotion and heritage districts. They can be "Disneyfied," we might say.

According to scholar Michael Hawkins, festivals reinforce ethnic group solidarity and help differentiate one group from another, but they also reflect ethnic commodification. Ethnic festivals provide a marketplace where ethnicity is packaged, sold, and consumed by both insiders and outsiders.[486] He describes ethnicity as a marketable commodity or product, in effect, the "commodification of culture." As another example of commodification of culture, one can even invent an ethnic place and "sell memory and place" as is being done in "America's Little Switzerland," New Glarus, Wisconsin.[487] Solvang, a small city in California, has used its Danish heritage in a deliberate and successful effort to promote tourism in its "Little Denmark." A study of the expression of ethnic identity by Italians in Reading, Pennsylvania, asks why this was happening fifty years after they initially settled the city.[488]

Such ethnic promotion can be a money-maker. Hawkins cites studies that show that about 15% of American tourists attend an ethnic or heritage festival annually and that the tourists who do so are older, more educated and more affluent than the general population. This pool of tourists in the United States is about 19 million people annually. Perhaps the best answer is that heritage promotion is a win-win for locals as well as visiting tourists. It helps promote and reinforce the culture not only to outsiders but to locals of that ethnic group as well. What better way for young Portuguese Americans to find out what that ethnicity means than to participate in a street festival on the *Dia de Portugal*?

As we have seen, first, second and later generation Portuguese Americans are taking increased pride in their Portuguese heritage by celebrating it and by sharing it with the non-Portuguese community through the media, through ethnic festivals and celebrations, and by constructing monuments and establishing museums. New museums and museum displays are being established. The Whaling Museum in New Bedford, now affiliated with the Smithsonian Institution, added permanent exhibits on Azorean and Cape Verdean whalemen (and has proposed a branch museum in Cape Verde). A museum of Madeiran culture was established in New Bedford and a Cape Verdean heritage museum in East Providence. In 2016, James G. DeMello, a local businessman, has bought a five-story building in downtown New Bedford with plans to make it into an International Center focused on Portuguese culture and Portuguese-oriented businesses tenants.[489] The national government of Portugal and the autonomous governments of the Azores and Madeira supports some of this cultural development through programs designed to perpetuate Portuguese heritage.

Local universities are very involved in cultural promotion in addition to offering courses in the Portuguese language and promoting Portuguese American student clubs. One of the largest local universities, the University of Massachusetts at Dartmouth (UMD), has established a Center for Portuguese Studies and a doctoral program in Portuguese Studies (Luso-Afro-Brazilian Studies and Theory). UMD frequently develops grant proposals and scholarly exchanges with Portugal and the islands, again often with substantial funding coming from the Portuguese and Azorean governments. Funds from private donors have helped transform part of

Figure 52
The Museum of Madeiran Heritage in New Bedford, adjacent to the Blessed Sacrament feast grounds. Exhibits feature art and fine crafts including embroidery, weaving, lace and pottery. The grounds include a miniature replica of a Madeiran house, a fountain, garden and grape arbor.

the UMD campus library into the Ferreira-Mendes Portuguese-American Archives. Brown University in Providence has a Department of Portuguese and Brazilian Studies that offers a doctoral program and a scholarly press, *Gávea-Brown,* that publishes books and a scholarly journal about topics of Portuguese American interest. Roger Williams University School of Law in Bristol, Rhode Island, 12 miles from Fall River, established the Portuguese-American Comparative Law Center. Bridgewater State University (BSU), 30 miles north of New Bedford has a Bridge Partnership Program to reach out to young Portuguese Americans and Cape Verdean students to help prepare them for college. BSU has signed an agreement with the Cape Verdean Ministry of Culture and has developed a leadership program for Cape Verdean students. An Azorean Heritage and Library, in conjunction with Bristol Community College, has been in the planning stages for a number of years (as of 2012) at a site in Fall River.[490] Although not affiliated with a college or university, the *Casa da Saudade* is a Portuguese public library and immigrant assistance center in New Bedford's South End. Established with a federal grant in 1971, the center has grown to 34,000 volumes and has special collections and special missions, such as to assist fishermen and their families.[491]

Private individuals of means are willing to make personal contributions to these efforts and Portuguese Americans in political and other leadership positions are willing to help initiate and energize these efforts. While hard data are not available, all indications are that the Portuguese community has finally come of age. The number of affluent individuals, politicians, and others in administrative positions, the "movers and shakers" who are of Portuguese ancestry, are more numerous than ever before in southeastern New England.

A PROPOSAL FOR A PORTUGUESE HERITAGE DISTRICT

With all this activity and the interest of private donors and governments, the stage is set and the time has come to take advantage of these opportunities to establish a Portuguese Heritage District or Park, a "Little Portugal" or "Portuguese Village," somewhere in the southeastern New England core community. Point Loma near San Diego is also proposing such a development.[492] A waterfront location in New Bedford or Fall River would be best because waterfront attractions have great tourist appeal. The attraction would consist of museums, exhibits, shops, restaurants and more. Not all of the attractions would have to be constructed from scratch; it may be possible to move some museums and to relocate some existing restaurants that are currently in hard-to-find locations; that is, locations difficult for out-of-town visitors to find at scattered sites in unfamiliar cities. The waterfront area around the *Portas da Cidade* in Fall River or a site at Fort Rodman in the south end of New Bedford could serve as a site for this development, but there are many other possible sites along the waterfronts of both New Bedford and Fall River.

There is a long history of proposing such a project. In 1999 Maximilian Ferro wrote about on-going interest in developing a vacant site in New Bedford as a cluster of Portuguese villages modeled after Disney's Epcot Center.[493] In 2007 developers proposed a residential complex called Howland Place built around a Portuguese cultural center at the vacant Goodyear Mill site in the south end of New Bedford.[494] The demolished mill site is bounded by Orchard, Swift and Bolton streets. Then in 2011, Dennis White wrote about the concept, citing Ferro's Epcot theme but attributing the revival of the idea to a former New Bedford City Councilor, Victor Pinheiro.[495] White proposed a waterfront site near Belleville Avenue and Washburn Street in New Bedford's north end. In 2015 newspaper reporter Michael J. Vieira wrote about developing Fall River's Columbia Street district as a "Little Portugal."[496]

The Village would feature a major Portuguese culture center or museum constructed with funding from federal and state grants, private donors and the Portuguese government. Local museums that already exist, such as the Cape Verdean museum and the Madeira museum, as well as an Azorean museum, could be incorporated in a single main building or in separate adjoining buildings. Outdoor spaces might be used for music and folk dancing. An adjacent three-decker could be furnished to offer a view of Portuguese American life at different eras, perhaps 1890s, 1930s and currently. (Many non-local visitors have never been inside a three-decker.) If a three-decker building is not nearby, one or more could be moved to the site. Perhaps part of the exhibit might be a recreation of an Azorean village with farm animals that would serve as a petting zoo. With the waterfront location, boats could be available for boarding. These boats might include replicas of a Portuguese caravel and other boats, such as a traditional coastal fishing boat from Nazare in Portugal or from the Azores. Harbor sight-seeing cruises or a harbor crossing ferry might leave from this site.

A variety of Portuguese restaurants would be available at the Village serving food ranging from snacks to fine restaurants offering *fado* in the evening. Street vendor stands or kiosks could sell favorites such as roasted sardines and fresh-baked malasadas. A Portuguese food store needs to be included. Gift shops would sell Portuguese-made goods and those made by local craftspeople including items such as cork handbags, pottery, clothing and traditional hand-crafted items such as Madeira lace. An art gallery could offer works of Portuguese and local Portuguese American artists. A wine shop would sell Portuguese wines and beers. The streets could be paved with black and white wavy tiles, as in parts of Lisbon and Rio de Janeiro. Perhaps a Portuguese-themed hotel might be built. New monuments may be erected at the Village or some existing monuments could be moved to the site.

If a waterfront site with new construction is too costly an objective, an existing area with many Portuguese businesses could be renovated for such a project. The Columbia Street Cultural District in Fall River, framed by the skyline of the Braga Bridge, is a possibility. This neighborhood centered around Santo Cristo church is the largest of Fall River's three Portuguese communities. The main street is already a vibrant Portuguese shopping district with stores, bakeries, and restaurants. It is the only one of the five major Portuguese neighborhoods in Fall River and in New Bedford where a deliberate attempt has already been made by civic authorities and neighborhood groups to develop heritage tourism. Black and white paving tiles decorate the street and some ornate lanterns and signage were added. But not much more was done to make the area attractive to tourists or to publicize it to outsiders. Critically, no designated parking is available; only street parking. An easy-to-find dedicated parking lot is a must for any serious effort at creating a major tourist attraction. Out-of-town visitors are not going to hunt for street parking in an unfamiliar urban environment. The Acushnet Avenue strip in New Bedford's North End, where that city's annual *Dia de Portugal* is held, with numerous Portuguese restaurants and stores, is another possibility ripe for conversion to a tourist attraction.

Once a Heritage District is established, a targeted, consistent, well-budgeted advertising campaign utilizing all media – social, print, broadcast – is necessary to make the project work. The population that would be most attracted to a major tourist site such as this is the population within an "easy day's drive." Those individuals include 14.5 million in New England itself, 20 million in New York State, 9 million in New Jersey, 8 million in eastern Pennsylvania (around Philadelphia, 5 hours away) and 4 million in metropolitan Montreal (6 hours away). This total of about 55 million people is more than enough to commercially support this attraction. And, of course, if we assume that half of the official estimate of 5 million Cape Cod visitors each year already pass through Providence, Fall River and New Bedford on their way to the Cape along I-195, the "Portuguese American Interstate Highway," that represents a base of 2.5 million tourists annually already passing through the area.[497] It is worth repeating that the Village must be led and designed with Portuguese American leadership and it must be creatively and consistently advertised with a proper budget. The huge tourist population already flowing through the cities is, counterintuitively, a problem: the tendency will be to say "build it and they will come." But the long-standing deteriorated condition of the Columbia Street "Official City Tourist Map" speaks volumes about that approach. Once constructed and properly advertised, visitors to "Little Portugal" or "Portuguese Village" would create jobs and the multiplier effect would spill over to the local economy. Tourists would have a good time, spend money, and learn about Portuguese culture; local residents would benefit from jobs and also experience renewed pride in their Portuguese heritage.

SUMMARY

We have seen that Portugal and the Portuguese Atlantic islands have long been a source of out-migration as people left rural poverty. They sought political freedom during the time of dictatorship and better economic opportunities. The Portuguese diaspora has sent people all over the world; not only to the United States, Canada, and Brazil but to Australia and to

Figure 53
The need for an adequate tourism promotion budget and an organized marketing plan is illustrated by this long-standing deteriorated tourist sign in the Columbia Street tourist district of Fall River.

many nations in Europe, Asia, and Africa. The Portuguese have tended to concentrate their settlement in relatively small areas compared to other immigrant groups, not only in the United States but in Canada and Australia as well.

In the United States, the Portuguese remain concentrated in relatively few states, especially those where settlement was initiated due to the whaling industry – the three states of southern New England, California, and Hawaii. The economic situation of Portuguese Americans in these states illustrates how, to some extent, "geography was destiny" for the Portuguese immigrants. Those arriving in Hawaii and California went into rural occupations but eventually did better economically than their East Coast cousins. Those arriving in southeastern New England experienced a continuous economic struggle with factory closings because most relied on manual labor for employment.

Over time there has been some expansion of Portuguese American settlement to New Jersey, New York, and Florida but that early clustering is still evident especially in New England where a few cities that had cores of settlement in the mid and late 1800s, such as New Bedford and Fall River, still house large numbers of those with Portuguese American ancestry and an even larger proportion of those born in Portugal. Within these cities, many Portuguese remain clustered in the same three-decker neighborhoods that housed their ancestors, an unusual scenario for American ethnic groups. It is likely that this neighborhood preservation is related to the slow economy of the area, the long-running loss of factory jobs, continued high unemployment and thus the lack of incentives for other immigrant groups to move in and displace the Portuguese.

The Portuguese Americans in southern New England remain handicapped by their origins, arriving from great poverty and extremely limited educational opportunities. During the periods of greatest immigration to the United States Portugal was one of the poorest and least educated nations of Europe and the Atlantic islands were even poorer and lesser educated. By measures of the 2010 Census Portuguese Americans have still not achieved equality on education, income or occupational status even compared to other European immigrant groups in the same metropolitan areas. Educational attainment is the key to increased economic opportunities and avoidance of the potential for downward assimilation into a perpetual underclass. Portuguese Americans have shown this can be achieved in California; it can likewise be achieved in southeastern New England now that the region has become part of the Boston-Providence metropolitan area job market.

Although immigration from Portugal has dramatically declined since around 1990, if the local economy improved due to new economic initiatives such as offshore wind or oil developments, or if a future natural disaster on the scale of the *Capelinhos* were repeated, immigration into southern New England could increase again. Meanwhile, Cape Verdean and Brazilian immigration are increasing not only in southeastern New England but in many other cities in eastern Massachusetts.

The landscape of the Portuguese Americans of southeastern New England remains a work in progress. It changes with the evolving tastes of new immigrants. As new (but fewer) immigrants arrive with greater amounts of exposure to American culture through the working of the global economy, immigrants are increasingly pre-adapted to American culture, or, more properly, to modern global culture, which is heavily influenced by American culture.

This global cultural exchange has been intensified in the islands by return migration from the United States. The days of rural isolation are long gone, even on the Portuguese islands. Folk costume is worn only for festivals. Young men and women arrive accustomed to wearing jeans and listening to American music and Portuguese rock groups. They may have tattoos and piercings and may have experimented with drugs. The monthly letters sent back home have been replaced by cell phone and Skype calls, text messages and yearly visits. Increased visitation back and forth, return migration, and the possibilities of dual citizenship have created a transnational culture with good and bad impacts upon Portugal and the islands.

Yet, immigrants do not arrive predisposed to abandon their rich Portuguese culture. There remains sufficient opportunity for the Portuguese community to re-shape its landscape. Portuguese signs and cultural symbols abound and we have seen how some of the displays, such as flags, shrines, and gardens, are not just an importation but a reaction to American culture. The on-going construction of monuments and museums and continuation of festivals and the establishment of new ones in the New England landscape are other examples of a vibrant culture. This production and preservation of culture have been enabled by the increased wealth of some members of the community and their generosity; by the rise of Portuguese Americans to positions of social and political prominence, and by financial assistance from Portuguese and Azorean governmental entities. The creation of a "Little Portugal" or "Portuguese Village" Heritage Park would be another way to reshape the landscape, to attract tourists and to create jobs.

Whatever the future and whatever the outcomes, with the increased cultural diversity provided by the increasing Brazilian and Cape Verdean arrivals, the Portuguese American cultural region will continue to evolve and to heighten the colors on the palette of the ethnic landscape of New England.

10
ENDNOTES

1. John Brinckerhoff Jackson, Discovering the Vernacular Landscape (New Haven; London: Yale University Press, 1984), 12.
2. Leo Pap, The Portuguese-Americans (Boston: Twayne Publishers, 1981); Jerry R Williams, And yet They Come: Portuguese Immigration from the Azores to the United States (Staten Island, N.Y.: Center for Migration Studies, 1982).
3. John Brinckerhoff Jackson, Discovering the Vernacular Landscape, 12.
4. Pap, The Portuguese-Americans; Williams, And yet They Come.
5. Williams, And yet They Come.
6. Carlos Teixeira and Victor M. P. Da Rosa, The Portuguese in Canada: Diasporic Challenges and Adjustment (University of Toronto Press, 2009).
7. Maria Beatriz Rocha-Trindade, "The Portuguese Diaspora in The Portuguese in Canada," in The Portuguese in Canada (University of Toronto Press, 2009), 11–44.
8. Ibid.
9. Rui Pena Pires et al., "Http://Observatorioemigracao.Pt/Np4/?NewsId=4093&fileName=OEm_Factbook_2014.Pdf," Portuguese Emigration Factbook 2014, December 2014, http://observatorioemigracao.pt/np4/?newsId=4093&fileName=OEm_Factbook_2014.pdf.
10. Wikipedia, "Immigration to France - Wikipedia, the Free Encyclopedia" (Wikipedia), accessed April 19, 2016, https://en.wikipedia.org/wiki/Immigration_to_France.
11. Wikipedia, "Demographics of Paris - Wikipedia, the Free Encyclopedia" (Wikipedia), accessed April 19, 2016, https://en.wikipedia.org/wiki/Demographics_of_Paris.
12. Niall McCarthy, "The Countries With The Most Native-Born People Living Abroad," Forbes, accessed January 23, 2016, http://www.forbes.com/sites/niallmccarthy/2016/01/15/the-countries-with-the-most-native-born-people-living-abroad-infographic/#64da12d5a9cc.
13. Hispanic Division Library of Congress, "Portuguese Settlement in the United States," accessed January 4, 2016, http://www.loc.gov/rr/hispanic/portam/settle.html.

14 Ibid.
15 Raphael Minder, "Azorean Diaspora Can't Resist the Powerful Pull of Home," The New York Times, June 4, 2015, http://www.nytimes.com/2015/06/05/world/europe/azores-diaspora-holy-christ-of-miracles.html.
16 Onésimo T. Almeida, "Portuguese-American Literature: Some Thoughts and Questions," Hispania, 2005, 733–738; Center for Portuguese Studies and Culture Center for Policy Analysis, "Education and Ethnicity in Southeastern Massachusetts II: 1980 to 2000: A Continuing Challenge" (University of Massachusetts, Dartmouth, 2005), https://www.umassd.edu/media/umassdartmouth/seppce/centerforpolicyanalysis/portuguese_education.pdf.
17 Nick Paumgarten, "Useless Beauty," The New Yorker, August 31, 2009.
18 Pap, The Portuguese-Americans, 9–12.
19 Library of Congress, "Portuguese Settlement in the United States."
20 Pap, The Portuguese-Americans.
21 Kingston Wm Heath, The Patina of Place: The Cultural Weathering of a New England Industrial Landscape: Knoxville: University of Tennessee Press, 2001), 165.2001
22 Williams, And yet They Come, 16–17.
23 Donald R Taft, Two Portuguese Communities in New England, (Arno Press, 1969), 113.
24 Center for Portuguese Studies and Culture Center for Policy Analysis, "Education and Ethnicity in Southeastern Massachusetts II: 1980 to 2000:A Continuing Challenge" (University of Massachusetts, Dartmouth, 2005), https://www.umassd.edu/media/umassdartmouth/seppce/centerforpolicyanalysis/portuguese_education.pdf.
25 Pap, The Portuguese-Americans, 83.
26 "Milestones: 1921–1936 - Office of the Historian," accessed April 13, 2017, https://history.state.gov/milestones/1921-1936/immigration-act.
27 Taft, Two Portuguese Communities in New England, 55.
28 Center for Policy Analysis, "Education and Ethnicity in Southeastern Massachusetts II: 1980 to 2000: A Continuing Challenge."
29 Ibid.
30 John Scofield, "A New Volcano Bursts from the Atlantic-Off Fayal, in Portugal's Verdant Azores, a Jack-in-the-Box Eruption Smothers Villages, Awes Visitors and Even Catches Whales," National Geographic 113, no. 6 (1958): 735–757.
31 Pap, The Portuguese-Americans.
32 Ibid., 94–99.
33 Stephen Castles and Mark J Miller, The Age of Migration: International Population Movements in the Modern World (Houndmills, Basingstoke, Hampshire: Macmillan, 1993).
34 Castles and Miller, The Age of Migration: International Population Movements in the Modern World, 284; See also Frederick W. Boal, "Immigration and Ethnicity in the Urban Milieu," in EthniCity, Geographic Perspectives on Ethnic Change in Modern Cities, Edited by CC Roseman, HD Laux and G. Thieme (Lanham, MD: Rowman & Littlefield, 1996), 283–304.
35 Williams, And yet They Come.
36 Luciano J Iorizzo and Salvatore Mondello, The Italian Americans, Third Edition (Youngstown, NY: Cambria Press, 2006), 76–77, http://search.ebscohost.com/login.aspx?direct=true&scope=site&db=nlebk&db=nlabk&AN=498749.
37 Pap, The Portuguese-Americans.
38 Ibid., 36.
39 Taft, Two Portuguese Communities in New England, 89.

40 Ibid., 88,99.
41 Pap, The Portuguese-Americans.
42 Taft, Two Portuguese Communities in New England,119–20.
43 Pap, The Portuguese-Americans, 85–87.
44 Ibid., 158.
45 Williams, And yet They Come; Jerry R Williams, In Pursuit of Their Dreams a History of Azorean Immigration to the United States (North Dartmouth, Mass: Center for Portuguese Studies and Culture, University of Massachusetts, Dartmouth, 2007).
46 Williams, And yet They Come, 83–91.
47 Ibid., 115–33.
48 Pap, The Portuguese-Americans, 74, 79, 83–91.
49 Williams, And yet They Come.
50 Ibid., 59–80.
51 Louise Lamphere, Filomena M. Silva, and John P. Sousa, "Kin Networks and Family Strategies: Working-Class Portuguese Families in New England," in Community, Culture and the Makings of Identity: Portuguese-Americans along the Eastern Seaboard (North Dartmouth, MA: Center for Portuguese Studies and Culture, University of Massachusetts Dartmouth, 2009), 361.
52 Taft, Two Portuguese Communities in New England.
53 Williams, And yet They Come, 66–71.
54 Peter Wise, "Portugal Faces 'perfect Demographic Storm,'"Financial Times, August 12, 2015. https://www.ft.com/content/657b9066-2df5-11e5-91ac-a5e17d9b4cff
55 Hans H. Leder, Cultural Persistence in a Portuguese-American Community (New York: Arno Press, 1981), 17.
56 Taft, Two Portuguese Communities in New England, 52.
57 Allen G Noble, To Build in a New Land: Ethnic Landscapes in North America (Baltimore, Md: Johns Hopkins Univ. Press, 1992), 21.
58 Taft, Two Portuguese Communities in New England, 59.
59 José Saramago, Raised from the Ground (Boston: Houghton Mifflin Harcourt, 2012).
60 Williams, And yet They Come, 64.
61 Taft, Two Portuguese Communities in New England, quoted in Leder, Cultural Persistence in a Portuguese-American Community, 18.
62 Williams, And yet They Come, 59–80.
63 Ibid.
64 Ibid.
65 David E Bertão, The Portuguese Shore Whalers of California, 1854-1904 (San Jose, CA: Portuguese Heritage Publications of California, 2006).
66 Williams, And yet They Come, 63, 73 and Taft, Two Portuguese Communities in New England, 91-94.
67 Pap, The Portuguese-Americans.
68 Sue Fagalde Lick, Stories Grandma Never Told: Portuguese Women in California (Berkeley, Calif.: Heyday Books, 1998).
69 Alfred Lewis, Home Is an Island. (New York: Random House, 1951).
70 Taft, Two Portuguese Communities in New England, 62–86.
71 Pap, The Portuguese-Americans, 45–46.
72 Kimberly DaCosta Holton et al., Community, Culture and the Makings of Identity: Portuguese-Americans along the Eastern Seaboard (North Dartmouth, Mass.: University of Massachusetts Dartmouth, Center for Portuguese Studies and Culture, 2009).

73. Marilyn Halter, Between Race and Ethnicity: Cape Verdean American Immigrants, 1860-1965 (Urbana: University of Illinois Press, 1993).
74. Ray Almeida, "Packet Trade," Cape Verde Home Page, 1978, http://www1.umassd.edu/specialprograms/caboverde/cvpacket.html.
75. Jason Deparle, "In a World on the Move, a Tiny Land Strains to Cope," The New York Times, June 24, 2007, http://www.nytimes.com/2007/06/24/world/africa/24verde.html.
76. Stanley Lieberson and Mary C. Waters, "The Location of Ethnic and Racial Groups in the United States," in Sociological Forum, vol. 2 (Springer, 1987), 780–810, http://link.springer.com/article/10.1007/BF01124384.
77. James Paul Allen and Eugene Turner, We the People: An Atlas of America's Ethnic Diversity (New York: Macmillan, 1988).
78. T. R. Balakrishnan and John Kralt, "Segregation of Visible Minorities in Montreal, Toronto and Vancouver," in Multi-Ethnic Canada: Identities and Inequalities (Toronto: Copp Clark Pitman, 1987), 138–57.
79. G. Hugo, "Diversity Downunder - the Changing Ethnic Mosaic of Sydney and Melbourne" (Rowman & Littlefield, 1996), https://thesis.library.adelaide.edu.au/dspace/handle/2440/31302.
80. Carlos Teixeira, "Residential Segregation and Ethnic Economies in a Multicultural City: The Little Portugal of Toronto," Landscapes of the Ethnic Economy, 2006, 63.
81. D'Vera Cohn and Rich Morin, "Who Moves? Who Stays Put? Where's Home?," Pew Research Center's Social & Demographic Trends Project, December 17, 2008, http://www.pewsocialtrends.org/2008/12/17/who-moves-who-stays-put-wheres-home/.
82. Thomas D. Boswell, "The Cuban-American Homeland in Miami," Journal of Cultural Geography 13, no. 2 (1993): 133–148.
83. Taft, Two Portuguese Communities in New England, 249–51.
84. Ira Sharkansky, The Portuguese of Fall River: A Study of Ethnic Acculturation (Weslayan University, 1960).
85. Dorothy Ann Gilbert, Recent Portuguese Immigrants to Fall River, Massachusetts: An Analysis of Relative Economic Success (New York: AMS Press, 1989), 171–75.
86. Ibid., 173–82.
87. Lamphere, Silva, and Sousa, "Kin Networks and Family Strategies: Working-Class Portuguese Families in New England," 358.
88. Gilbert, Recent Portuguese Immigrants to Fall River, Massachusetts.
89. Pap, The Portuguese-Americans, 157.
90. James Fonseca, "The Portuguese American Community of New Bedford, Mass.," Proceedings, New England - St. Lawrence Valley Geographical Society 6 (1976).
91. David Ward, Poverty, Ethnicity, and the American City, 1840-1925: Changing Conceptions of the Slum and the Ghetto (Cambridge [England]; New York: Cambridge University Press, 1989).
92. Wilbur Zelinsky, "Seeing Beyond the Dominant Culture," in Understanding Ordinary Landscapes (New Haven: Yale University Press, 1997), 160.
93. Allen G. Noble, "The Immigrant Experience in the Nineteenth Century and Afterwards," in Noble, To Build in a New Land, 399–406
94. Ibid., 401–2.
95. Williams, And yet They Come, 23–29.
96. O. Louis Mazzatenta, "New England's 'Little Portugal,'" National Geographic Magazine 147, no. 1 (January 1975): 90–109.
97. Marc Monroe Dion, "Frenchcame.Pdf," Keeley Library Resources, accessed October 8, 2016, http://www.sailsinc.org/durfee/frenchcame.pdf.
98. Taft, Two Portuguese Communities in New England.

99   Sam Roberts, "New York's Little Italy, Littler by the Year," The New York Times, February 21, 2011, http://www.nytimes.com/2011/02/22/nyregion/22littleitaly.html.
100 Heath, The Patina of Place, 2001, 165.
101 Noble, To Build in a New Land.
102 Heath, The Patina of Place, 2001, 165.
103 Alice R. Clemente, "Of Love and Remembrance–the Poetry and Prose of Frank X. Gaspar," Gavea-Brown: A Bilingual Journal of Portuguese-American Letters and Studies 21 (2000): 25–43.
104 Michael P. Conzen, "Ethnicity on the Land," in The Making of the American Landscape (Boston: Unwin Hyman, 1990), 226, 248.
105 Richard H. Schein, "The Place of Landscape: A Conceptual Framework for Interpreting an American Scene," Annals of the Association of American Geographers 87, no. 4 (December 1, 1997): 660–80, doi:10.1111/1467-8306.00072.
106 Roland Barthes, Annette Lavers, and Colin Smith, Elements of Semiology (New York: Hill and Wang, 1968).
107 Steven D. Hoelscher and Robert C. Ostergren, "Old European Homelands in the American Middle West," Journal of Cultural Geography 13, no. 2 (March 1, 1993): 87–106, doi:10.1080/08873639309478391.
108 Albert Benedict and Robert Kent, "The Cultural Landscape of a Puerto Rican Neighborhood in Cleveland, Ohio," in Hispanic Spaces, Latino Places: Community and Cultural Diversity in Contemporary America, 2004, 187–205.
109 Inés M. Miyares, "Changing Latinization of New York City," in Hispanic Spaces, Latino Places: Community and Cultural Diversity in Contemporary America, 2004, 145–166.
110 Christopher L Salter, The Cultural Landscape (Belmont CA: Duxbury Press, 1971), ii.
111 Lesley Head, Cultural Landscapes and Environmental Change (London: Arnold, 2000).
112 Jackson, Discovering the Vernacular Landscape.
113 Peirce F. Lewis, "Axioms for Reading the Landscape: Some Guides to the American Scene," in The Interpretation of Ordinary Landscapes (New York, 1979), 11–32.
114 Paul Groth, "Frameworks for Cultural Landscape Study," in Understanding Ordinary Landscapes, 1997, 3–21.
115 Lawrence Halprin, "Nature into Landscape into Art," in Landscape in America (Austin: University of Texas Press, 1995), 242–43.
116 Lewis, "Axioms for Reading the Landscape: Some Guides to the American Scene."
117 Donald W. Meinig, "The Beholding Eye: Ten Versions of the Same Scene," in The Interpretation of Ordinary Landscapes: Geographical Essays (New York: Oxford University Press, 1979), 33–48.
118 J. B. Jackson, "Goodbye to Evolution," Landscape 13 (Winter 1963): 1, cited by D. Meinig, "Reading the Landscape: An Appreciation of WG Hoiskins and JB Jackson," in The Interpretation of Ordinary Landscapes (New York: Oxford University Press, 1979), 196–244.
119 Yolanda Prieto, "Cuban Women in the US Labor Force. Perspectives on the Nature of Change," in Latina Issues: Fragments of Historia, 1999, 163–76.
120 Meinig, "Reading the Landscape," 215.
121 Ibid., 215, 227.
122 Alan Noble, "Finns in northern Minnesota," in Noble, To Build in a New Land.
123 Noble, To Build in a New Land, 23.
124 Conzen, "Ethnicity on the Land," 234–38.
125 Heath, The Patina of Place, 2001.

126 Joseph A Conforti, Imagining New England: Explorations of Regional Identity from the Pilgrims to the Mid-Twentieth Century (Chapel Hill; London: University of North Carolina Press, 2006); Joseph A Conforti, Another City upon a Hill a New England Memoir. (North Dartmouth, MA: Tagus Press at UMass Dartmouth, 2013).
127 Heath, The Patina of Place, 2001, 137–38
128 Ibid., 129.
129 Gilbert, Recent Portuguese Immigrants to Fall River, Massachusetts, 140–42.
130 John Brinckerhoff Jackson, "Pueblo Architecture and Our Own," Landscape 3, no. 2 (1953): 1953–54, cited by Meinig, "Reading the Landscape," 217.
131 James Rojas, "The Latino Landscape of East Los Angeles," NACLA Report on the Americas 28, no. 4 (1995): 32.
132 Teixeira and da Rosa, The Portuguese in Canada.
133 Terry G Jordan-Bychkov and Lester Rowntree, The Human Mosaic: A Thematic Introduction to Cultural Geography, 5th ed. (New York: Harper & Row, 1990).
134 Bela Feldman Bianco, "Multiple Layers of Time and Space: The Construction of Class, Ethnicity, and Nationalism among Portuguese Immigrants," in Community, Culture and the Makings of Identity: Portuguese-Americans along the Eastern Seaboard (North Dartmouth, MA: Center for Portuguese Studies and Culture, University of Massachusetts Dartmouth, 2009), 64.
135 Daniel D. Arreola, "Mexican American Housescapes," Geographical Review 78, no. 3 (1988): 302.
136 Geoffrey Jellicoe and Susan Jellicoe, The Landscape of Man: Shaping the Environment from Prehistory to the Present Day (New York: Viking Press, 1975), 217.
137 Ibid., 23.
138 Jim Dunbar, "City's Three Deckers Are Special," Herald News, March 4, 1990.
139 Gilbert, Recent Portuguese Immigrants to Fall River, Massachusetts, 159–62.
140 Thomas Muller, Immigrants and the American City, 1993, 105, 153, 207–17
141 David Lowenthal, "Past Time, Present Place: Landscape and Memory," Geographical Review, 1975, 8.
142 Zelinsky, "Seeing Beyond the Dominant Culture," 159.
143 Joseph Wood, "Vietnamese American Place Making in Northern Virginia," Geographical Review 87, no. 1 (1997): 64.
144 D. W Meinig and John Brinckerhoff Jackson, The Interpretation of Ordinary Landscapes: Geographical Essays (New York: Oxford University Press, 1979), 3.
145 William Q Boelhower, Through a glass darkly: ethnic semiosis in American literature (New York ; Oxford: Oxford university press, 1987), cited by Reinaldo Francisco Silva, "Frank Gaspar's The Holyoke: Childhood as Catalyst for Portuguese-American Writing," Frank X. Gaspar, accessed January 6, 2016, http://www.frankgaspar.com/articles/silva.html.
146 Mary V Dearborn, Pocahontas's Daughters: Gender and Ethnicity in American Culture (New York: Oxford University Press, 1986), cited by Silva, "Frank Gaspar's The Holyoke: Childhood as Catalyst for Portuguese-American Writing."
147 Francis Millet Rogers, "The Contribution by Americans of Portuguese Descent to the US Literary Scene," in Ethnic Literatures Since 1776: The Many Voices of America (Lubbock: Texas Tech University, 1978), cited by Silva, "Frank Gaspar's The Holyoke: Childhood as Catalyst for Portuguese-American Writing."
148 Almeida, "Portuguese-American Literature."
149 Francisco Cota Fagundes, "Portuguese Immigrant Experience in America in Autobiography," Hispania, 2005, 701–712.

150 Wilbur Zelinsky, The Cultural Geography of the United States (Englewood Cliffs, N.J.: Prentice Hall, 1992).
151 John Brinckerhoff Jackson, The Necessity for Ruins, and Other Topics (Amherst: University of Massachusetts Press, 1980), 34, 35.
152 Dolores Hayden, "Urban Landscape History: The Sense of Place and the Politics of Space," in Understanding Ordinary Landscapes (New Haven: Yale University Press, 1997), 127.
153 Donna Huse and Jim Sears, "Urban Cottage Gardens of the Portuguese Community," in Portuguese Spinner: An American Story : Stories of History, Culture and Life from Portuguese Americans in Southeastern New England (North Dartmouth, MA: Spinner Publications, 1998), 139–41.
154 Darrell Kastin, The Conjurer and Other Azorean Tales (North Dartmouth, MA: Tagus Press at UMass Dartmouth, 2012), http://site.ebrary.com/id/10628396.
155 Huse and Sears, "Urban Cottage Gardens of the Portuguese Community," 141.
156 Reinaldo Silva, "The Ethnic Garden in Portuguese-American Writing," The Journal of American Culture 28, no. 2 (June 1, 2005): 192, doi:10.1111/j.1542-734X.2005.00163.x.
157 Ibid., 191–93.
158 Ibid., 192.
159 Huse and Sears, "Urban Cottage Gardens of the Portuguese Community," 156.
160 Frank Gaspar, "Frank X. Gaspar - Poet, Novelist | Poems | Ernestina The Shoemaker's Wife," accessed December 27, 2015, http://www.frankgaspar.com/poems/Ernestina.html.
161 Wilbur Zelinsky, Nation into State: The Shifting Symbolic Foundations of American Nationalism (Chapel Hill: University of North Carolina Press, 1988).
162 Elaine Rubinstein-Avila, "Brazilian Portuguese in Massachusetts's Linguistic Landscape: A Prevalent yet Understudied Phenomenon," Hispania, 2005, 873–880.
163 Benedict and Kent, "The Cultural Landscape of a Puerto Rican Neighborhood in Cleveland, Ohio."
164 Huse and Sears, "Urban Cottage Gardens of the Portuguese Community."
165 Pap, The Portuguese-Americans, 157.
166 Frank Gaspar, Leaving Pico: A Novel (Hanover, NH: University Press of New England, 1999).
167 Pap, The Portuguese-Americans, 157, 220.
168 Charles Howland, "Feelings of Powerlessness, Self Concept and Acculturation in Portuguese Immigrant Mothers (Massachusetts)" (Electronic Thesis or Dissertation, 1982), http://portuguese-diaspora-studies.com/index.php/ijpds/thesis/view/84.
169 Michael P. Conzen, "American Homelands: A Dissenting View," in Homelands: A Geography of Culture and Place across America, 2001, 238–270.
170 Michael P. Conzen, "Culture Regions, Homelands, and Ethnic Archipelagos in the United States: Methodological Considerations," Journal of Cultural Geography 13, no. 2 (March 1, 1993): 13–29, doi:10.1080/08873639309478386.
171 D. W. Meinig, "The Mormon Culture Region: Strategies and Patterns in the Geography of the American West, 1847–1964," Annals of the Association of American Geographers 55, no. 2 (June 1, 1965): 191–219, doi:10.1111/j.1467-8306.1965.tb00515.x.
172 D. W Meinig, Southwest: Three Peoples in Geographical Change, 1600-1970 (New York: Oxford University Press, 1971).
173 Richard L Nostrand, The Hispano Homeland (Norman: University of Oklahoma Press, 1992), http://search.ebscohost.com/login.aspx?direct=true&scope=site&db=nlebk&db=nlabk&AN=14927.

174 John Cater and Trevor Jones, Social Geography: An Introduction to Contemporary Issues (London; New York; New York: E. Arnold ; Distributed in the USA by Routledge, Chapman, and Hall, 1989), 142.
175 Karl B. Raitz, "Ethnic Maps of North America," Geographical Review 68, no. 3 (1978): 335–50, doi:10.2307/215051.
176 Allen G. Noble, "Rural Ethnic Islands," in Ethnicity in Contemporary America: A Geographical Appraisal, Edited by JO McKee, vol. 241, 1985, 257.
177 Conzen, "American Homelands."
178 Daniel D. Arreola, "Urban Ethnic Landscape Identity," Geographical Review 85, no. 4 (1995): 518–34, doi:10.2307/215923.
179 Conzen, "American Homelands."
180 Iorizzo and Mondello, The Italian Americans.
181 Noble, To Build in a New Land, 18.
182 M.Gloria de Sa and David Borges, "Context or Culture? Portuguese-Americans and Social Mobility," in Community, Culture and the Makings of Identity: Portuguese-Americans along the Eastern Seaboard (North Dartmouth, MA: Center for Portuguese Studies and Culture, University of Massachusetts Dartmouth, 2009), 265–90.
183 Conzen, "American Homelands."
184 Jordan-Bychkov and Rowntree, The Human Mosaic.
185 Almeida, "Portuguese-American Literature"; Center for Policy Analysis, "Education and Ethnicity in Southeastern Massachusetts II: 1980 to 2000: A Continuing Challenge."
186 Pap, The Portuguese-Americans, 182.
187 Rita Duarte Marinho, "Portuguese-Americans in the Political Process: A Quarter-Century Retrospective," in Portuguese-Americans and Contemporary Civic Culture in Massachusetts (North Dartmouth, MA: Center for Portuguese Studies and Culture, University of Massachusetts Dartmouth, 2002), 161.
188 Pap, The Portuguese-Americans, 176–82.
189 Maria Gloria Mulcahy, "Brazilians in New Bedford and Fall River" (Brown University), accessed December 26, 2015, http://www.brown.edu/Departments//Sociology/faculty/hsilver/immigneng/pubs/mulcahy.pdf.2015, http://www.brown.edu/Departments//Sociology/faculty/hsilver/immigneng/pubs/mulcahy.pdf.}","plainCitation":"Maria Gloria Mulcahy, "Brazilians in New Bedford and Fall River" (Brown University
190 Rubinstein-Avila, "Brazilian Portuguese in Massachusetts's Linguistic Landscape."
191 Noble, To Build in a New Land.
192 Robert Clifford Ostergren, A Community Transplanted: The Trans-Atlantic Experience of a Swedish Immigrant Settlement in the Upper Middle West, 1835-1915 (Madison, Wis.: University of Wisconsin Press, 1988).
193 "Church Attendance," Wikipedia, the Free Encyclopedia, May 3, 2016, https://en.wikipedia.org/w/index.php?title=Church_attendance&oldid=718505879.
194 Taft, Two Portuguese Communities in New England, 31–32.
195 Leder, Cultural Persistence in a Portuguese-American Community, 33.
196 Taft, Two Portuguese Communities in New England, 338–39.
197 Caroline Brettell, Men Who Migrate, Women Who Wait: Population and History in a Portuguese Parish (Princeton, N.J.: Princeton University Press, 1986), 59–61.
198 Pap, The Portuguese-Americans, 178–80.
199 Barry W Wall, Bearing Fruit by Streams of Waters: A History of the Diocese of Fall River (Strasbourg: Editions du Signe, 2003), 24.
200 Ibid., 96.
201 Ibid., 29–30.

202 Matt Camara, "St. John's Closes after 140 Years While Parishioners Press Forward with Appeal," Southcoasttoday.Com, November 5, 2012, http://www.southcoasttoday.com/apps/pbcs.dll/article?AID=/20121105/news/211050309.
203 Wall, Bearing Fruit by Streams of Waters, 38.
204 Ibid., 37–38.
205 Ibid., 88.
206 Ibid., 38, 47, 87–90.
207 Taft, Two Portuguese Communities in New England, 338.
208 Wall, Bearing Fruit by Streams of Waters, 91.
209 Ibid., 47.
210 Stephen L. Cabral, "History and Traditions of the Feast of the Blessed Sacrament," accessed December 28, 2015, http://www.newbedford.com/festa.html.
211 Paul Erling Groth and Todd W Bressi, Understanding Ordinary Landscapes (New Haven: Yale University Press, 1997).
212 Hayden, "Urban Landscape History," 130.
213 João Leal, "Travelling Rituals: Azorean Holy Ghost Festivals in Southeastern New England," in Community, Culture and the Makings of Identity: Portuguese-Americans along the Eastern Seaboard. Dartmouth, MA, Center for Portuguese Studies and Culture, University of Massachusetts (Dartmouth), 2009, 127–144, http://ceas.iscte.pt/artigos/leal_2005_traveling.pdf.
214 Ibid.
215 Pap, The Portuguese-Americans, 190–97.
216 Leal, "Travelling Rituals," 128.
217 Lurdes da Silva, "A Lenten Pilgrimage," O Jornal, April 12, 2000.
218 Pap, The Portuguese-Americans, 197–201.
219 R. Meyer, "Strangers in a Strange Land: Ethnic Cemeteries in America," in Ethnicity and the American Cemetery (Bowling Green, Ohio: Bowling Green State University Popular Press, 1993), 3.
220 David Lowenthal, The Past Is a Foreign Country (Cambridge [Cambridgeshire]; New York: Cambridge University Press, 1985), 323.
221 Ray F. Wyrick, "Cemetery Travelogues: VIII Havana," Park and Cemetery 3 (January 1929): 299–310, cited in John Matturri, "Windows in the Garden: Italian-American Memorialization and the American Cemetery," in Ethnicity and the American Cemetery (Bowling Green, Ohio: Bowling Green State University Popular Press, 1993), 14–35.
222 Meyer, "Strangers in a Strange Land," 1.
223 Ibid., 11.
224 Matturri, "Windows in the Garden," 25–27.
225 Barthes, Lavers, and Smith, Elements of Semiology.
226 Noble, To Build in a New Land, 23–24.
227 Kate A. Berry, "Latino Commerce in Northern Nevada," in Hispanic Spaces, Latino Places: Community and Cultural Diversity in Contemporary America, 1st ed. (Austin: University of Texas Press, 2004), 225–38.
228 I thank Florbela Rebelo Gomes, "Linguistic Question," March 28, 1997, for assistance with these grammar questions.
229 Pap, The Portuguese-Americans, 206.
230 Gilbert, Recent Portuguese Immigrants to Fall River, Massachusetts, 251.
231 Fernanda Ferreira at Bridgewater State University in southeastern Massachusetts, has written a fascinating study of the reactions of introductory Portuguese language students' first exposure to learning grammatically correct Portuguese and their comparisons of it to the various dialects they learned at home. Fernanda L. Ferreira, "That's Not How My Grandmother Says It: Portuguese Heritage

Learners in Southeastern Massachusetts," Hispania 88, no. 4 (2005): 848–62, doi:10.2307/20063214.

232   Jackson, Discovering the Vernacular Landscape, 148.
233   M. Isabel Valdés and Marta H Seoane, Hispanic Market Handbook: A Definitive Source for Reaching This Lucrative Segment of American Consumers (New York: Gale Research, 1995).
234   Arreola, "Mexican American Housescapes," 309.
235   Benedict and Kent, "The Cultural Landscape of a Puerto Rican Neighborhood in Cleveland, Ohio," 205.
236   Pap, The Portuguese-Americans, 211.
237   John Lewis, "Tainted Love," The Guardian, April 27, 2007, sec. Music, http://www.theguardian.com/music/2007/apr/27/worldmusic.
238   Kimberly DaCosta Holton, Performing Folklore: Ranchos Folclóricos from Lisbon to Newark (Bloomington: Indiana University Press, 2005).
239   Katherine Brucher, "Viva Rhode Island, Viva Portugal! Performance and Tourism in Portuguese-American Bands," in Community, Culture and the Makings of Identity: Portuguese-Americans along the Eastern Seaboard (North Dartmouth, MA: Center for Portuguese Studies and Culture, University of Massachusetts Dartmouth, 2009), 203–26.
240   B. J Graham, G. J Ashworth, and J. E Tunbridge, A Geography of Heritage: Power, Culture, and Economy (London; New York: Arnold ; Oxford University Press, 2000), 193–96.
241   B. J. Godfrey, "New Urban Ethnic Landscapes," in Miyares, I.; Airriess, C. Contemporary Ethnic Geographies in America. Rowman & Littlefield, 2007, 333, 337.
242   Daryl Gonyon, "Letter: A Salute to Mariano S. Bishop, Fall River's Noted Labor Leader - Opinion - The Herald News, Fall River, MA - Fall River, MA," September 8, 2015, http://www.heraldnews.com/article/20150908/OPINION/150906994.
243   Abdoolkarim Vakil, "Nationalizing Cultural Politics: Representations of the Portuguese 'Discoveries' and the Rhetoric of Identitarianism, 1880-1926," in Nationalism and the Nation in the Iberian Peninsula: Competing and Conflicting Identities, Oxford: Berg (Oxford [England]; Washington, D.C.: Berg, 1996), 41–42.
244   Joanne Maddern, "The Battle for Annie Moore: Sculpting an Irish American Identity at Ellis Island National Monument," in Heritage, Memory and the Politics of Identity: New Perspectives on the Cultural Landscape, Aldershot: Ashgate, 2007, 42–49, http://lib.imps.ac.ir/pdfTemp/9780754640127.pdf#page=50.
245   Katherine Vaz, Saudade (New York: St. Martin's Press, 1994). But it is interesting to note that it has been noted that "Every language, it seems, now has a special word for home sickness that its speakers claim to be radically untranslatable…" Marcel Proust and Joachim Neugroschel, The Complete Short Stories of Marcel Proust (New York: Cooper Square Press, 2001), 20.
246   Jackson, The Necessity for Ruins, and Other Topics, 91.
247   Ibid., 92–97.
248   Deborah Allard, "Open Arms: Gates Monument Welcomed to Fall River's Landscape," Herald News, July 23, 2006.
249   Stephen Mills, "Moving Buildings and Changing History," in Heritage, Memory and the Politics of Identity: New Perspectives in the Cultural Landscape, 2007, 109–119.
250   Pap, The Portuguese-Americans, 230.
251   Arreola, "Urban Ethnic Landscape Identity," 525.

252 Massachusetts Foundation for the Humanities, "Pilgrim Monument Completed in Provincetown," Mass Moments, 2009, http://massmoments.org/moment.cfm?mid=242.
253 John Collier, Provincetown, Massachusetts. City..., 1 negative : safety, April 1942, Library of Congress Prints and Photographs Division Washington, DC 20540, http://photogrammar.yale.edu/records/index.php?record=owi2001004231/PP.
254 Manuel Luciano da Silva, "The Portuguese Discovery Monument at Brenton State Park Is Falling Apart," 2000, http://www.dightonrock.com/portuguese_discovery_monument_at.htm.
255 Pap, The Portuguese-Americans, 18, 59–60.
256 Heath, The Patina of Place, 2001, 165.
257 Michael Gagne, "Durfee Students' Mural Tells History of Fall River through Tiles," O Jornal, March 11, 2016.
258 Daniel D. Arreola, "Mexican American Exterior Murals," Geographical Review 74, no. 4 (1984): 409–24, doi:10.2307/215024.
259 Anthony King, "The Politics of Vision," in Understanding Ordinary Landscapes (New Haven: Yale University Press, 1997), 140–41.
260 Feldman Bianco, "Multiple Layers of Time and Space: The Construction of Class, Ethnicity, and Nationalism among Portuguese Immigrants," 73.
261 Williams, And yet They Come, 138.
262 Graham, Ashworth, and Tunbridge, A Geography of Heritage.
263 DaCosta Holton, Performing Folklore.
264 John R Short, Human Geography: A Short Introduction (New York: Oxford University Press, 2015).
265 Alejandro Portes and Min Zhou, "The New Second Generation: Segmented Assimilation and Its Variants," The Annals of the American Academy of Political and Social Science 530, no. 1 (November 1, 1993): 74–96, doi:10.1177/0002716293530001006; Min Zhou, "Segmented Assimilation: Issues, Controversies, and Recent Research on the New Second Generation," The International Migration Review 31, no. 4 (1997): 975–1008, doi:10.2307/2547421.
266 Marilyn Halter, Shopping for Identity: The Marketing of Ethnicity (New York: Schocken Books, 2000), 78–79.
267 Portes, Alejandro, and József Böröcz. "Contemporary immigration: theoretical perspectives on its determinants and modes of incorporation." International migration review (1989): 606-630.
268 Zhou, "Segmented Assimilation."
269 Caroline R. Nagel, "Rethinking Geographies of Assimilation," The Professional Geographer 61, no. 3 (July 6, 2009): 400–407, doi:10.1080/00330120902941753.
270 Wilbur Zelinsky and Barrett Lee, "Heterolocalism: An Alternative Model of the Sociospatial Behaviour of Immigrant Ethnic Communities," International Journal of Population Geography 4 (1998): 281–98.
271 Milton Myron Gordon, Assimilation in American Life: The Role of Race, Religion, and National Origins. (New York: Oxford University Press, 1964), cited in Caroline R. Nagel, "Rethinking Geographies of Assimilation," The Professional Geographer 61, no. 3 (July 6, 2009): 400–407, doi:10.1080/00330120902941753.
272 Herbert J. Gans, "Symbolic Ethnicity and Symbolic Religiosity: Towards a Comparison of Ethnic and Religious Acculturation," Ethnic and Racial Studies 17, no. 4 (October 1, 1994): 577–92, doi:10.1080/01419870.1994.9993841.
273 Herbert J. Gans, "Symbolic Ethnicity: The Future of Ethnic Groups and Cultures in America," Ethnic and Racial Studies 2, no. 1 (January 1, 1979): 1–20, doi:10.1080/01419870.1979.9993248.

274 Peter Kivisto, Dag Blanck, and Swenson Swedish Immigration Research Center, eds., American Immigrants and Their Generations: Studies and Commentaries on the Hansen Thesis after Fifty Years (Urbana: University of Illinois Press, 1990), 191–203.
275 Michael Novak, The Rise of the Unmeltable Ethnics; Politics and Culture in the Seventies. (New York: Macmillan, 1972).
276 Halter, Shopping for Identity, 78–79.
277 Gans, "Symbolic Ethnicity," 8–9.
278 Hoelscher and Ostergren, "Old European Homelands in the American Middle West," 87.
279 Halter, Shopping for Identity, 14.
280 Hoelscher and Ostergren, "Old European Homelands in the American Middle West," 90–91.
281 Kivisto, Blanck, and Swenson Swedish Immigration Research Center, American Immigrants and Their Generations, 191–203.
282 "Census Ancestry Changes Reflect Changing America - 3_news.Pdf," accessed July 11, 2016, http://www.incontext.indiana.edu/2002/sep-oct02/articles/3_news.pdf.
283 Leder, Cultural Persistence in a Portuguese-American Community.
284 Pap, The Portuguese-Americans, 126.
285 Leder, Cultural Persistence in a Portuguese-American Community.
286 Ibid.
287 Gilbert, Recent Portuguese Immigrants to Fall River, Massachusetts, 2.
288 Ibid
289 Oscar Handlin, Boston's Immigrants: 1790-1880 : A Study in Acculturation (Cambridge, Mass.; London: The Belknap Press of Harvard University Press, 1991) and Oscar Handlin, The Uprooted. (New York: Grosset & Dunlap, 1951), cited by Gilbert, Recent Portuguese Immigrants to Fall River, Massachusetts, 163–64.
290 Pap, The Portuguese-Americans, 123, 129.
291 N. Fogg, K. McCabe, and A. Sum, "School Enrollment, Employment, English Speaking Proficiency, Income Adequacy, and Parenthood Indicators for 16-21 Year Old Young Adult Residents of communities in Regional Competitiveness Councils and Local Workforce Investment Areas in Massachusetts, 2000. Northeastern University, Center for Labor Market Studies," accessed May 3, 2009, http://www.commcorp.org/p21/pdf/YouthIndicatorsPackage2.pdf.
292 Ric Oliveira, "Fishing's Deadly Dark Side," Southcoasttoday.com, July 14, 1996, http://www.southcoasttoday.com/apps/pbcs.dll/article?AID=/19960714/News/70312047. See also Rory Nugent, Down at the Docks (New York: Pantheon Books, 2009).
293 Massachusetts Governor's Office, "$1.25M Granted to Combat Youth Violence, Gang Activity," Governor of Massachusetts, June 18, 2015, http://www.mass.gov/governor/press-office/press-releases/fy2015/1-25m-granted-to-combat-youth-violence-gang-activity.html.
294 Curt Brown, "2014 FBI Stats: New Bedford Most Violent City in Mass.; Fairhaven and Wareham Also Rank in Top 40," Southcoasttoday.Com, October 1, 2015, http://www.southcoasttoday.com/article/20151001/NEWS/151009906.
295 Immigration and Customs Enforcement, "ICE Deportations: Gender, Age, and Country of Citizenship," accessed January 1, 2016, http://trac.syr.edu/immigration/reports/350/.
296 Pap, The Portuguese-Americans, 121–22.
297 Susan James et al., "An Inquiry Into the 'Agonies' (Agonias) of Portuguese Immigrants From the Azores," Hispanic Journal of Behavioral Sciences 27, no. 4 (November 1, 2005): 547–64, doi:10.1177/0739986305281084.

298 Charles Reis Felix, Through a Portagee Gate (North Dartmouth, Mass.: Center for Portuguese Studies and Culture, University of Massachusetts Dartmouth, 2004).
299 Charles Reis Felix, Da Gama, Cary Grant, and the Election of 1934 (North Dartmouth: University of Massachusetts Dartmouth, Center for Portuguese Studies and Culture, 2005), 45–47.
300 Center for Policy Analysis Center for Portuguese Studies and Culture, "Portuguese Americans in the Power Structure" (University of Massachusetts Dartmouth, 2005), http://www.portstudies.umassd.edu/docs/power_structure050920.pdf.
301 Clyde W Barrow, Shawna E. Sweeney, and David Borges, "Portuguese-Americans in Southeastern Massachusetts: Opinions on Social and Cultural Issues," in Portuguese-Americans and Contemporary Civic Culture in Massachusetts (North Dartmouth, MA: Center for Portuguese Studies and Culture, University of Massachusetts Dartmouth, 2002), 123–46.
302 "The Portuguese American Citizenship Project," accessed January 1, 2016, http://www.portugueseamerican.org/about.html.
303 Howland, "Feelings of Powerlessness, Self Concept and Acculturation in Portuguese Immigrant Mothers (Massachusetts)."
304 Clyde W Barrow, "The Political Culture of Portuguese-Americans in Southeastern Massachusetts," in Community, Culture and the Makings of Identity: Portuguese-Americans along the Eastern Seaboard (North Dartmouth, MA: Center for Portuguese Studies and Culture, University of Massachusetts Dartmouth, 2009), 291–315.
305 Irene Bloemraad, "Citizenship, Naturalization and Electoral Success: Putting the Portuguese-American Experience in Comparative Context," in Community, Culture and the Makings of Identity: Portuguese-Americans along the Eastern Seaboard (North Dartmouth, MA: University of Massachusetts Dartmouth, 2009), 27–49, http://dare.uva.nl/record/464051.
306 Center for Policy Analysis, "Education and Ethnicity in Southeastern Massachusetts II: 1980 to 2000: A Continuing Challenge."
307 Bloemraad, "Citizenship, Naturalization and Electoral Success," 47.
308 Ric Oliveira, "Why Will Flanagan Won," O Jornal, November 6, 2009.
309 Felix, Da Gama, Cary Grant, and the Election of 1934.
310 Duarte Marinho, "Portuguese-Americans in the Political Process: A Quarter-Century Retrospective," 169.
311 Center for Portuguese Studies and Culture, "Portuguese Americans in the Power Structure."
312 Michael W. Freeman, "Proposed Area Seems Catered to Ethnic Group," Herald News, July 18, 2001.
313 Carlos Teixeira and Robert A. Murdie, "The Role of Ethnic Real Estate Agents in the Residential Relocation Process: A Case Study of Portuguese Homebuyers in Suburban Toronto," Urban Geography 18, no. 6 (August 1, 1997): 497–520, doi:10.2747/0272-3638.18.6.497.
314 Ann Bookman, "Unionization in an Electronics Factory: The Interplay of Gender, Ethnicity, and Class," in Community, Culture and the Makings of Identity: Portuguese-Americans along the Eastern Seaboard (North Dartmouth, MA: Center for Portuguese Studies and Culture, University of Massachusetts Dartmouth, 2009), 386.
315 Pap, The Portuguese-Americans, 158.
316 Cristiana Bastos, "Revisiting: Two Portuguese Communities in New England – Lecture," Portuguese American Journal, accessed January 9, 2016, http://portuguese-american-journal.com/revisiting-two-portuguese-communities-in-new-england-lecture/.

317 Onésimo T. Almeida, "Media-Made Events: Revisiting the Case of Big Dan's," in Community, Culture and the Makings of Identity: Portuguese-Americans along the Eastern Seaboard (North Dartmouth, MA: Center for Portuguese Studies and Culture, University of Massachusetts Dartmouth, 2009), 247–62.
318 Joseph R. LaPlante, "Portuguese Know How to Make a Point with Noise," Standard Times, October 15, 2006.
319 "Vigilant Against Deportation: Mother's Day Vigil Draws Hundreds to New Bedford for Teary Demonstration," O Jornal, May 17, 2000.
320 Peter Pereira, "Portuguese President Appeals for Close Ties, Preservation," Standard Times, June 26, 2007.
321 Alan Freeland, "The People and the Poet: Portuguese National Identity and the Camões Tercentenary (1880)," in Heritage, Memory and the Politics of Identity: New Perspectives on the Cultural Landscape (Ashgate, 2007), 53.
322 DaCosta Holton et al., Community, Culture and the Makings of Identity.
323 Freeland, "The People and the Poet," 53.
324 Feldman Bianco, "Multiple Layers of Time and Space: The Construction of Class, Ethnicity, and Nationalism among Portuguese Immigrants," 85.
325 DaCosta Holton et al., Community, Culture and the Makings of Identity.
326 Brockmann, M. (2002). Towards a model of quality of life for older ethnic minority migrants in Germany, Austria and the UK. European Societies, 4 (3), 285-306.
327 Leder, Cultural Persistence in a Portuguese-American Community, 108–12.
328 Ibid., 134-35.
329 Ibid., 76–77.
330 Lick, Stories Grandma Never Told.
331 M. Estellie Smith, "The Portuguese Female Immigrant: The 'Marginal Man,'" The International Migration Review 14, no. 1 (1980): 77–92, doi:10.2307/2545062.
332 Lick, Stories Grandma Never Told, 138.
333 Ibid., 60–61.
334 Leder, Cultural Persistence in a Portuguese-American Community, 23
335 Lick, Stories Grandma Never Told, 83, 105, 185.
336 Leder, Cultural Persistence in a Portuguese-American Community, 23–24.
337 Ibid., 26–31.
338 Marie Price and Courtney Whitworth, "Soccer and Latino Cultural Space: Metropolitan Washington Fútbol Leagues," in Hispanic Spaces, Latino Places, 2004, 167–86.
339 John R. Gillis, "Memory and Identity. The History of a Relationship," in Commemorations. The Politics of National Identity, JR Gillis (Princeton, N.J.: Princeton University Press, 1994), 10.
340 Taft, Two Portuguese Communities in New England, 33.
341 Susan J Ferguson, Race, Gender, Sexuality, and Social Class: Dimensions of Inequality and Identity, SAGE Publications 2016.
342 Miguel Moniz, "The Shadow Minority: An Ethnohistory of Portuguese and Lusophone Racial and Ethnic Identity in New England," in Community, Culture and the Makings of Identity: Portuguese-Americans along the Eastern Seaboard. North Dartmouth: University of Massachusetts Dartmouth, 2009, 409–430.
343 Carolyn L. Karcher, "Melville's 'The 'Gees': A Forgotten Satire on Scientific Racism," American Quarterly 27, no. 4 (1975): 421–42, doi:10.2307/2712330.
344 Reinaldo Francisco Silva, "Mark Twain and the 'Slow, Poor, Shiftless, Sleepy, and Lazy' Azoreans in The Innocents Abroad," The Journal of American Culture 26, no. 1 (March 1, 2003): 17–23, doi:10.1111/1542-734X.00070.
345 Benedict Thielen, "This Is My Own, My Native Land," Harper's Magazine, April 1937.

346 Taft, Two Portuguese Communities in New England.
347 Joe Burns, "Pride and Prejudice Motivated 'Porky,'" The Provincetown Banner, June 19, 1997.
348 Arthur Rose, Portage Hill and a People: A Tribute to the Portuguese People (Gloucester, MA: Sea Shore Literary, 1991).
349 Laurinda C Andrade, The Open Door, (New Bedford, Mass: Reynolds-De Walt, 1968), 94, 211.
350 Conforti, Another City upon a Hill a New England Memoir.
351 Gilbert, Recent Portuguese Immigrants to Fall River, Massachusetts, 104–5.
352 Adeline Becker, "The Role of the School in the Maintenance and Change of Ethnic Group Affiliation," in Community, Culture and the Makings of Identity: Portuguese-Americans along the Eastern Seaboard (North Dartmouth, MA: Center for Portuguese Studies and Culture, University of Massachusetts Dartmouth, 2009), 317–34.
353 Barrow, Sweeney, and Borges, "Portuguese-Americans in Southeastern Massachusetts: Opinions on Social and Cultural Issues," 129.
354 Daniel Georgianna and Roberta Hazen Aaronson, The Strike of '28 (New Bedford, Mass.: Spinner Publications, 1993).
355 DaCosta Holton et al., Community, Culture and the Makings of Identity.
356 Lick, Stories Grandma Never Told.
357 James A. Geschwender, Rita Carroll-Seguin, and Howard Brill, "The Portuguese and Haoles of Hawaii: Implications for the Origin of Ethnicity," American Sociological Review 53, no. 4 (1988): 515–27, doi:10.2307/2095846.
358 Ibid., 518–21.
359 Williams, And yet They Come, 83–91.
360 Pap, The Portuguese-Americans, 74, 79.
361 Jim Mackinnon, "Brenton Point Monument Stirs up Ocean Drive Residents," The Newport (R.I.) Daily News, March 11, 1989; Chris Aleixo, "Did the Portuguese Explorers Monument Sneak in behind Newport's Back?," Newport This Week, April 20, 1989, v. 16, no. 16 edition.
362 J. Phillip Thompson and Alethia Jones, "Race, Immigration and Planning Lecture Notes," MIT Open Courseware, 2016, http://ocw.mit.edu/courses/urban-studies-and-planning/11-947-race-immigration-and-planning-spring-2005/lecture-notes/lect8_rev.pdf.
363 Pablo Vila, Crossing Borders, Reinforcing Borders: Social Categories, Metaphors, and Narrative Identities on the U.S.-Mexico Frontier (Austin: University of Texas Press, 2000), 73, 111–24, 131, 180–81.
364 Lick, Stories Grandma Never Told, 173.
365 "University Press of New England | Gaspar Interview," An Interview with Frank X. Gaspar, accessed January 1, 2016, http://www.upne.com/features/gasparQ&A.html.
366 Gilbert, Recent Portuguese Immigrants to Fall River, Massachusetts.
367 Pap, The Portuguese-Americans, 156–62.
368 Herald News Staff, "'Greenhorn' writer apologizes," The Herald News, January 29, 1998, sec. Local, 3.
369 Anna Brown and Eileen Patten, "Statistical Portrait of the Foreign-Born Population in the United States, 2012," Pew Research Center's Hispanic Trends Project, April 29, 2014, Table 5, http://www.pewhispanic.org/2014/04/29/statistical-portrait-of-the-foreign-born-population-in-the-united-states-2012/.
370 Caroline Brettell, "Current Trends and Future Directions in Portuguese-American Studies," in Community, Culture and the Makings of Identity: Portuguese-Americans along the Eastern Seaboard (North Dartmouth, MA: Center for

Portuguese Studies and Culture, University of Massachusetts Dartmouth, 2009), 557.
371 Leder, Cultural Persistence in a Portuguese-American Community, 7.
372 Ibid, 154.
373 Susan James et al., "An Inquiry Into the 'Agonies' (Agonias) of Portuguese Immigrants From the Azores," Hispanic Journal of Behavioral Sciences 27, no. 4 (November 1, 2005): 547–64.
374 Clémence Jouët-Pastré and Leticia J. Braga, "Community-Based Learning: A Window into the Portuguese-Speaking Communities of New England," Hispania 88, no. 4 (2005): 863–72, doi:10.2307/20063215; M. Estellie Smith, "Portuguese Enclaves: The Invisible Minority.," ERIC, March 1973, http://eric.ed.gov/?id=ED076720; Bloemraad, "Citizenship, Naturalization and Electoral Success."
375 Taft, Two Portuguese Communities in New England, 17.
376 Iorizzo and Mondello, The Italian Americans, 53.
377 United States and Central Intelligence Agency, The CIA World Factbook 2014 (New York: Skyhorse Publishing, Inc., 2013), http://public.eblib.com/choice/publicfullrecord.aspx?p=1321087.
378 Taft, Two Portuguese Communities in New England, 137–93.
379 Robert Higgs, "Race, Skills, and Earnings: American Immigrants in 1909," The Journal of Economic History 31, no. 02 (June 1971): 420–428, doi:10.1017/S002205070009094X.
380 Russell Bourne, The View from Front Street (New York: W. W. Norton, 1989).
381 Frank Gaspar, The Holyoke (North Dartmouth, MA: Center for Portuguese Studies and Culture, University of Massachusetts Dartmouth, 2007).
382 Frank Gaspar, Mass for the Grace of a Happy Death (Tallahassee, Fla.: Anhinga Press, 1995).
383 Frank Gaspar, A Field Guide to the Heavens (Madison: University of Wisconsin Press, 1999).
384 Gaspar, The Holyoke.
385 Gaspar, A Field Guide to the Heavens.
386 Pap, The Portuguese-Americans, 136–40.
387 "Photogrammar," accessed January 11, 2016, http://photogrammar.yale.edu/.
388 Williams, And yet They Come.
389 Hispanic Division Library of Congress, "Twentieth-Century Arrivals from Portugal Settle in Newark, New Jersey," The Portuguese in the United States, accessed December 24, 2015, http://www.loc.gov/rr/hispanic/portam/arrivals.html; Pap, The Portuguese-Americans, 85–90.
390 Pap, The Portuguese-Americans, 158.
391 Ibid., 85.
392 Williams, And yet They Come, 84–86.
393 Ilma Ribeiro Silva, "Rumors and Dreams of Eldorado That Are Bringing Brazilians to America," Brazil Sun, August 21, 2007.
394 Halter, Shopping for Identity, 102. Halter quotes Joseph Machado on the renewal of Portuguese ethnicity in California post-1960's and on the role that electronic communication and real estate played in improving conditions for Portuguese Americans in that state.
395 Almeida, "Portuguese-American Literature."
396 Sherman, L. (2009, April 14). U.S. Cities Where It's Hardest to Get By. Forbes.com. http://www.forbes.com/2009/04/14/cities-city-top-lifestyle-real-estate-cities-united-states.html Accessed Sunday May 3, 2009.

397 Kathryn Dill, "The Best And Worst Cities For Finding A Job In 2016 - Forbes," January 6, 2016, http://www.forbes.com/sites/kathryndill/2016/01/06/the-best-and-worst-cities-for-finding-a-job-in-2016/.
398 Ross J. Gittell, Renewing Cities (Princeton University Press, 2014).
399 "Bureau of Labor Statistics Data," accessed April 30, 2017, https://data.bls.gov/timeseries/LNS14000000.
400 "Workforce Development," accessed April 30, 2017, http://lmi2.detma.org/lmi/Laborarea_comparison.asp.
401 Autonomous Region of the Azores, "Assumptions and Context for the Action Plan 2014-2020," Autonomous Region of the Azores, June 2013, http://ec.europa.eu/regional_policy/archive/activity/outermost/doc/plan_action_strategique_eu2020_acores_en.pdf.
402 "DocumentingServices.NET," Madeira Economy, accessed January 1, 2016, https://documentingservice.net/madeira.php.
403 Dulce Maria Scott, "Portuguese Americans' Acculturation, Socioeconomic Integration, and Amalgamation," Sociologia, Problemas e Practicas 61 (2009): 41–64.
404 Maria da Gloria Mulcahy, "The 'Portuguese Problem' and Economic Development," Standard-Times, September 2005.
405 de Sa and Borges, "Context or Culture? Portuguese-Americans and Social Mobility," 268, 287.
406 Center for Policy Analysis, "Education and Ethnicity in Southeastern Massachusetts II: 1980 to 2000: A Continuing Challenge."
407 Gilbert, Recent Portuguese Immigrants to Fall River, Massachusetts, 130.
408 OECD, Education at a Glance 2013 (Paris: Organization for Economic Co-operation and Development, 2013), http://www.oecd-ilibrary.org/content/book/eag-2013-en.
409 Charles Forelle, "A Nation of Dropouts Shakes Europe," Wall Street Journal, March 25, 2011, sec. Business, http://www.wsj.com/articles/SB10001424052748704076804576180522989644198.
410 Center for Policy Analysis, "Education and Ethnicity in Southeastern Massachusetts II: 1980 to 2000: A Continuing Challenge."
411 Ibid.
412 Grace M Anderson, Networks of Contact: The Portuguese and Toronto (Waterloo, Ont.: Wilfrid Laurier University, 1974); Pap, The Portuguese-Americans, 154–55.
413 de Sa and Borges, "Context or Culture? Portuguese-Americans and Social Mobility."
414 Norbert F. Wiley, "Ethnic Mobility Trap and Stratification Theory, Social Problems 15 (1968 1967): 147; Geschwender, Carroll-Seguin, and Brill, "The Portuguese and Haoles of Hawaii," 525.
415 Pap, The Portuguese-Americans, 130–55.
416 Center for Policy Analysis, "Education and Ethnicity in Southeastern Massachusetts II: 1980 to 2000: A Continuing Challenge."
417 M. Reibel, "Immigrants at Work," in Contemporary Ethnic Geographies in America, Rowman & Littlefield (Lanham: Rowman & Littlefield, 2007), 359.
418 Department of Unemployment Assistance Massachusetts Executive Office of Labor and Workforce Development, "Labor Force, Employment and Unemployment Massachusetts and Cities and Towns," Labor Force, Employment and Unemployment, November 2015, 48–51, http://lmi2.detma.org/lmi/town_comparison.asp.
419 de Sa and Borges, "Context or Culture? Portuguese-Americans and Social Mobility," 285.

420 Gilbert, Recent Portuguese Immigrants to Fall River, Massachusetts, cited in M.Gloria de Sa and David Borges, "Context or Culture? Portuguese-Americans and Social Mobility," in Community, Culture and the Makings of Identity: Portuguese-Americans along the Eastern Seaboard (North Dartmouth, MA: Center for Portuguese Studies and Culture, University of Massachusetts Dartmouth, 2009), 289.
421 Nugent, Down at the Docks.
422 Pap, The Portuguese-Americans, 133–34.
423 Ibid., 56–57.
424 http://www.upne.com/features/gasparQ&A.html University Press of New England, An Interview with Frank X. Gaspar.
425 John Dyer, "Scallops Bringing Decent Living to New Bedford Fishermen - The Boston Globe," BostonGlobe.Com, December 1, 2013, https://www.bostonglobe.com/business/2013/12/01/scallops-bringing-decent-living-new-bedford-fishermen/P9WxPWhm05vYN5xaBSZY8I/story.html.
426 Jack Spillane, "Portuguese Fishermen Wonder How to Be Loved in America," Southcoasttoday.Com, June 11, 2007, http://www.southcoasttoday.com/apps/pbcs.dll/article?AID=/20070611/NEWS/706110342/-1/news0704.
427 Jerome Krase, "The Present/Future of Little Italies," Brooklyn Journal of Social Semiotics Research 1, no. 1 (1999): 1–22.
428 Maria da Gloria Mulcahy, "Assimilation and Future Perspectives," in Portuguese Spinner (New Bedford, MA: Spinner Publications, 1998), 273–81.
429 Shawna E. Sweeney, "Portuguese Language Instruction in Massachusetts Public Schools, Colleges, and Universities," in Portuguese-Americans and Contemporary Civic Culture in Massachusetts (North Dartmouth, MA: Center for Portuguese Studies and Culture, University of Massachusetts Dartmouth, 2002), 147–58.
430 Will Richmond, "What Does a Shrinking Portuguese Population Mean for Fall River?," The Herald News, August 15, 2010.
431 Ibid.
432 Reibel, "Immigrants at Work," 363.
433 Algarve Daily News, "Regional Breakdown of Portugal's Unemployment Problem," Algarve Daily News, April 23, 2015, http://algarvedailynews.com/news/5420-regional-breakdown-of-portugal-s-unemployment-problem.
434 Eurostat, "Fertility Statistics - Statistics Explained," Eurostar Eurostat, E.U. European Commission, March 2016, http://ec.europa.eu/eurostat/statistics-explained/index.php/Fertility_statistics.
435 Governo dos Acores, "Azores Lead Birth Rate in Portugal," Governo Dos Acores, September 11, 2008, http://www.azores.gov.pt/Portal/en/entidades/pgra/noticias/Azores+lead+birth+rate+in+Portugal.htm.
436 Williams, And yet They Come, 115–33.
437 Pap, The Portuguese-Americans, 83–84.
438 Center for Policy Analysis, "Education and Ethnicity in Southeastern Massachusetts II: 1980 to 2000: A Continuing Challenge."
439 The exact figures of those reporting Portuguese among multiple ancestries according to the American Community Survey conducted by the Census Bureau are as follows: 1990, 1,148,857; 2000, 1,173,691 and 2010, 1,442,897.
440 Willams, And yet They Come, 115-33
441 Ibid.
442 Noble, To Build in a New Land, 400.
443 Ibid.
444 Warren A. Reich, Jennifer M. Ramos, and Rashmi Jaipal, "Ethnic Identity

and Interethnic Dating in Portuguese Young Adults," Asian Journal of Social Psychology 3, no. 2 (August 1, 2000): 153–61, doi:10.1111/1467-839X.00060.
445   James P. Allen and Eugene Turner, "Spatial Patterns of Immigrant Assimilation*," The Professional Geographer 48, no. 2 (May 1, 1996): 141, doi:10.1111/j.0033-0124.1996.00140.x.
446   Conzen, "Ethnicity on the Land," 241.
447   Rubinstein-Avila, "Brazilian Portuguese in Massachusetts's Linguistic Landscape."
448   Conzen, "Ethnicity on the Land," 240–41.
449   Williams, And yet They Come, 81.
450   Migration Policy Institute, "State Demographics Data | Migrationpolicy.Org," accessed December 24, 2015, http://www.migrationpolicy.org/data/state-profiles/state/demographics/MA.
451   "Brazilians Showcase Their Rise in Boston," Boston.Com, accessed April 25, 2017, http://www.boston.com/news/local/massachusetts/articles/2010/06/05/brazilians_showcase_their_rise_in_boston/.
452   Ilma Ribeiro Silva, "Rumors and Dreams of Eldorado That Are Bringing Brazilians to America," Brazil Sun, August 21, 2007.
453   Marilyn Halter, "Diasporic Generations: Distinctions of Race, Nationality and Identity in the Cape Verdean Community, Past and Present," in Community, Culture and the Makings of Identity: Portuguese-Americans along the Eastern Seaboard (North Dartmouth, MA: Center for Portuguese Studies and Culture, University of Massachusetts Dartmouth, 2009), 530.
454   Dan Adams, "Immigrants Commemorate Anniversary of New Bedford Raid," BostonGlobe.Com, March 10, 2013, https://www.bostonglobe.com/metro/2013/03/10/immigrants-commemorate-anniversary-new-bedford-raid/Bd2uvh9zjWDhpCgPGGrNoJ/story.html.
455   "Entry/Exit Overstay Report: Fiscal Year 2015 - FY 15 DHS Entry and Exit Overstay Report.Pdf," accessed July 5, 2017, https://www.dhs.gov/sites/default/files/publications/FY%2015%20DHS%20Entry%20and%20Exit%20Overstay%20Report.pdf.
456   Maria Gloria Mulcahy, "Brazilians in New Bedford and Fall River," paper at http://www.brown.edu/Departments/Sociology/faculty/hsilver/immigneng/pubs/mulcahy.pdf
457   Gaspar, Mass for the Grace of a Happy Death.
458   Brettell, Men Who Migrate, Women Who Wait, 84.
459   Taft, Two Portuguese Communities in New England, 101.
460   Williams, And yet They Come, 78–80.
461   David Jacobson, Place and Belonging in America (Baltimore: Johns Hopkins University Press, 2002), 182–86, http://site.ebrary.com/id/10021584.
462   Pap, The Portuguese-Americans, 68.
463   Taft, "Two Portuguese Communities in New England," 118.
464   Williams, And yet They Come, 78–80.
465   Ibid.
466   Jacobson, Place and Belonging in America, 182–86.
467   Pap, The Portuguese-Americans, 48–49.
468   Williams, And yet They Come, 134–39.
469   Robert C Smith, Mexican New York: Transnational Lives of New Immigrants (Berkeley: University of California Press, 2006), http://hdl.handle.net/2027/heb.31542.
470   Roger Waldinger et al., "Divergent Diasporas : the Chinese Communities of New York and Los Angeles Compared," Revue européenne de migrations

internationales 8, no. 3 (1992): 91–115, doi:10.3406/remi.1992.1339.
471 The deportation of such persons by the United States and Canada, many of them young people who do not speak Portuguese, is considered a human rights issue by the government of Portugal. The approximately 500 deportees in the Azores were the subject of the film Jorge Paixao da Costa, Devolvidos (2000), 2000, http://www.cinemagia.ro/filme/devolvidos-299760/.
472 Sara Rimer, "By the Sea, the Specter of Drugs and AIDS," The New York Times, March 24, 1997, sec. U.S., http://www.nytimes.com/1997/03/24/us/by-the-sea-the-specter-of-drugs-and-aids.html.
473 Office of HIV/AIDS Massachusetts Department of Public Health, "What Is the Geographic Distribution of the HIV/AIDS Epidemic in Massachusetts?," December 2012, http://www.mass.gov/eohhs/docs/dph/aids/2012-profiles/geographic-distribution.pdf.
474 Deparle, "In a World on the Move, a Tiny Land Strains to Cope."
475 Office of the Press Secretary The White House, "The President's Trip to Europe: Portugal, Germany, Russia, Ukraine," U.S.-Portugal Bilateral Issues, May 30, 2000, http://clinton4.nara.gov/WH/New/Europe-0005/factsheets/us-portugal-bilateral-issues.html.
476 Immigration and Customs Enforcement, "ICE Deportations: Gender, Age, and Country of Citizenship."
477 Jennette Barnes, "Deportees Struggle to Find New Life in the Old Country," Southcoasttoday.Com, October 8, 2006.
478 "Prevention Deportation Program Launched – Azores," Portuguese American Journal, April 19, 2011, http://portuguese-american-journal.com/prevention-deportation-program-launched-azores/.
479 Graham, Ashworth, and Tunbridge, A Geography of Heritage, 201.
480 Michael Hawkins, "Ethnic Festivals, Cultural Tourism, and Pan-Ethnicity," in Contemporary Ethnic Geographies in America, Lanham, MD: Rowman and Littlefield (Lanham: Rowman & Littlefield, 2007), 378.
481 Conzen, "Ethnicity on the Land."
482 Charles A. Stansfield, "Heritage Districts: The Role of Epitome Districts" (Association of American Geographers, Charlotte NC, 1996).
483 Zelinsky, "Seeing Beyond the Dominant Culture," 160.
484 Arreola, "Urban Ethnic Landscape Identity," 519.
485 Ibid., 531.
486 Hawkins, "Ethnic Festivals, Cultural Tourism, and Pan-Ethnicity."
487 Steven D Hoelscher, Heritage on Stage: The Invention of Ethnic Place in America's Little Switzerland (Madison, Wis.: University of Wisconsin Press, 1998).
488 Joan Saverino, "Italians in Public Memory: Pageantry, Power, and Imagining the Italian American, The Italian American Review," Italian American Review 8 (Autumn/Winter 2001): 83–111.
489 Lurdes da Silva, "Santander Building Sold, to Become DeMello International Center," O Jornal, March 11, 2016.
490 Jo C. Goode, "Fall River Portuguese Heritage Museum Still in the Planning Stage - News - Wicked Local - Boston, MA," Herald News, August 12, 2012, http://www.wickedlocal.com/article/20120812/News/308129780.
491 Maria da Gloria Mulcahy, "The Immigrants Assistance Center," in Portuguese Spinner (New Bedford, MA: Spinner Publications, 1998), 104–9.
492 Dave Schwab, "Is Little Portugal the next Big Thing in Point Loma?," SDNews.Com, August 31, 2016, http://sdnews.com/view/full_story/27259930/article-Is-Little-Portugal-the-next-big-thing-in-Point-Loma-?instance=most_popular1.
493 Maximilian Ferro, "The Art of Public Display: More on New Bedford and the

Portuguese Village," The South Coast Insider, May 1999, sec. Urban Living.
494   Aaron Nicodemus, "Developers Propose 'Portuguese Village' for Goodyear Site," Southcoasttoday.Com, September 21, 2007, http://www.southcoasttoday.com/apps/pbcs.dll/article?AID=/20070921/news/709210366.
495   Dick White, "Little Portugal, This Is Your Time to Shine," Southcoasttoday.Com, January 11, 2011, http://www.southcoasttoday.com/apps/pbcs.dll/article?AID=/19990223/news/302239994.
496   Michael J. Vieira, "Fall River's Little Portugal," Coastalmags.Com, August 31, 2015.
497   Victor Gautam, "Cape Cod and the Islands: Working Toward a Sustainable Year-Round Economy," From the Field, accessed January 3, 2016, http://www.massbenchmarks.org/publications/issues/vol2i3/6.pdf.

Made in the USA
Coppell, TX
12 November 2021